SAMURAI
INVASION

SAMURAI INVASION

JAPAN'S KOREAN WAR
1592-98

STEPHEN TURNBULL

CASSELL&CO

DEDICATED WITH AFFECTION AND RESPECT TO
THE PEOPLE OF JAPAN AND KOREA

ACKNOWLEDGEMENTS

To the Royal Armouries, Leeds; to Bill Dwyer, for suggesting the title; to
Professor Brian Bradford, for supplying vital source material; to Professor Jurgis
Elisonas, for his helpful comments and suggestions; to Jo, for navigating our
hire car round Korea with a map printed only in Korean script and never once
getting lost!

Cassell & Co
Wellington House, 125 Strand, London WC2R 0BB

Copyright © Stephen Turnbull 2002

First published in Great Britain by Cassell 2002

Stephen Turnbull has asserted his right to be identified as the Author of this Work.

A catalogue record for this book is available from the British Library

ISBN 0-304-35948-3

Printed and bound in Slovenia by DELO tiskarna
by arrangement with Prešernova družba d.d., Ljubljana

CONTENTS

'The dread of the tiger is so universal as to
warrant the Chinese proverbial saying,
"The Korean hunts the tiger one half of the year,
and the tiger hunts the Korean the other half".'

Isabella Bird, *Korea and her Neighbours* (1897)

PROLOGUE

As the 15th day of the fourth lunar month was set aside as the memorial service day for the Queen consort of King Sŏngjong, it was unthinkable that Yi Sun-sin, Left (i.e. Eastern) Naval Commander of Chŏlla province, should attend his office.

If any work should arise out of Yi's share of the important responsibility for the maritime defence of Korea, then it would have to be done very discreetly, but in fact there had been little to occupy him recently. He had spent the last two days practising his archery, and the day before that had watched the test firing of cannon from the deck of the newly built vessel that was his pride and joy. They called it a turtle ship, and it was almost ready for commissioning into the Korean Navy.

As even archery practice was forbidden on a national memorial service day the sun was going down on a very uneventful period of time, when a messenger arrived from Yi's colleague Wŏn Kyun, the Right (Western) Naval Commander of Kyŏngsang province to the east, with the news that 90 Japanese vessels were lying off Pusan, Korea's principal port. Wŏn Kyun, a man not noted for either his judgement or his imagination, had concluded somewhat optimistically that the ships were on a trade mission, but almost immediately another despatch arrived. This was from the Left Naval Commander of the same area, reporting that a further 350 Japanese ships had now entered Pusan harbour, and that he and Wŏn Kyun were monitoring their movements. Even Wŏn Kyun had now realised that they were probably dealing with a very serious development in the relations between Korea and Japan.

Fearing the worst, Yi Sun-sin put his Chŏlla fleet on full alert before retiring for the night with a very troubled mind. At 10 a.m. the following morning he received very bad news. Pusan had fallen to a Japanese attack with the slaughter of the entire garrison and a massacre of the inhabitants. Next day came the news of the capture of Tongnae, the mountain fortress that lay on the main road to the north of Pusan. It was now evident that this was not just another pirate raid but a full-scale invasion of Korea, and the Japanese were heading rapidly for Seoul.

chapter one

KOREA AND JAPAN

JAPAN'S Korean War of 1592–8, which devastated the Korean peninsula and gravely damaged the resources of Ming China, is so little known in the western world that it is often not even dignified with the title of a war. Instead the truce period of 1593–7, during which Japan both occupied and terrorised parts of Korea while sporadic fighting continued, is conventionally ignored, and the seven years' war is divided into two separate episodes to become 'the Japanese Invasions of Korea', or simply given the name of the man who masterminded the enterprise, and called 'Hideyoshi's Invasions of Korea'. It therefore joins the invasions of the Japanese islands of Shikoku and Kyushu as just one more campaign by Toyotomi Hideyoshi (1536–98), who unified all Japan under his sword and then carried his aggression just that little bit further, in an expression that makes the long and bloody conflict sound little more than a larger version of the pirate raids that Japan had inflicted upon Korea for centuries.

Whatever its name, the war of 1592–8 was fought between Korea, a country that had known no war other than border raids and pirate attacks for two centuries, and Japan, which had known nothing but war for five. The conflict soon dragged into its maw the empire of the Ming, whose army came to Korea's assistance across the Yalu river. It is therefore important to stress that although almost all the fighting was done in Korea, none was ever intended to take place there. To Hideyoshi, whose manifest destiny was to rule the Four Seas (a vague expression of personal intent that included India), the achievement of universal monarchy was always going to begin with a war against China. Centuries later, when Japan was once again to harbour designs of imperial grandeur, the title of the resulting Sino-Japanese War also totally ignored the suffering inflicted upon the Korean nation that by accident of geography happened to stand in the way. For Hideyoshi in 1592 it was no more than a happy coincidence that made the tip of the Korean peninsula the nearest point between Japan and the Asiatic mainland. From Tsushima to Pusan it was a mere thirty miles by sea, a fact which the Yuan dynasty of China had used in

Opposite: Map of Korea during the Chosŏn dynasty showing the pre-modern provinces in 1592, (excluding Cheju island), and the Japanese islands of Tsushima and Iki.

Korea under the Chosŏn Dynasty

N

Hoeryŏng

Tumen River

HAMGYŎNG

Yalu River

P'YŎNGAN

Ch'ŏngchŏn

Ŭlju

Hamhŭng

Anju

Provincial border

KANGYŎN   Province

Wŏnju   Important towns and locations

Taedong River

P'yŏngyang

HWANGHAE

KANGWŎN

Haeju

Seoul

Wŏnju

KANGHWA ISLAND

Han River

KYŎNGGI

CH'UNGCH'ŎNG

Choryŏng Pass

Naktong River

Kongju

Taegu   Kyŏngju

Chŏnju

KYŎNGSANG

0   25   50 miles

CHŎLLA

Chinhae   Pusan

KŎJE ISLAND

TSUSHIMA

IKI

Empress Jingū leads the invasion of Korea. This painted scroll depicts the legendary event that was held to provide a precedent for Hideyoshi's operation. Jingū, who is pregnant with the future Emperor Ōjin, to be deified as Hachiman Dai Bosatsu – the god of war – is dressed in a magnificent suit of armour. Koreans are shown falling into the sea around her. (Private Collection)

the thirteenth century when they launched the abortive Mongol invasions of Japan. With Toyotomi Hideyoshi this convenient invasion route was to be used in reverse.

To Hideyoshi, therefore, Korea was merely the road to China, an obstacle that by negotiation or force of arms could be converted into a strategic asset. But in the past it had been so much more, because through Korea had flowed a steady stream of Chinese and Korean culture that had permeated and enriched Japanese society, from superlative bronze Buddhist sculptures to highly prized bowls for the tea ceremony. It may well be that many of the invaders of 1592 would have acknowledged a considerable cultural debt to the peninsula, but in terms of the overall goal of military conquest the pivotal event in the long history of Japanese/Korean relations was the cherished story of how Korea had submitted to Japanese aggression once before. This legendary operation had been carried out by the Empress Jingū, who had led an invasion of Korea in about AD400 while she was pregnant, and the son born to her was later to be deified as Hachiman the god of war. By contrast, the Korean version of the tale saw Jingū as a Korean warrior princess who had actually conquered Japan, but to Hideyoshi's enthusiastic followers her mystical campaign, which ended in Korea's submission and homage, provided an unquestioned historical precedent that was frequently to be invoked in justification of Japan's new incursions.[1]

KOREAN SOCIETY IN 1592

Prior to the time of Hideyoshi the only attacks on Korea by Japan had been carried out by bands of pirates, and it was to the north — not the south — that Korea had tended to look when anticipating foreign invasion. Separated from China by the Yalu and Tumen rivers which provided its border with Manchuria, Korea had suffered much from this direction. The Mongol horde had swept into Korea this way during the thirteenth century, forcing the

Korean King into exile on Kanghwa island and finally extracting submission only when he had seen his country devastated around him. In time the Mongol curse was to pass from Korea, and with it the Koryŏ dynasty who had suffered their depredations, ushering in a welcome time of peace under the Chosŏn (or Yi) dynasty, which was to rule Korea until 1910.

The Chosŏn dynasty of Korea and the Ming dynasty of China were both founded during the fourteenth century, and had much in common. Both represented the final overthrow of a Mongol yoke, and the Confucian ideals to which both aspired meant that Korea respected China, which was so much larger both in population and in territory, while China respected Korea for the great skills its officials displayed in the Chinese classics. As a result, unlike the long misery of the Mongol incursions into Korea during the later years of the Koryŏ dynasty, the Ming honoured Korean independence and never interfered with Korean politics, and for three centuries these two nations who shared a common border carried out no aggressive acts against each other. Both countries were also very wary of the Jurchens of eastern Manchuria who would periodically raid across both borders. The Jurchens had long since lost their empire of Jin to the Mongols, and were now divided into small tribal states. In time they would rise again as the Manchus, and sweep away both the Ming dynasty and Korean independence, but for now they represented just an additional challenge to the seaborne incursions periodically inflicted on both China and Korea from Japan.

By the time of the Japanese invasion in 1592 the Chosŏn dynasty had been ruling Korea for two centuries. As it had been the old regime of the Koryŏ dynasty who had submitted to a Mongol conquest, it was with a suitably patriotic and reforming zeal that the military commander Yi Sŏngyye (King Tae'jo) had set up the new dynasty. The philosophical rationale that lay behind his reforms was Confucianism. Confucian scholars had been intimately involved in the political movement that had led to the overthrow of Koryŏ, and their moral outrage at the shortcomings of Koryŏ society ensured that their primary objective would be the replacement of that dynasty's discredited aristocracy by a new meritocracy based on knowledge of the Confucian classics. These writings emphasised a limited monarchy, though one to which absolute loyalty was due, under whom might be found equal opportunity for men of moral rectitude who administered government services with honesty and probity.

The first practical outcomes of these ideals were enacted shortly after the founding of Chosŏn in 1392. Government administration was centralised, and success in civil service examinations was made mandatory for the achievement of office. An examination system had existed under Koryŏ, and included military exams which covered personal combat expertise as well as studies of military texts. These were continued under Chosŏn and laid the foundations for the regular recruitment of military officials. Unfortunately for the development of Korea's army, the civil examinations carried much greater prestige, but neither variety were to prove sufficient in ensuring the disappearance of Koryŏ's aristocracy.

The term used for the class that had dominated Koryŏ society was yangban, an expression that originally meant the 'two files' of officials (one civil, the other military), who lined up in front of the throne during a royal audience. Apart from a few families who were eliminated because of their support for the old Koryŏ regime, most of the yangban succeeded in making the transition from one dynasty to another with their landed wealth and social positions intact, the new examination system proving a by-no-means insurmountable obstacle. High office was now theoretically open to all yang'in (freemen), but in practice the yangban had the easiest access to both schools and offices. So instead of a new ruling elite based on upwardly mobile freemen, the Chosŏn dynasty settled into a more familiar pattern of yangban rule, the Chosŏn version being a hybrid between the new ideals of a meritocratic bureaucracy and the old Koryŏ style of a hereditary aristocracy.[2]

The influence of education through the examination system and long political stability ensured that there were many men of talent and great learning to be found among the yangban ranks who made a huge contribution to Korea in science, art, literature and warfare. The reign of King Sejong between 1418 and 1450, for example, was a golden age for Chosŏn that saw innovations ranging from the creation of han'gŭl, Korea's own alphabet, to the production of accurate rain gauges two centuries before they were introduced in Europe.[3] Although exempt from conscription to military service, many yangban made great contributions in the martial field as well, with important developments such as fine cannon and the establishment of a formidable navy. Yet, as in most societies, there were also many who enjoyed the great privileges that rank always brought while giving nothing in return. To such men politics and individual prestige were intimately linked, and no victory on a battlefield could compare to a victory gained in the corridors of the Korean court.

Apart from examinations, one other means by which the first Chosŏn king tried to curtail yangban power was by increasing the influence of the monarchy at their expense, but King Tae'jo's benevolent Confucian ideals were not shared by all his successors, and on several occasions the aggrandisement of power into royal hands did not automatically ensure its wise and restrained use. For example, King T'aejong (ruled 1401–18) manipulated the succession in his own favour, while King Sejo (ruled 1455–68) usurped the throne from his nephew. Yet while Confucianism stressed loyalty to the throne it could also provide the moral justification for the overthrow of monarchs. Thus it was that when Korea was faced with a succession dispute in 1545 one yangban

Admiral Yi Sun-sin as a yangban. The yangban were the aristocrats of Chosŏn dynasty Korea, and the famous admiral is shown here dressed in the typical white yangban costume with the characteristic hat in the Korean Folk Village near Suwŏn. Behind him is a replica of the screen presented to Yi by Ming China.

clan created political havoc by banishing and having executed the members of the rival faction. Thirty years later during the reign of King Sŏnjo (ruled 1567–1608), a similar factionalism arose over the appointment of an official in the Ministry of Personnel. The rival claimants were supported by two groups of yangban, known as the Easterners and the Westerners, over the location of their homes in the capital. King Sŏnjo did little to quieten the factionalism, and even made it worse by switching allegiance from one side to the other at whim, so that by the time of the Japanese invasion the factionalism had become firmly entrenched and had also developed a disturbing hereditary element that was to cause major problems for King Sŏnjo's successors. As will be demonstrated in the pages which follow, the rivalry between the factions was to have a marked influence on the decision-making process during the years leading up to the war with Japan.

At the other end of the Korean social spectrum from the yangban lay the slaves. By 1592 slaves made up one-third of all Korean society and two-thirds of the population of Seoul, which had become the Chosŏn dynasty's capital at the time of its foundation. Most of the slaves were owned by yangban, and a yangban measured his wealth as much by the number of slaves he owned as by the amount of land he controlled. Slavery as an institution had such a long history of being an integral part of Korean society and of its economy that it

The beautifully recreated Korean village scene at the Korean Folk Village near Suwŏn.

Yu Sŏng-nyong, the Prime Minister of Korea during the war against Japan, as depicted in a Japanese illustration which shows him pleading with the Ming for aid. (ETK detail)

was seldom challenged or even questioned. Nor did Confucianism do any more towards the condemnation and abolition of the practice than did contemporary Christianity, an attitude demonstrated most clearly when the Confucian and anti-Buddhist founding fathers of Chosŏn dissolved Buddhist monasteries and seized their lands. With the temple properties came 80,000 slaves, but instead of granting them their freedom they merely made them government slaves.

On several occasions in Korean history slaves were to take advantage of political or military turmoil to burn the slave registers. Within a few days of the flight of King Sŏnjo from Seoul in the face of the Japanese advance in 1592 slaves and refugees would attack the Changyewŏn (Slave Agency) and destroy all its records, but there were other ways for a slave to gain his freedom, because, like yangban, slaves were normally excluded from military service. The exceptions arose in times of national emergency, when attacks by Jurchens or pirate raids on the coasts regularly revealed a serious shortage of men for military duties. In 1554 and 1555 the government recruited slaves for service in the north and granted them their freedom in return, until the protests of their former owners made the government restrict liberation to those who had actually taken part in combat.

It is estimated that as many as 20–30,000 slaves gained their freedom through fighting the Japanese from 1592 onwards. In 1593 slaves were even allowed to take the military examinations. Warrants for this, and for granting freedom, were supposed to be handed out by provincial officials to slaves after counting the number of Japanese heads the prospective candidate presented, but it was a system open to abuse from both sides. The officials sold the warrants for profit, and dishonest slaves cut the heads from Korean beggars who had already died of natural causes.

KOREA'S PREPARATIONS FOR DEFENCE

Hideyoshi's warlike intentions against Korea were suspected by the Koreans for several years prior to 1592, and there exists a valuable eyewitness account of the defence preparations made at this time. It is entitled *Chingbirok* (Record of Reprimands and Admonitions), and was written by Yu Sŏng-nyong, who occupied several important government positions immediately prior to the outbreak of hostilities and was Prime Minister of Korea during the war itself. Yu was actively engaged in the diplomatic exchanges with Japan that sought to avert war, and then took part in the peace negotiations. The curious title of his work is explained by the remorse he felt at being somehow personally responsible for the disaster that had overtaken his country, and he introduces his record as follows:

> An unworthy person like me, who receives an important government position at a time of peregrination and lawlessness, but was unable to uphold the tottering and support the falling, cannot expiate his crime even by death . . . I constantly thought about the events of former days, and there has never been a moment when I did not feel unbearable shame.[4]

Yu Sŏng-nyong's regret for bad judgements and missed opportunities went back to Korea's failure to repel a Jurchen attack in 1582. The scholar official Yulgok had reviewed Korea's lamentable performance and concluded that 'the nation's strength has been so sapped that I fear before the decade is out a landslide of a disaster may befall us.'[5] He went on to recommend that both slaves and the sons of yangban by their concubines should be recruited to swell the ranks with an aim of producing an army of 100,000 men. Of these, 20,000 would be stationed in the capital and 10,000 in each province. Yulgok was of the Western Faction, which almost inevitably assured that his proposal would be rejected by the then dominant Eastern Faction as represented by Yu Sŏng-nyong, a decision Yu later bitterly regretted. Some recruitment did go ahead, but the planned regional deployment was never carried out and the actual recommendation itself was regarded as so unimportant that it was not officially recorded.

In 1588 a provincial governor urged that twenty islands off the south coast should be made into military bases. Two years later another official proposed fortifying the islands off Pusan in case of a surprise Japanese attack. Both suggestions came to nothing, as did the dramatic recommendation in 1588 by a certain Cho Hŏn of the Western faction that Korea should launch a pre-emptive strike against Japan, an audacious proposal that led to his banishment and replacement by an Easterner.

As the Japanese threat grew steadily more believable, the influential Yu Sŏng-nyong eventually changed his views and became a powerful voice arguing for a strengthening of Korea's defences, but in the bitter factionalism of the Korean court counter-arguments were always brought forward for purely political reasons. A good example may be found in the objections to Yu's insistence on the need to repair fortresses. Castle building, which involved forced labour on a massive scale was very unpopular at every level of society, as Yu noted in *Chingbirok*:

> At that time we had been at peace for many years and were accustomed to both internal and external tranquillity. The people therefore disliked this forced labour. Murmurs of discontent filled the streets.[6]

A factional opponent of Yu's supported this popular feeling, but argued against the proposed fortress building programme in a curiously self-contradictory statement:

> In front of Samga is the stream Chŏngjin, which blocks the way. Can the Japanese fly across? Why is the labour of the people used wastefully? Moreover, if 10,000 li of ocean cannot hold back the Japanese, then to wish only one piece of sash-like water will be impassable to the Japanese is indeed ridiculous. [7]

More worrying to Yu was the fact that similar attitudes towards defence issues were shared by several of the Korean generals, of whom, he reckoned, 'not one in a hundred knew the methods of drilling soldiers'.[8] As late as the spring of 1592, when the Japanese invasion fleet was preparing to set sail, General Sin Rip, who held the post of Tosunbyŏnsa (General Circuit Defence Commander) was sent on a tour of inspection of Kyŏnggi and Hwanghae provinces. Sin Rip set off with an ostentatious train that, in its expression of effortless personal superiority, exemplified the yangban class at its worst. 'Everywhere he had people killed to display his authority,' wrote Yu, 'and the provincial magistrates were terrified.' Sin Rip eventually returned to Court with a cursory assessment of the weaponry available to the troops, but with no plan of how they might be used. Yu records their subsequent conversation:

> I asked him, 'Sooner or later there will be a war, and since you are responsible for military affairs, what do you think about the power of the enemy today? Is he strong or weak?' Rip treated this question extremely lightly and appeared completely free from anxiety. I said, 'That is not the right attitude. Formerly the Japanese depended on short weapons alone, but now they are supplied with muskets which are effective at a distance. We can't treat the matter lightly.' Rip hastily said, 'Even if they have muskets, they can't hit anyone with them.' [9]

Sin Rip, the Korean general famous for the immortal statement, 'Even if they (the Japanese) have muskets, they can't hit anyone with them.' He is about to flee to Ch'ungju, where he was killed. (ETK detail)

As appointment to high rank depended far more on patronage and social connections than on skills in warfare, and knowledge of military strategy counted for nothing compared to expertise in the Confucian classics, men such as Sin Rip prospered while talented leaders such as the famous Admiral Yi Sun-sin languished in small provincial commands. It took ten years for Yi to reap the just rewards of his military successes against the Jurchens by being promoted (at Yu Sŏng-nyong's recommendation) to Left Naval Commander of Chŏlla province in 1585, but even then, noted Yu in disgust, 'Others were distrustful of such a rapid rise in station.'

Yet some of the generals who were to come in for withering criticism from Yu Sŏng-nyong had in the past shown a genuine ability to learn from their mistakes and to make changes. The much maligned Yi Il (1538–1601), who was to lose the crucial battle of Sangju in 1592, had been appalled by the disarray of the troops stationed in northern Hamgyŏng when he defeated the Jurchens there in 1583. As well as reorganising the local garrisons, he carried out the important reform of delegating to the Hamgyŏng provincial commander the responsibility of reacting appropriately to a raid across the border, rather than waiting idly by until a superior commander was sent from the capital. The practice of sending commanders from Seoul also concerned Yu Sŏng-nyong. '...visiting generals gallop down to the provinces on the spur of the moment,' he wrote in *Chingbirok*. 'They are acquainted with neither the conditions in the province where they are sent nor the valour or timidity of the soldiers there. They shun the arts of war. We will certainly regret this later.' [10]

This centralised command scheme effectively dated from 1488, when it had replaced the earlier 'chin'gwan' system of local responsibility. Faced by the Japanese threat in 1591 Yu argued strongly for a return to a modified version of the local model, which had originally fallen into disrepair because men had tended to be sent to garrisons at some distance from their homes, thus leading to great personal hardship and a consequent high risk of non-compliance. There had also been problems with the provincial magistrates who were given authority to train their troops in peacetime, and to organise and lead them to victory in wartime. Most of the appointees were more interested in tax collection and far too ready to accept payment (rendered in the form of cloth) in lieu of military service.

Strangely enough, the chaotic nature of Korean military thinking during the century leading up to the Japanese invasions had actually meant that both systems were to be found in operation at various places at the same time, and had therefore allowed the opportunity for the two models of command to be tested and thereby compared. In 1510, during the so-called 'Three Ports Incident' when Japanese residents in Korea revolted, a problem was revealed with the decentralised chin'gwan system when the provincial organisation proved to be so inflexible that country garrisons could not easily be moved even to ports in the same province. The centralised alternative provided different problems as Yi Il discovered in 1583 but, ironically, he had originally been one of the greatest enthusiasts for the system, even though it had failed against a large Japanese pirate raid of 1555. On that occasion the troops were mobilised, then left waiting with no leader until the enemy advanced, at which point they all ran away before the commander arrived on the scene after his four-day journey from Seoul.

The most valuable lesson that should have been learned from both failures was that neither system was capable of converting the garrison soldiers into an effective army because the troops involved were almost totally untrained,

Front and rear view of a popular type of Korean armour as worn by officers. The coat is of reinforced cloth with a scale armour overlay.

unorganised and ill-disciplined. Unfortunately for Korea, this point was either not picked up or not acted upon and, looking back during the period of truce after a much bigger disaster had overtaken his country in 1592, Yu Sŏng-nyong summed up his views of the state of the Korean army as follows:

> Basically, they do not know anything about fighting, and they have no units such as platoons, squads, banners or companies to which they are attached. They are in confusion and without order, make a big racket and run around in chaos, not knowing what to do with their hands, feet, ears or eyes. And then all of a sudden these men are placed in the midst of arrows and stones where they have to fight to the death . . .[11]

'If it is like this in peacetime,' he asked after quoting a similar comment from his colleague Cho Hŏn, who had observed better practices in China, 'what could we do during wartime?'

Some reforms were carried out nevertheless. In 1589 a military training centre was established at Andong in the strategic Kyŏngsang province, and local peasants were required to undergo six months of training every year, yet even at this late stage an understandable reluctance to abandon agriculture for military service meant that most recruits were either too old or too young. The generals sent to lead such men therefore had to augment these forces by recruiting other troops as they proceeded, and would often enlist a motley crew of retired army officers, bored or adventure-seeking yangban, slaves eager for freedom or Buddhist monks. Yet in spite of all the negative experience gained this would still be the system that would creak into motion when the Japanese landed in 1592, and 1595 was to see Yu Sŏng-nyong still arguing for a return to what he saw as the golden age of the chin'gwan system.

The Korean army was therefore very primitive by Japanese standards, and this was further reflected in its equipment. The basic design of a suit of Korean armour consisted of a three-quarter-length heavy coat worn over an inner garment that resembled a divided apron, with trousers and leather boots. By the Koryŏ Period lamellar armour had been introduced, the lamellae being added either to the outside of the coat or inside it, or stitched inside the lining. The final version was the studded coat, whereby the heads of rivets, which held in place small plates inside the armour, protruded from its outside surface to give an appearance very similar to brigandine. Officers would also sport a bright coloured sash or belt over coats of red or blue, but the usual appearance for most wearers was of dull brown fabric of cotton or hemp.

The Korean helmet consisted of a simple rounded conical bowl made from

A Korean helmet in the collection of the Royal Armouries, Leeds. The bowl is of lacquered iron, and the neck guard is of cloth reinforced with metal plates on the inside, riveted through.

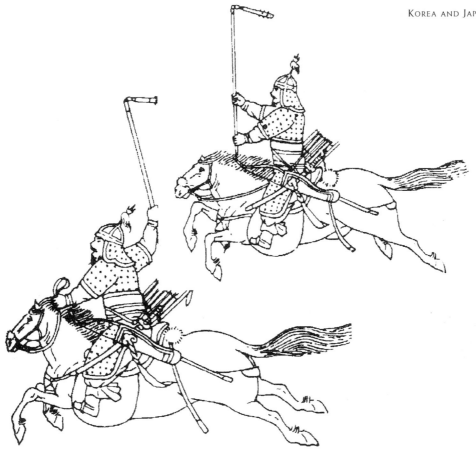

four main pieces riveted together and secured round the brow. A neck guard of lamellae or brigandine was suspended from it in three sections, and decoration in the form of feathers could be flown from the helmet point. Officers' helmets could be lacquered black and ornamented with gold and fur. Korean foot soldiers wore no armour at all, just their traditional white clothes with a sleeveless black jacket and a belt, but a felt hat gave some small protection in battle.

Many Korean swords were two-edged, straight-bladed weapons, although curved swords like Japanese katana were also made, and actual Japanese models were imported. By contrast, Korean polearms showed considerable Chinese influence. Their use was most prized from the back of a horse, so we see cavalrymen armed with tridents, long straight spears and glaives with heavy curved blades much wider than a Japanese naginata. Unique to Korea, however, was the flail, a rounded hardwood stick, painted red and four feet long, to which was attached a shorter and heavier mace-like shaft studded with iron nails or knobs. The attachment was provided by a short length of chain. The flail was highly regarded, and successful candidates for the military examinations had to gallop along a trench and knock over a certain number of artificial heads. Foot soldiers were armed with all the above varieties of polearm except the flail.

A flail in action from horse-back. The flail, which was effectively a long-handled mace for a cavalryman, was a weapon almost unique to Korea, and many Korean generals placed great faith in it.

Prowess at archery was also greatly valued, and the celebrated Admiral Yi Sun-sin was an accomplished archer. The ordinary Korean bow was a composite reflex bow, made from mulberry wood, bamboo, water buffalo horn and cow sinew spliced together. It had a pronounced negative curve, against which the bow had to be pulled in order to string it. A Japanese source from the time of the 1592 invasion claims that Korean bows were the one thing in which the Koreans were superior to the Japanese, because their range was 500 yards against the Japanese longbow's range of 350 yards.

The one thing the Korean army could be really proud of was its artillery. In addition to the cannon that were mounted on Korean warships or on the walls of castles, an army in the field could boast multiple rocket launchers firing volleys of steel-tipped arrows or darts, which were devastating against close formation troops if timed correctly. Otherwise it lacked armoured infantry, long spears and arquebuses, as well as proper organisation, combat experience, trained officers and a clear chain of command, and this was an army that was to face an invasion by one of the contemporary world's most sophisticated military machines.

As to the state of the fortresses where these wretched garrisons were located, we noted earlier the reluctance of the Korean population to be press-ganged into repairing walls. There was an equal unwillingness to follow the official rule to 'strengthen the walls and clear the countryside', which meant that on the outbreak of hostilities the local people should leave their homes and fields and take their families, their possessions and their grain to the shelter of their nearest fortress. Anyone who failed to comply would be automatically assumed to be a collaborator with the enemy and could face execution. The weakness of the system was that most of the fortresses were not walled towns but sansŏng (mountain castles), which were often so far away from their homes that the civilians buried everything in the nearby hills and stayed in their villages or hid nearby. Alternatively, the policy was followed to the letter, leaving the fields and roads denuded of people and allowing an invader a free and unopposed passage.

One result of the popular mistrust of the sansŏng was that when people were made to repair the walls of their nearest refuge the work was frequently shoddy, so that a ten-day period of impressed labour was often followed by the collapse of the new wall soon after it was finished. Admiral Yi Sun-sin's War Diary contains several examples. Early in 1592 the embankment of the moat in Yŏsu had crumbled 'four arm-spans wide' and had to be repaired.[12] A month later we read that 'the stone cutters constructed the embankment of the moat very badly, and the stone walls crumbled in many places. I ordered the reconstruction under penalty of heavy flogging.'[13] A further month later Yi reports that the newly built walls of Namhae had 'crumbled nine arms spans wide'.[14] That the stone cutters were not professional masons is illustrated by a separate entry of how 'Pak Mongse, a local sailor residing under the city wall, pretended to be a stone-cutter and went to the quarry but played with his neighbour's dog, so I ordered him flogged with 80 blows'. [15]

Some of the blame for this lay in the basic design of the sansŏng. As Yu Sŏng-nyong was later to observe when one mountain castle after another fell to the Japanese, the Korean people were unskilled when it came to the location and construction of walls. Japanese castles were characterised by excavations that literally carved up a mountain into a series of horizontal and interlocking enceintes that allowed for an excellent field of fire from sloping stone walls that were built firmly into the sculpted hillsides. Korean walls, by contrast, were vertical constructions of small flat stones that followed the contours of the mountain in a snake-like fashion as if they were miniature versions of the Great Wall of China. The overall height was therefore inevitably restricted, as was the capacity to erect turrets or corner towers, nor was there much use made of protruding turrets to allow crossfire as was to be found in the grander and better-designed Chinese version of a serpentine mountain fortress. Only in the major walled towns such as Seoul and Chinju were formidable walls to be found.

The overstretched and often unsteady walls of the sansŏng therefore symbolised Korean society on the eve of the Japanese war. Their thin defences sheltered a peaceful nation that was politically stable, rich in learning and proud of its cultural achievement, but was also a society almost paralysed by complacency and self-interest and weakened by factional infighting. The cracks in the walls had been exposed by border raiders and pirates, and never was the neglect to be more clearly demonstrated than in the government's woeful lack of military preparation against the most ruthless and professional army in contemporary Asia.

The fortress of Chukjusansŏng, typical of the simple serpentine style of the traditional Korean castle wall. Many of the sansŏng (mountain fortresses) that faced the Japanese would have had this simple construction of low, vertical stone walls.

力

chapter two

JAPAN AND KOREA

ONE of the factors underlying the Korean attitude to Japan was a serious underestimation of Japan's strength, a miscalculation that operated at two levels. The first error arose from Korea's observations of the turmoil of Japan's long civil wars, which the yangban contrasted with the stability and unity they enjoyed in their Confucian paradise. The second mistake was to argue that, even if an invasion should happen, either Korea's navy would prevent it from landing, or the Korean army would drive it back into the sea.

The history of Japan's past century and a half made both attitudes perfectly understandable. Since the end of the Gempei War in the twelfth century Japan had been ruled by a warrior class under the military dictator or Shogun, a process that appeared to have guaranteed not peace and tranquillity but the continuation of civil war. The first Shogunal dynasty, that of the Minamoto, had not lasted long, and the new stability that appeared to have been given to Japanese society by the establishment of the Ashikaga Shogunate in 1336 was tested by the Nanbokuchō Wars (fought between the supporters of rival emperors) and then mortally wounded by the Ōnin War of 1467–76. Following this disastrous conflict Japan had dissolved into a country of rival daimyō (warlords). In time the more powerful daimyō conquered and absorbed lesser fry, until by the mid-sixteenth century the civil wars that would have come to the attention of Korean observers were very large-scale affairs. The picture thus presented to the outside world was that Japan was a nation in conflict with itself, a point illustrated most keenly to the Korean mind by the clear failure by any centralised Japanese administration to control the Japanese pirates that periodically ravaged Korea's shores. That a nation so divided could consider attacking another was therefore unthinkable.

Unfortunately for Korea in 1592 such an attitude was just a few years out of date. Had they looked more deeply, they would have perceived a new unity within Japan that put to shame the factional divisions in Korea. Also, and this was the crucial point, the newly discovered unity had been achieved by war, and the war had been conducted by the man who was presently planning to invade Korea.

THE RISE OF HIDEYOSHI

In the two decades before his invasion began, Toyotomi Hideyoshi had experienced a rise to power that was unequalled by anyone else in Japanese history. His father had been a peasant farmer who had served as an ashigaru (foot soldier) until a bullet wound invalided him out. Hideyoshi, then called Tokichirō, followed in his father's footsteps and served the daimyō Oda Nobunaga (1534–82) as the latter grew to become the first of Japan's great unifiers. Nobunaga had an eye for talent, and rewarded Tokichirō's successive military accomplishments by rapid promotion, until by the time of Nobunaga's murder in 1582 Hideyoshi was one of his most trusted generals.[1]

Toyotomi Hideyoshi, as portrayed in later life. This hanging scroll in the Hyōgo Prefectural Art Museum, Himeji is probably a very good likeness of the Taikō as he would have appeared at the time of the Korean campaign.

A suit of Japanese armour said to have been worn during the Korean campaign by a retainer of the Matsuura. It is in the Matsuura Museum, Hirado, and bears the mon (badge) of the Matsuura as a helmet crest and also on the sashimono (back flag). This is typical of the straightforward 'battledress' armours that would have been worn by the Japanese troops in Korea.

Hideyoshi heard the news of Nobunaga's assassination while he was besieging the castle of Takamatsu on the Inland Sea. Realising that the news would encourage the castle's defenders he kept it secret and arranged a negotiated settlement, then hurried back towards Kyoto, where he defeated the usurper Akechi Mitsuhide at the decisive battle of Yamazaki. The triumph associated with being Nobunaga's avenger gave Hideyoshi the opportunity to fill the power vacuum which Nobunaga's death had left, and during the next two years Hideyoshi was to challenge and defeat all other rivals, including Nobunaga's surviving sons, in a series of brilliant military campaigns. At Shizugatake in 1583 he surprised his rival by a forced march, and at Komaki in 1584 he successfully employed an earthwork defensive line covered by arquebuses. By 1585, with his political rivals eliminated, Hideyoshi was able to begin extending the boundaries of Nobunaga's former conquests, taking in the island of Shikoku and the provinces of western Japan. The Shikoku campaign involved a successful sea crossing, and in 1587 Hideyoshi conquered the great southern Japanese island of Kyushu in a huge and well-coordinated campaign that was to provide a model for the Korean expedition. The defeat of the Hōjō in 1590, which involved mobilising the largest army ever seen in Japan, led to most of the northern daimyō submitting without a fight, so that by 1591 the 'Period of Warring States' was effectively over, and Japan was reunited under the sword of a former foot soldier.

Hideyoshi's rise from the ranks was undoubtedly one of the reasons why he inspired such loyalty and confidence in his followers. Most of his generals were men like him. Several of them had served in the armies of daimyō defeated by Hideyoshi, and had then rushed to pledge service to this consummate general who had allowed them to retain their heads. Somehow Hideyoshi had a perfect grasp of when to be ruthless with those he had conquered and when to be generous. The sectarian rabble of the Negoro temples were massacred in the same year that the defeated ruler of Shikoku island was allowed to retain his lands in return for a pledge of allegiance. Those who followed him were also richly rewarded, and were eager to share in further conquests.

In private life this ruthless leader of armies composed numerous tender and affectionate letters to friends and relatives. In this personal correspondence there is always great concern expressed for the recipient's health, just as Hideyoshi himself was also obsessively concerned with his own well-being and his need to produce an heir, a matter to which we will return. As for Hideyoshi's appearance, contemporary observers note his small, wizened stature and his total lack of aristocratic features on a monkey-like head, yet as his power grew Hideyoshi had taken on aristocratic trappings on a grander scale than any ruler before him. The lavish decoration of his castles, gardens

and palaces, the use of gold leaf for sliding screens and the ostentation of his costume spoke of a Renaissance prince, and above all there was Hideyoshi's passion for the tea ceremony. In his hands this exquisite practice that encapsulated all that was subtle and unworldly in Japanese culture became a tool both of self-expression and of political diplomacy. The tea ceremony Hideyoshi held for the emperor of Japan in a gold-plated tea room was the height of flamboyance, but this was the exception. Otherwise through tea ceremonies Hideyoshi communed with nature and with his rivals. Alliances were made and broken in Hideyoshi's mind while his hands fondled a priceless tea bowl, the utensil that was the key to the aesthetic performance and was, as often as not, made in Korea.

The Japanese sword, or katana, one of the decisive weapons possessed by the invading forces, and used to its most noticeable effect at the battle of Pyŏkje in 1593.

One result of his extensive military operations in Japan was that the army which Hideyoshi was able to commit to the conquest of distant lands was highly trained, vastly experienced, and composed of virtually professional soldiers. Both samurai and foot soldiers wore stout iron armour and helmets, and all ranks were armed with the formidable and legendary Japanese sword. The samurai carried spears as their primary weapon, while the foot soldiers were divided into corps of archers, spearmen and arquebusiers, the latter weapon providing the biggest difference in weapon type from the Korean experience. The Japanese troops were reliable and highly disciplined, and controlled on the battlefield by flags and drums. Above them was a recognised and trusted chain of command that led up to Toyotomi Hideyoshi, the master of siegecraft, logistics and large-scale troop movement, who aroused a fanatical loyalty and commitment in his men.

THE JAPANESE PIRATES

The second Korean misunderstanding about Japan, that an invasion could be easily repulsed, was based on the argument that any Japanese action would be no more than an extension of the pirate raids which Korea had successfully resisted in the past. There was good reason for such optimism, because Korea possessed a navy that was technologically advanced and strategically superior to Japan's own seaborne capacity. It had served them well in the past against Japanese incursions, and would surely do so again.

The Koreans called the Japanese pirates waegu, which was rendered into Japanese as wakō, the 'brigands from the country of Wa'.[2] During the thirteenth century the main Japanese pirates' nest had been in the north-west of Hizen province in Kyushu. They were known as the Matsuura-tō, from their location, and three hundred years later one of their descendants, Matsuura Shigenobu, his family now both legitimated and ennobled, was to become one of the spearheads of the Japanese invasion of Korea. Back in 1227 some exemplary beheading and the subsequent Mongol invasions of Japan gave Korea a century of respite from the Matsuura-tō, until the confusion of the Nanbokuchō Wars between rival emperors in the fourteenth century gave free rein to the wakō to start again. During the ten years between 1376 and 1385 there were 174 recorded wakō raids on Korea. Some of these expeditions amounted to miniature Japanese invasions of Korea, with as many as 3,000 wakō penetrating far from the coast, ravaging Kaesŏng, the Koryŏ capital, and even pillaging as far north as P'yŏngyang. In addition to looting property the wakō became slave traders, taking the well-established Korean tradition of slave-owning to its logical conclusion by shipping their captives back to Japan.

On several occasions the Korean navy hit back. In 1380 over 500 Japanese ships were set ablaze at the mouth of the Kŭm river, while three years later Admiral Chŏng Chi, in command of 47 ships, chased away more than 100 Japanese ships with gunfire. In 1389 a successful raid was carried out against the pirates based on the Japanese island of Tsushima, but the most important influence against the wakō was political, because in 1392, the same year in which the Chosŏn dynasty was founded, Japan acquired a new Shogun. His name was Ashikaga Yoshimitsu, and in addition to the achievements for which he is best known – the reconciliation between the rival Southern and Northern Courts and the building of the Kinkakuji or Golden Pavilion in Kyoto – Yoshimitsu accepted from the Ming emperor the title of 'King of Japan'. Yoshimitsu thereby formally assumed the status of subject of the Ming, and restored a situation that the Chinese reckoned to have existed first during the Han dynasty until being grievously sundered by acts of piracy and war. The benefit to Yoshimitsu and to Japan was trade, which was henceforth to be carried out under the tally system which legitimated voyages that, in the eyes of the Ming at any rate, brought 'tribute' to the court of the Son of Heaven.[3]

By the time of Ashikaga Yoshimitsu's accession the haughty wakō had already extended their activities to China, so the newly licensed trade agreements with the Ming provided the stability that both governments needed to deal with piracy. In a dramatic incident in 1419 a large wakō fleet was ambushed off Liaodong and perhaps a thousand Japanese pirates were relieved of their heads. At the same time diplomatic discussions took place between

Matsuura Shigenobu, daimyō of Hirado, whose family had a long connection with Korea through piratical activity. From a painted portrait scroll in the Matsuura Historical Museum, Hirado.

the Chosŏn court and the Ashikaga Shogun on ways to curb the wakō by more peaceful means. One result was a report from the Korean ambassador Pak Sŏ-saeng in 1429 recommending a direct approach to the particular Japanese daimyō who controlled the territories where the pirates lurked. After all, as another ambassador reported in a curiously generous memorandum in 1444, these people lived in a barren land that constantly threatened them with starvation, so piracy was only natural to them.

Among the devices designed to win the hearts and minds of those who had influence over the wakō was the granting to cooperative daimyō of official titles, accompanied by appropriate stipends, and the issue of copper seals, possession of which had the similar effect of legitimating trade that was enjoyed on a larger scale by the Shogun through the tribute system. Not surprisingly, the family who benefited most from these arrangements were the Sō, whose territories lay closest to Korea. They were based on Tsushima, an island only thirty miles from the Korean shore yet 150 miles from the Japanese mainland. Tsushima had been the first place to be attacked during the Mongol invasions in 1274 and 1281, an action in which the Sō's ancestors had participated most heroically. The island was also a pirates' lair, but in response to entreaties from the Chosŏn court the daimyō of Tsushima concluded the so-called Kakitsu Treaty with Korea in 1443. Not only were the Sō allowed to sponsor 50 vessels a year for the Korea trade, they were also given the responsibility of overseeing every Japanese ship that went to Korea, a checkpoint system that proved to be highly lucrative for them. In 1461 Sō Shigetomo asked for, and received, the investiture by the Korean court of the title of governor of Tsushima, an honour that further served to increase the Sō's own feelings of self-importance, and helped to persuade the Koreans that Tsushima was actually part of their country. The devastating roles that future members of the Sō were to play in Korea could then hardly be guessed at.

As a result of these diplomatic efforts piratical activities diminished and trading links between Japan and Korea developed in ways that, on the surface, promised nothing but peaceful relations, but had within them seeds of conflict every bit as threatening as a violent wakō raid. The most important development was the establishment of Japanese trading posts within Korea itself. By the end of the fifteenth century Japanese communities were flourishing in the three ports (samp'o) located in present-day Pusan, Chinhae and Ulsan, where they were officially permitted to reside. Their populations grew rapidly, and a census of 1494 revealed, to the concern of the Chosŏn court, that these trading posts now contained nine times the number of Japanese households than had originally been allowed. Exempt from Korean taxes, the Japanese residents traded, farmed, fished and worshipped with great enthusiasm and energy, making themselves thoroughly at home and very rich.

So successful were these Japanese settlements that they began to pose a major economic threat to Korea's own trade, but it was only when the pirate heritage of their inhabitants began to show through that the Korean authorities were forced to crack down. Attacks on Korean ships, arson, and a raid on Kadŏk island marred the first decade of the sixteenth century, and by 1510 such conduct could no longer be officially ignored. Amid threats of reprisals against this outrageous Japanese behaviour the Korean government contacted the Sō daimyō, to whom many of the Japanese residents paid the only taxes demanded from them, and ordered him to bring an end to the illegal activities of the settlers, or else all the Japanese residents of the Three Ports beyond the official maximum would be expelled.

The Japanese reaction was an uprising disguised as a spontaneous riot during which the Korean magistrates' offices in Chinhae and Pusan were seized. Meanwhile an army sent from Sō, who was a far from disinterested observer of the scene, did nothing to quell the riot and attacked Kŏje island instead. The hinterland of the Three Ports was then ravaged like a wakō raid of old, after which the Japanese combined their forces in Chinhae with the intention of compelling the Korean government to back down. Instead the Korean army attacked them. Although cumbersome to organise because of difficulties in moving men from the garrison fortresses to the ports, the chin'gwan defence system that depended upon local responsibility served its purpose, and the Japanese insurgents were defeated with a loss of 295 heads. The Japanese trading posts were sacked, and the survivors fled to Tsushima.

It says something about the great service that the Sō had previously provided to Korea that relations with the island of Tsushima were restored within two years of this alarming incident. The Sō, unsurprisingly, had their wings clipped, with the number of licensed ships reduced and Japanese settlement restricted to Chinhae, although Pusan was restored as a treaty port in 1521. Frustrated in their trade, some other Japanese, although not the Sō, resumed their piratical activities, which actually helped the Sō's cause by reminding the Koreans how much they needed them as policemen of the seas.

Korea was also granted a temporary respite from piracy for a different reason, because the wakō had begun to turn their attentions towards China once again, with 467 incidents being recorded for the 1550s alone. By this time,

The area round present-day Chinhae as shown on a Korean map from the time when it was one of the 'Three Ports' in which Japanese resided and traded. The square at the top is the walled town of Ungch'ŏn. The rectangles indicate Buddhist monasteries.

however, there were as many Chinese pirates involved in the raids as there were Japanese and, like their fourteenth-century predecessors, slaves formed part of the booty. A new wave of piratical activity came to Korea in 1555 when a massive raid was launched against the coast of Chŏlla by 70 ships from the Gotō archipelago and from the Matsuura area. This action, the last of the large-scale wakō incursions, proved almost to be a dress rehearsal for the Japanese invasion of Korea. On the one side could be seen the collapse of Korean resistance. Left waiting for their commander to arrive from Seoul, the Korean troops gave in as the Japanese advanced, and by the time the general arrived he had no army to lead, just runaway soldiers hiding in the forests and no one left in reserve. On the Japanese side there was a more ironic precedent, because the sons of these same pirate chiefs would be back in Korean waters in less than half a century, pirates no longer, but transformed into the loyal and legitimate navies of the Japanese daimyō, in whose service they would provide the transport, the warships and some of the fiercest fighters for the greatest wakō raid of all: Hideyoshi's invasion of Korea.

JAPAN'S PREPARATIONS FOR WAR

Hideyoshi's desire to extend his domestic conquests overseas was no spur of the moment decision, but an idea that had been growing in his mind while his military strength was developing to a level that made such a plan feasible. The first expression of Hideyoshi's intention to extend his conquests to Korea and China is sometimes dated as early as 1577, though this is on the basis of an anecdote of doubtful provenance. At the time Hideyoshi was merely a subordinate general subduing the Mōri daimyō on behalf of his master Oda Nobunaga, so to request permission to extend his conquests overseas was somewhat presumptive. The anecdote is recorded as something of a jest, which is how Nobunaga apparently received it, and if it did happen it certainly does not seem to have upset the very strong relationship of trust that existed between the two men. In fact the earliest reliable statement of such an intent comes not from Hideyoshi but from Nobunaga himself, who was slowly conquering Japan and expressed an aim to subdue China too. This was shortly before he was murdered, in 1582.

By 1585 Hideyoshi, whose ancestry barred him from assuming the title of Shogun, had become Kampaku (Regent) and acquired the family name of Toyotomi, and as his internal campaigns moved slowly towards their intended goal we read a number of authentic references to the grand design that would succeed them. When Father Gaspar Coelho, the Vice-Principal of the Jesuit mission in Japan, was received by Hideyoshi in 1585, the latter disclosed to him his plans for overseas expansion, and asked for two Portuguese ships to be made available, a request that was politely refused. Two years later, while setting off on the Kyushu campaign, Hideyoshi told his companions of his intention to 'slash his way' into Korea, China and the lands beyond.

In 1588 Hideyoshi enacted the first of two ordinances that were to have an indirect influence on the conduct of the war. This was the famous 'Sword Hunt', by which all weapons were to be confiscated from the peasantry and placed in the hands of the daimyō and their increasingly professional armies. By this act the means of making war was forcibly removed from anyone of whom Hideyoshi did not approve, because the Sword Hunt was much more than a search of farmers' premises. Minor daimyō whose loyalty was suspect, religious institutions who had the capacity for armed rebellion and recalcitrant village headmen were all purged in an operation that has parallels with Henry VIII's Dissolution of the Monasteries. The victims were told that the swords, spears and guns thus collected would not be wasted, but would be melted down to make nails for the enormous image of The Buddha that Hideyoshi was erecting in Kyoto. The nation would therefore benefit from the operation in two ways. It would be spiritually blessed, and would be freed from the curses of war and rebellion which had caused such disruption and suffering in the past.

It is more than likely that the majority of the weapons seized were not actually destroyed but stored ready for future campaigns, but less well known was another edict issued on the same day as the Sword Hunt. It was aimed not at the tillers of land but at those who fished the sea, particularly those whose catches were other than fish. In their case the local representatives of the daimyō were not specifically looking for weapons (though this is implied) but sought instead to obtain written oaths that no seafarer should engage in piracy. If any daimyō should fail to comply with the order and allow pirates to stay and practise their craft, then his fief would be confiscated. By this order the long and dishonourable Japanese wakō tradition came to an abrupt yet peaceful end.

The Separation Edict which followed in 1591 did not explicitly mention seafarers, but its intentions towards them were no less clear for that. The peasants had now been disarmed, and there was to be a total separation between the military function and the productive (i.e. agricultural) function:

If there should be living among you any men formerly in military service who have taken up the life of a peasant since the seventh month of last year, with the end of the campaign in the Mutsu region, you are hereby authorised to take them under surveillance and expel them . . .

. . . if any peasant abandons his fields . . . not only should he be punished but the entire village should be brought to justice with him. Anyone who is not employed either in military service or in cultivating land shall likewise be investigated by the local authorities and expelled. [4]

The Separation Edict therefore defined the distinction between samurai and farmer that was to continue throughout the Tokugawa Period. It also allowed the potential for a reign of terror to be inflicted upon any local population who did not comply with Hideyoshi's wishes, a situation that was to apply almost immediately with the forced recruitment of peasants and fishermen for the forthcoming Korean campaign. Yet the Separation Edict had changed the nature of such recruitment for ever. No longer could a peasant like Hideyoshi enlist as a foot soldier and rise to be a general. From now on a peasant who was forced (or even volunteered) to do his duty would not carry out that function with a sword or gun in his hand, but with a cripplingly heavy pack on his back. To the leader of a modern army such as Hideyoshi such a restriction on military manpower was a matter of no concern. He had troops in easy sufficiency and, because of the increased sophistication associated with weaponry, an untrained and undrilled peasant handed an arquebus or a long-shafted spear would be a liability rather than an asset. In a similar way the seafarers who had seen their piratical livelihood replaced by fishing and manning ferryboats would do their duty in China only as boatmen and crew members. This rigid separation between soldiers and labourers was to become a noticeable feature of the Korean campaign.

THE KOREAN ROAD TO CHINA

With the fall of Kunoe castle to Hideyoshi's general Gamō Ujisato in 1591 the campaigns of the domestic arena were complete, and plans for an overseas expedition could begin in earnest. The purely military preparations will be described in the chapter which follows, but by then Hideyoshi's representatives had already been engaged in long and ultimately fruitless negotiations with the Korean government seeking to enlist that country's help in the grand design. As noted earlier, Hideyoshi's goal was the conquest of China, not Korea, and the role that Korea might play in the affair was regarded as being subject to negotiation.

Hideyoshi's desire was that the Chosŏn court should pay him homage, thereby opening the road to China for his armies. Such a bloodless Korean submission was not, however, a sudden expression of megalomania on Hideyoshi's part, but the logical extension of a sound policy that had borne fruit on many occasions during his Japanese campaigns. The process had worked like this. The targeted daimyō was invited to pay homage to Hideyoshi. Should he refuse, there was war. When he accepted, either prior to his crushing defeat or afterwards, the daimyō was likely to see himself re-invested in his territories in return for a pledge of loyalty. As noted earlier, Hideyoshi was a generous victor, so that mass acts of suicide or battles to the death were rare events during his campaigns. Date Masamune, the powerful daimyō of northern Japan, had submitted in this way without firing a shot. As Korea was the key to a successful invasion of Ming China a similar expression of submission followed by cooperation had to be assured before the Japanese armies could march through unmolested.

It was also perfectly logical that the incumbent daimyō of Tsushima, Sō Yoshinori, who in Hideyoshi's view had some vague influence over Korea, should be the agent of a familiar and hitherto successful procedure. Sō therefore became Hideyoshi's middleman, partly because of his geographical location and the family's long-established links with Korea, but also for another extraordinary reason. Hideyoshi's stupendous ignorance of the countries he was planning to invade extended to the more remote areas of Japan as well, and included the strange belief, based no doubt on a misinterpretation of the privileged situation that the Sō had enjoyed for a century, that Korea was in some way subject to Tsushima. Sō would thereby have the ability to command the Korean monarch to come to Japan and offer homage.

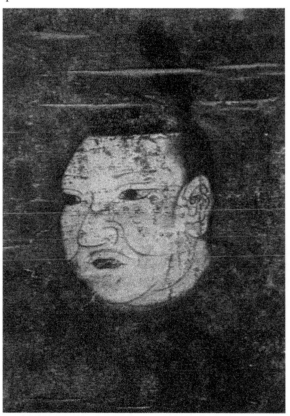

Hideyoshi's order to Sō Yoshinori in 1587 to deliver an ultimatum to the Chosŏn king to submit or be conquered caused the Sō family great apprehension. The Sō had most to lose from the disruption of trade that a war with Korea would bring, even if it could be argued that they also had most to gain from the large-scale wakō-like pillage that would surely come in its wake. But a more important factor for them was that the Sō did not share Hideyoshi's delusions about the probable Korean response. They saw instead the wider picture of the traditional amity between China and Korea, and were also convinced that Korea would reject any hint that she should accept vassalage to Japan. The friendly relations currently enjoyed between Chosŏn and Ming also made it most unlikely that Korea would cooperate in any way with a Japanese attempt to invade China. That there was Confucian filial respect on Korea's part towards its 'parent' China, there can be no doubt, even if this may have been tinged with a little fear, but this would be

Sō Yoshitomo, daimyō of Tsushima, who played an important diplomatic role prior to the invasion and was first to land when the attack finally happened, from a portrait scroll in the Historical Museum on Tsushima.

counterbalanced by a confidence that, should Korea be attacked, Ming China would honour its 'child', and would certainly come to its assistance. In short, there was not the slightest possibility that Korea would agree to support Hideyoshi's plans in any form.

By contrast, the mere existence of Hideyoshi's aggressive intentions towards China clearly showed that the filial piety with which Korea idealised the Ming did not hold sway in the Japanese mind. Hideyoshi was determined to continue into the Asiatic mainland the process that was steadily coming to fruition in northern Japan. The Sō therefore decided to play for time, and gained two years by obfuscation around the safety of the sea passage, until by 1589 a frustrated Hideyoshi again commanded the Sō to produce results, adding to this letter an ominous warning about an immediate invasion of Korea should the assurance of support not be forthcoming.

It was therefore with a heavy heart that Sō Yoshitomo (whose name can also be read as Yoshitoshi), and who had by now succeeded his father, decided to go to Korea in person along with a Buddhist monk named Gensō as his chief negotiator. The Korean minister Yu Sŏng-nyong took part in the subsequent talks, and recorded his impressions in *Chingbirok*. 'Yoshitomo was young and fierce,' he wrote of his opposite number, 'and the other Japanese feared him. Prostrating themselves, they crawled before him, not daring to gaze upwards.'[5]

Sō, however, disguised from the Koreans the true nature of the task with which Hideyoshi had entrusted him, claiming that his visit was merely to improve good relations between the two countries. It is quite clear that the Koreans did not believe him, and suspected that he was on a spying mission. The Korean government therefore proposed a test of Japan's sincerity. A few years previously there had been a minor wakō raid on Sonchuk island off the Chŏlla coast. A Korean pirate called Sal Pae-dong had returned to Japan with the wakō and had since acted as guide for more raids. The return of Sal Pae-dong and his fellow renegades would be an ample expression of Japan's good faith. It is doubtful whether the Koreans expected the Japanese to comply, yet within ten days the pirate band were delivered to Korea and shortened by the length of their heads. Apart from anything else, the speed of the operation showed that the Japanese authorities knew exactly where the pirates were and cared little for them.

The Korean bluff having been called, Yu Sŏng-nyŏng was given the difficult task of compiling a reply to Hideyoshi. The gracious and amicable request for envoys to be sent to Japan from the King of Korea (as Sō had conveniently disguised the call for homage) seemed innocuous enough. To accept the invitation at face value would also enable the Korean ambassadors to do some intelligence gathering of their own, so King Sŏnjo invested the first Korean

envoys to Japan for many years. The factional rivalry at Court, of course, necessitated the appointment of one ambassador from the dominant Westerners (Hwang Yun-gil), and a deputy from the Eastern faction (Kim Sŏng-il), together with a secretary called Hŏ Sŏng.[6]

As the Embassy made ready to leave during the third lunar month of 1590 there was a ceremonial exchange of gifts. Such rituals were part and parcel of the ambassadorial life, but in a strangely symbolic way one of the presents from Japan to Korea silently conveyed the gist of the undeclared and threatening message with which Sō had been entrusted. The gift was a gun, a state of the art Japanese arquebus of a design originally copied and then improved from the Portuguese originals brought to Japan in 1543. At that time the Japanese smiths had been speedily set to work to mass produce such weapons for the daimyō's armies, and in 1575 3,000 arquebuses had won the battle of Nagashino for Oda Nobunaga, a pivotal event in Japanese history which Toyotomi Hideyoshi had witnessed with his own eyes.

The Japanese gift was the first arquebus to be seen in Korea, but their reaction to the weapon was very different from the enthusiasm showed by the Japanese in 1543. Complacent perhaps because of the quality of their cannon, which surpassed Japanese specimens, the arquebus was inspected, admired, sent off to the royal arsenal and forgotten about. It was a missed opportunity that was to cost Korea dearly. In contrast to their fine cannon, Korean personal firearms only existed in the form of short-barrelled and inefficient sŭngja, Chinese-style hand guns that were almost identical to the

The Japanese arquebus was the other decisive weapon of the invaders. The design was far superior to the Chinese-style hand guns used by the Korean army. These examples are in Himeji castle.

ones the Japanese had instantly abandoned for the European arquebus half a century earlier. To add further irony, arquebuses had first been used in anger by the Japanese during wakō raids on China in 1548. During the discussions only the lone voice of Yu Sŏng-nyong argued that the new acquisition should provide a prototype for their mass production for the Korean army. Once again, as in his plans for castle repair, Yu was ignored, and Korea was doomed to face devastating Japanese firepower with little of their own with which to reply.

So the embassy departed, and first arrived on Japanese territory on the island of Tsushima. Here the deputy envoy Kim Sŏng-il began to test the limits of Korean authority on that island, and also tried to assert himself at the expense of his factional rival. Sō Yoshitomo had arranged a banquet, and arrived in a palanquin. Kim Sŏng-il appeared to be very insulted by this, and claimed that as Tsushima was a vassal state of Korea, Sō should have followed Korean court etiquette and alighted from his palanquin outside the gate, rather than inside it. Not wishing to upset his guests, Sō blamed the palanquin bearers for the error and had them both beheaded on the spot. After this, wrote Yu Sŏng-nyong (who was dependent upon the proud Kim Sŏng'il for the information), the Japanese held the same Kim Sŏng-il 'in awe'. [7]

When the embassy finally arrived in Kyoto they were lodged in the Daitokuji temple and spent the next few months waiting for the opportunity to meet Hideyoshi, who was otherwise engaged with the protracted siege of Odawara and the destruction of the powerful Hōjō family. This operation, involving 200,000 soldiers in the largest troop movement ever seen in Japanese history, was a masterpiece of logistics, and must have convinced Hideyoshi that a similar operation could be carried out as smoothly in Korea.

Hideyoshi was informed of the presence in Japan of the envoys as he made his triumphal progress back to Kyoto. He was certainly never told that the Koreans had come to pay homage, but as that was his firm belief about the purpose behind the visit, then neither Sō nor anyone else dared let him think otherwise. Two more months passed before the Koreans were ushered into Hideyoshi's august presence. The fare was simple, and the resulting formalities were few. A letter was presented from the King of Korea containing bland felicities, and the usual gifts were exchanged. As later comments by Hideyoshi himself would confirm, the mere presence of the ambassadors had convinced him that the Koreans had come to do homage and had agreed to be the vanguard of his attack upon China, so there was not much to discuss with them.

Needless to say, nothing of the sort had been intended by the ambassadors, who were puzzled by the lack of formality at the reception and also surprised by Hideyoshi's peasant-like appearance. 'Hideyoshi was short and common looking,' wrote Yu Sŏng-nyong following Kim Sŏng-il's return, 'the colour of his face was dark black, and nothing marked him as unusual except that they say if he opened his eyes slightly, his eyeballs gleamed and a ray of light shone upon people.' After an exchange of pleasantries the meeting degenerated into farce. Hideyoshi left the room, then returned dressed in simple clothes and carrying his infant son Tsurumatsu, who proceeded to urinate all over him. With that undiplomatic, yet somehow strangely appropriate comment, the historic embassy was concluded.

The puzzled Koreans were therefore left with nothing to take back to their King. In response to messages Hideyoshi claimed that there had been insufficient time to draft a reply to King Sŏnjo's letter, and suggested that the ambassadors should return without one. Not unnaturally, they refused, and waited twenty days at the port of Sakai before a letter was composed, but its tone was regarded as so insulting to the Korean King that it was sent back for redrafting.

The final version of the letter addressed to the King of Korea was the first overt statement of Hideyoshi's intentions to be set in writing for the information of his intended victims. He began by acknowledging his humble origins (which the ambassadors had already suspected), but claimed in effect that his mother was merely acting as an agent for something truly miraculous, because he was actually conceived 'when the wheel of the sun entered his mother's womb', a revelation revealed to her in a dream. As the sun illuminates the universe, so it was Hideyoshi's destiny to spread his fame throughout the world, and the speed of his success in Japan was proof of that. The letter continued:

> In this world human existence, however long it may be, has rarely attained a hundred years since ancient times. Why should I gloomily spend my life here? I shall invade the Great Ming, although it is a country far away and divided from ours by mountains and seas, and will have the customs and manners of our country adopted in the four hundred provinces, bestowing on the people the benevolent imperial government of our country for millions of years to come. This is the plan I have in mind.

The letter then moved on to the role of Korea in this great enterprise, and revealed the extent of Hideyoshi's erroneous beliefs about the purpose of the diplomatic mission and Korea's future part in the forthcoming war:

> That your country is the first to come and pay homage to our Court shows that whoever looks far into the future will have no sorrow, but I shall not forgive even distant countries and islands in the middle of the seas if they are late in coming.

> When I proceed to China, if you, as the head of your army, will join us, the ties between our neighbouring countries will be further strengthened. I have no other desire than to have the glory of my name known in the three countries.

> We have received the tribute according to the list. [8]

Anticipating what the Korean reaction would be to this bombshell, Sō sent his former colleague Gensō to Korea along with the Korean envoys to try to soften the impact by insisting that the word 'tribute', which referred to the exchange of diplomatic gifts, was a scribe's error, and that the homage referred to was that of Korea paying homage to the Ming, as Hideyoshi would himself later do. But no one was fooled, and of the military role intended for the Korean army, little could be done to contradict its implications, although the Japanese envoys suggested that Hideyoshi would actually be satisfied with the guarantee of a safe passage through Korea for his armies, or even (and here they were clutching at straws), that the paragraph was a clumsy metaphor for the act of smoothing a path for the resumption of friendly relations.

Yu Sŏng-nyong was present when the two ambassadors returned to Korea. According to his account Hwang Yun-gil, the senior ambassador from the Western Faction, reported frankly that 'the horrors of war were a certainty'. Unfortunately, the factional rivalry between him and his deputy Kim Sŏng-il led the latter to contradict his colleague's conclusions and warnings almost as a matter of course. For whatever personal political reasons, he interpreted Hideyoshi's letter in the same bland and reassuring tone that the Japanese envoys had suggested to them, and claimed that Korea had nothing to fear from Japan. The Eastern Faction, as represented by Kim Sŏng-il, was now in the ascendancy at Court. It therefore became the party of denial, and initially convinced the King that no special action need be taken. Yu Sŏng-nyong, however, was greatly concerned. Hideyoshi was clearly planning to send troops to China through Korea, so, at the very least, the Ming should be informed:

> If we conceal this and do not inform the Emperor, we will not be acting in accordance with our vows of loyalty. Indeed, if these robbers really plan to invade China, others may inform the Emperor. Then the Celestial Court will unjustly suspect that we have concealed this business because we are in accord with the Japanese. [9]

Yu was quite correct about China's likely conclusions when other reports of Japan's intentions began to reach the Ming before Korea had a chance to report for itself. Korea then hastily sent messages of its own, and any suspicions about Korean collusion were diplomatically quashed. By now King Sŏnjo was convinced that the Eastern 'doves' were wrong, and the Western 'hawks' were correct, and ordered a military inspection of Korea's three southern provinces. Kim Su was sent to Kyŏngsang, Yi Kwang went to Chŏlla and Yun Sŏn-gak was despatched to Ch'ungch'ŏng. It was at this point that the fortress repair programme, which caused such opposition from the local people, was proposed.

At the same time the Korean government sent a reply to Hideyoshi's letter via the monk Gensō. The missive was courteous, but stated bluntly that, in view of the long history of friendship between the two countries, to allow an army to pass through Korea to attack China was quite unthinkable. Gensō delivered the message to Sō Yoshitomo, who was so concerned about the effects of its contents on Hideyoshi that he prevented it from going any further than Tsushima, and made a personal last-ditch visit to Korea, arriving in Pusan in the summer of 1591. He urged the Koreans to mediate between Japan and China and, having done his best, waited on his ship for ten days for a more helpful reply that he could pass on – but none came.

For the next few months, and almost until the war's first shot was fired, Sō Yoshitomo shouldered the personal burden of believing that he was the only one who really understood the situation. Even at the last minute, when the invasion fleet dropped anchor to rest overnight in preparation for a dawn attack on Pusan, Sō landed and took a letter to the governor asking for that same free passage through Korea that had always been Japan's primary aim. With this final refusal the whole diplomatic farce came to an end. A huge military machine had been cranking into a motion that was now virtually unstoppable, and as successive orders to his generals over the past few months had made clear, Hideyoshi was little concerned whether the Koreans would cooperate or not. Hideyoshi was going to conquer China. That was a fact of history. In order to reach China the army had to go through Korea. That was a fact of geography. If the Koreans would spearhead the attack or guide his soldiers, then so be it. If they were willing only to guarantee free passage along their roads, then so be it. If they did neither they would be slaughtered, and so be it. In that case what had always been intended as a Sino-Japanese War would unfortunately have to begin with a Korean War.

chapter three

THE YEAR OF THE DRAGON

WHILE Sō's negotiations for a safe passage through Korea were continuing, Toyotomi Hideyoshi made plans for the attack on China that would be conveyed along its roads. To allow himself the time to take personal command of the venture he resigned from his post of Kampaku in 1591 and appointed his nephew Hidetsugu in his stead. Hideyoshi then took the title of Taikō, by which he was to be known for the rest of his life.

The campaign was to be the largest ever mounted in Japanese history up to that point. When the invasion began the expeditionary force totalled a quarter of a million men, a vast host that drained the military resources of the daimyō, as it was no doubt intended to. But long before a single soldier, horse or bag of beans had been loaded on to the transport fleet, the Kyushu lords had already had to supply men and materials for the construction of the massive invasion base which rose from the rice fields near present-day Karatsu in just over six months. Nagoya castle, completed in the early spring of 1592, the 'Year of the Dragon' according to the Chinese calendar, was an enormous fortress encircled by an inner and an outer bailey built in traditional Japanese style with cyclopean sloping stone walls and lavish decoration within. The daimyō built their own headquarters around it, transforming a remote peninsula with little strategic value into a huge garrison town and armed camp. While Nagoya was being built roads and bridges were constructed or repaired to allow easy communications between it and the rest of Japan. Vast quantities of gold and silver coins were minted to pay for it all, and enough rice was commandeered to feed almost half a million mouths.

THE MUSTER ROLL

The numbers of men who took part in the invasion are well documented, although there are small discrepancies between different sets of figures which are largely explained by the inclusion or omission of reserve corps from the

Opposite: Map of the first invasion in 1592, showing the initial advance from Pusan through Seoul and on to P'yŏngyang. Katō Kiyomasa's crossing of the peninsula towards Hamgyŏng province is also shown, along with the pacification process in Kangwon province conducted by the Fourth Division.

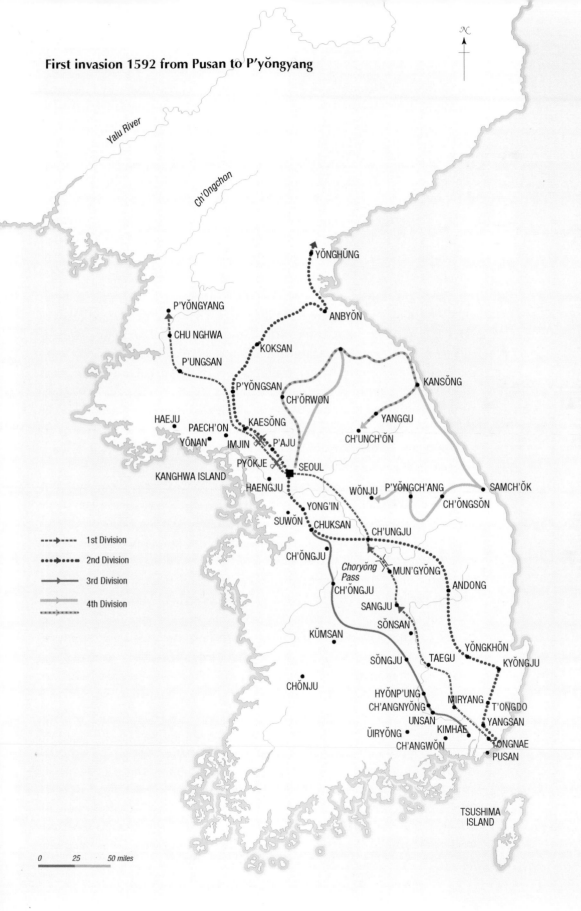

First invasion 1592 from Pusan to P'yŏngyang

Yalu River

Ch'Ongchon

YŎNGHŬNG

P'YŎNGYANG

CHU NGHWA

ANBYŎN

P'UNGSAN

KOKSAN

P'YŎNGSAN

KANSŎNG

CH'ŎRWON

HAEJU

YANGGU

PAECH'ON

KAESŎNG

P'AJU

YŎNAN

IMJIN

CH'UNCH'ŎN

PYŎKJE

SEOUL

KANGHWA ISLAND

HAENGJU

WŎNJU

P'YŎNGCH'ANG

SAMCH'ŎK

YONG'IN

CH'ŎNGSŎN

SUWŎN

CHUKSAN

CH'UNGJU

CH'ŎNGJU

Choryŏng
Pass

MUN'GYŎNG

ANDONG

CH'ŎNGJU

KŬMSAN

SANGJU

SŎNSAN

YŎNGKHŎN

SŎNGJU

TAEGU

KYŎNGJU

CHŎNJU

HYŎNP'UNG

MIRYANG

CH'ANGNYŎNG

T'ONGDO

UNSAN

YANGSAN

ŬIRYŎNG

KIMHAE

CH'ANGWŎN

TONGNAE

PUSAN

TSUSHIMA
ISLAND

- - -▶ 1st Division
••••▶ 2nd Division
——▶ 3rd Division
——▶ 4th Division

0   25   50 miles

various lists. The most reliable source, an order of battle sent by Hideyoshi to Mōri Terumoto dated 3m 13d, gives an overall structure of vanguard, main body, rearguard and reserves, and is set out in Appendix I. Hideyoshi's plans envisioned that a bridgehead would be established at Pusan by the First Division under Konishi Yukinaga, who was to be joined by the Second Division under Katō Kiyomasa for the drive north. The final vanguard unit, the Third Division under Kuroda Nagamasa, were to attack to the west of Pusan across the Naktong river. They were to be joined within a few days by the Fourth, Fifth, Sixth and Seventh Divisions totalling 84,700 men, while the Eighth and Ninth Divisions of 21,500 men were to be held in immediate reserve on the islands of Tsushima and Iki respectively.

The number of troops in the above nine divisions totalled approximately 158,800, all of whom – except for the Ninth Division, the Iki rearguard of 11,500 men – were moved forward to Tsushima as the jumping-off point. There was also a sizeable rearguard left in reserve in Japan, named in some accounts as the Tenth Division, while Nagoya castle was garrisoned by 27,000 troops under Hideyoshi's personal command, together with over 70,000 men supplied by the eastern daimyō who stayed in reserve in the castle town. Even those who did not expect to see their forces cross the seas suffered some disruption with the stationing of thousands more as the final rearguard near Kyoto. A whole nation was at war.

The overall figures for the army do not reveal the impact the mobilisation had on individual daimyō, and it is only when the figures are broken down that enormous discrepancies within the quota system are revealed. The first point to note is the wide variation in the supply of men between the daimyō of western and eastern Japan. In an interesting analysis the historian Nukii Masayuki divided the map of Japan into western and eastern daimyō at Kyoto, so that Wakasa, Ōmi, Iga and Ise are in the eastern half.[1] His figures showed that out of a total of 101 named daimyō on the map, 59% made the crossing to Korea while 41% did not. Fifty-three fiefs lie to the west of Kyoto and 48 to the east, and here there is the greatest difference. Out of the western daimyō 46 (87%) served in Korea while only seven (13%) did not, while for the eastern territories 14 (29%) served in Korea while 34 (71%) did not.

The percentages serving increase the further to the west one looks, and on Kyushu only one named daimyō out of 22, Terazawa Hidetaka (1563–1633), stayed in Japan. Terazawa held the important post of Governor of Nagasaki, but his exemption may also have been a compensation for the fact that his fief was Karatsu, a large part of which had just disappeared under the castle town of Nagoya! Yet even Terazawa missed only the initial invasion, because records note him being absent in Korea during 1596.[2] The proportion of men to be supplied against a daimyō's income was also greater in the west than in the east. Daimyō from Kyushu and Shikoku had to supply six men per 1,000 koku. The Chūgoku (western Honshu) lords supplied five per 1,000 while the quota for some fiefs was as little as two per 1,000 koku.[3]

It was obviously easier for a daimyō based nearer to Nagoya to supply troops than for one from the far north of Japan, but there were other considerations, some political, others geographical. A number of the Kyushu lords were not natives of the island but had been granted fiefs on its rich agricultural soil because Hideyoshi knew they were loyal soldiers and had depended upon them in the past. Both his vanguard leaders fell into this category. Katō Kiyomasa (1562–1611) hailed from Hideyoshi's home village in Owari and had received the fief of Kumamoto in 1585 following the disgrace of Sasa Narimasa, while Konishi Yukinaga (?–1600) was the son of a medicine dealer from Sakai, and had been given the fief of southern Higo following the Kyushu campaign in 1587.

In vivid contrast the Shimazu of Satsuma, who had lived in Kyushu for centuries, had little choice but to respond to Hideyoshi's call to arms as it was Hideyoshi who had defeated them in 1587 and then generously allowed them to retain their ancestral lands. Other ancient Kyushu daimyō such as Nabeshima of Saga and Matsuura of Hirado were particularly valuable because of the long association, legitimate or otherwise, that they had with Korea, and the newcomer Katō Kiyomasa had noted without a touch of irony that 'a great many of the people of the Hizen coast had been over on bahan (i.e. wakō) business and are quite used and attached to China'.[4]   Into this category fell Sō Yoshitomo of Tsushima, who had tried so hard to avoid a war with Korea and would be the first to land on Korean soil when the invasion began. For historical reasons Kyushu also had the greatest concentration of Christian daimyō, and the First Division included the 'Kirishitan' contingents of Konishi, Sō, Ōmura and Arima, a fact which, as Elisonas notes wryly, gave the undertaking 'the air of a bizarre crusade'.[5]

Kyushu, therefore, shouldered the burden of invading its near neighbour, and when we break the figures down even further the fine structure of these daimyō's armies is revealed. Gotō Sumiharu (?–1595), who held the fief of Fukue on the Gotō archipelago, had an assessed income of 140,000 koku, which would require him to supply 840 men for the Korean campaign. Family records show that he actually led only 705, the majority of whom were not fighting samurai, as illustrated in Table 1.[6]

Several points may be noted from the Gotō figures. First, as the samurai attendants, who acted as grooms and weapon carriers, would be armed warriors, a strict distinction may be made between Gotō's 220 fighting men and his 485 noncombatants. The labourers and boatmen were the peasants and former pirates (for which the Gotō islands had been notorious) who had

Table 1: Troops supplied by Gotō Sumiharu in 1592

TROOP TYPE	MEN	HORSES
Fighting Troops		
Samurai-taishō (general)	1	1
Bugyō (commissioners) for army, flags, supplies, bows and long spears	5	5
Messengers	3	3
Inspectors	2	2
Mounted samurai	11	11
Foot samurai	40	
Samurai's attendants	38	
Ahigaru	120	
SUB TOTAL	220	
Supportive Functions		
Priests, doctors, secretaries	5	5
Labourers	280	
Boatmen	200	
TOTAL	485	
GRAND TOTAL	705	27

been disarmed by the Sword Hunt of 1587 and classified by the Separation Edict of 1591. If such a pattern was common throughout the other daimyō then it is evident that about 68% of a typical daimyō's manpower quota might be filled by labourers and transport staff rather than pure combat troops. It is also interesting to note that of the 32% of the Gotō force who were fighting men, only 27 out of the 220 (12%) were mounted samurai. This figure probably reflects the decline in mounted fighting that had been apparent since the battle of Nagashino, and is unlikely to indicate any particular decision relating to the Korean campaign.

Another daimyō whose military service quota has been preserved in a written record is Shimazu Yoshihiro (1535–1619) of Satsuma, who had been ordered by Hideyoshi to take over the domain from his brother Yoshihisa in 1587. The number of men Yoshihiro took to Korea in 1592 as part of the Fourth Division is recorded in the main muster rolls as 10,000. The family records state that the number to be supplied was 15,000, but as the Shimazu were in straitened circumstances following their recent defeat they may simply have been unable to make up the full number. The records show an army consisting of 600 samurai (of whom as many as possible were required to supply horses) and 3,600 ashigaru, the latter being divided into 1,500 arquebusiers, 1,500 archers, 300 spearmen (of which 200 are specified as nagaeyari, the long spears akin to European pikes) and 300 flag bearers. Even on the basis of the 10,000 he is believed to have actually supplied, these numbers account for only 36% of the force, implying that the remaining 64% were labourers, a figure very similar to the data for Gotō Sumiharu.[7]

As a later chapter will illustrate, materials relating the second invasion of 1597 clearly show that the impressed labourers went unwillingly to Korea and were treated cruelly when they arrived, and there is evidence that some peasants absconded in 1592 instead of joining a daimyō's forces. A similar opposition to Hideyoshi's intentions may also have been considered at a higher social level, but by and large the daimyō kept their feelings to themselves and followed him as loyally as they had always done. Some may have grumbled about the drain on their resources of building Nagoya and of their fears on being sent abroad, for which the promise of lands in China was but a vague and distant recompense, but only one open mutiny is known to have occurred. This was the Umekita rebellion, which involved 2,000 troops and happened in Satsuma when Shimazu Yoshihiro was assembling his army. The affair is mentioned in the family records of the Iriki family of Satsuma, who were retainers of the Shimazu. A certain Iriki-in Shigetoki was unwell and sent a relative called Tōgō Shigekage to serve in his stead. The account continues:

> At that time, one Umekita Kunikane, starting after Lord Yoshihiro for Korea, moored ships at Hirado in Hizen, and perhaps fearing punishment for his tardiness, suddenly changed his mind and began a rebellion . . . Unexpectedly (Tōgō) Shigekage also followed Umekita's forces and invaded Higo . . . (Shimazu) Yoshihisa, who was at Nagoya, hearing this event at once reported it; and receiving a strict command, went down to the province with Hosokawa Yūsai and punished the Umekita party. Kunikane was defeated and died at Sashiki in Higo province, and Shigekage and his seventy-five men were killed at several places. Iriki-in Shigetoki, obeying a strict order, killed Shigekage's father and relatives of the former's followers.[8]

The execution of Tōgō Shigekage's innocent father was no doubt intended as a warning to anyone else who dared to disobey the orders of a daimyō. To drive home the point to a wider audience than would have witnessed this act in a small corner of Satsuma province, the wife of the ringleader Umekita Kunikane was taken into the garden of Nagoya castle and burned to death in front of the assembled invasion leaders. There was no further trouble after this.

With all dissent crushed, with Nagoya castle finished and with the greatest army Japan had ever seen equipped and assembled, their supreme commander, the Taikō Toyotomi Hideyoshi, made a stately progress from Kyoto to the

Shimazu Yoshihiro, who provided the largest contingent in the Fourth Division of the invading army, shown in aggressive mood before the battle of Sach'ŏn in 1598. His mon (badge) appears on his breastplate and on the maku (field curtains). (ETK detail)

military boom town that was to provide the realisation of his greatest dream in that auspicious Year of the Dragon. Eyewitness accounts record the splendour of his retinue and the magnificence of the armour, weaponry and accoutrements of those who followed in his train. Hideyoshi himself was dressed in full yoroi-style armour with a long sword slung from his belt and a somewhat anachronistic bow held in his left hand. His mounted bodyguard wore the finest of costumes, and rode horses that sported their own suits of armour. Behind them were paraded 66 long banners, one for each of the Japanese provinces now unified for the first time in a century under Hideyoshi's rule, and each bearing Hideyoshi's mon (badge) of a paulownia flower, a motif originally bestowed upon the Ashikaga Shoguns by the Emperor of Japan. His followers did their best to emulate their master's high standards of flamboyance, and an enthusiastic description comes from the brush of a retainer of Date Masamune from distant Sendai, who paints a vivid picture of 'Date's dandies'. Even the lowly foot soldiers of Date's bodyguard wore golden helmets with three-foot-high crowns shaped like witches' hats, a contingent made all the more splendid by the knowledge that their elaborate equipment was not intended to be used in combat but would merely adorn the reserve garrison at Nagoya for almost the entire war.[9]

In Nagoya castle Hideyoshi entertained the waiting daimyō with tea ceremonies and Noh performances as he put the finishing touches to his master plan, and the chronicles of the Matsuura family record his final review of the troops immediately before the armada set sail from Nagoya to make their attack preparations on the island of Tsushima:

Toyotomi Hideyoshi watches the departure of his fleet. Hideyoshi is seated on a camp stool. His 'thousand gourd' standard appears to his right, while another samurai holds a banner bearing the paulownia badge. The mon on the sails of the ships identify the commanders. (ETK)

At noon that day His Highness the Taikō came to the harbour. He raised his golden fan and urged his followers on. A bell was rung as a signal from the boat of the Commanding General (Ukita) Hideie, and at that moment Konishi Yukinaga's and Katō Kiyomasa's ships sprang forward like two outstretched hands.[10]

As a later chapter will illustrate, the rivalry between Konishi and Katō made the analogy with outstretched arms somewhat optimistic, but the enthusiastic chronicler then goes on to invoke the mystical precedent of Empress Jingū that was to underwrite the whole operation:

Hōin (Matsuura Shigenobu) wore an eboshi [cap] and robe over his armour and held up a heihaku [Shintō offering made of paper] and with the banners on his ship turned to face in the direction of the Iwashimizu (Hachiman Shrine), he made obeisance three times, fired off his cannons simultaneously and raised a war cry three times. A messenger came from the Taikō and enquired about the reason for it. It was reported back, 'The precedent is the occasion in ancient times when the Empress Jingū conquered the Three Kingdoms, and on Shigenobu's ship Hachiman is worshipped and enshrined.' The Taikō heard this and was much pleased, and afterwards graciously praised him.[11]

Thus thrice blessed by his commander in chief, by the god of war, and by history itself, this descendant of the wakō pirates sailed off to follow in his ancestors' footsteps.

BLITZKRIEG IN KOREA

The First Division, who were destined to share the greatest samurai honour of being the first into battle, were a hardened and experienced mixture of Kyushu Christians, ex-pirates and Hideyoshi loyalists. Leading them was Konishi Yukinaga, the daimyō of southern Higo. His unfortunate later life, which involved choosing the wrong side before Sekigahara and being executed after it, has robbed posterity of any portrait of him or any mementoes of his earlier and glorious career. It had been his political talents rather than his military skills that had first brought Konishi to Hideyoshi's attention, when he had been employed by his master Ukita Naoie in negotiating the bloodless surrender of the Ukita domains to Hideyoshi. Loyal service during the Kyushu campaign earned him the fief of Uto in Higo province, where the site of his castle, a grassy mound topped by a modern statue, provides his only memorial, although the Uto tower which now graces his rival's castle at Kumamoto is said to have once been Konishi's castle keep. He was baptised in 1583, and is known in the Jesuit accounts as Dom Agostinho (Augustin).

Konishi's 7,000 men made up the largest unit in the First Division, closely followed by the 5,000 men under Sō Yoshitomo, whose knowledge of Korea and its people was unequalled by anyone in Japan. He too was a Christian daimyō, having been baptised as Dario, and was married to Konishi Yukinaga's daughter. Matsuura Shigenobu (1549–1614), who brought 3,000 men, was not a Christian but was tolerant of its presence in his domain of Hirado island, and there were many Christians in his ranks. The Matsuura, whose ancestors had been among Japan's first and most feared pirates, had actively courted the European trade that Christianity promised, and his father Takanobu had tried to persuade the Portuguese to make Hirado their main port, a venture in which he was ultimately unsuccessful when Nagasaki was ceded to the Jesuits by

Konishi Yukinaga, the Commander of the First Division, as depicted on his statue on the site of his castle at Uto, Kumamoto Prefecture. Yukinaga's unfortunate fate following the battle of Sekigahara in 1600 has robbed posterity of any contemporary likeness of him.

Ōmura Sumitada in 1580. In 1592 the son of Sumitada, Ōmura Yoshiaki (1568–1615), who had been baptised as Sanche, was to be found fighting beside the Matsuura in the First Division with 1,000 men, along with Arima Harunobu (Dom Protásio) with 2,000 men, and Gotō Sumiharu from Fukue in the island chain that bore his surname, whose 700-strong army was analysed above.

The First Division left Tsushima at 8.00 a.m. on the 12th day of the 4th lunar month of Bunroku I, which was 23 May 1592 on the Gregorian calendar, and were bowled across the straits of Tsushima by a strong following wind that deposited them safely and unmolested off Pusan at 5.00 p.m. on the same day. The fleet then dropped anchor off Chŏryŏng island where they waited in readiness for a dawn attack. Sō Yoshitomo alone disembarked with his final plea for a safe conduct through Korea. With the Koreans' final rejection he returned to his ship to await the morning and the assault on Pusan.

The port of Pusan was, and still is, Korea's southern gateway. It lies on a huge natural harbour in a bay dotted with islands, defended to the west by the Naktong river, and surrounded by high and wooded hills. Pusan had seen the departure of the Mongol invasions of Japan in 1274 and 1281, and was to

The attack on Pusan. The Japanese invaders are shown assaulting the front gate of the fortress, which was part of the overall city wall. (ETK)

provide the last foothold on the peninsula for the retreating UN forces in 1950. In 1592 the first shots of the invasion were to be fired against Pusan castle, a tiny part of which survives today as a wooded hilltop park several miles from the modern shoreline. Dividing their forces, Konishi and Sō led simultaneous attacks against the main castle and a subsidiary harbour fort called Tadaejin, a strategy planned because of Sō's local knowledge. Unlike the Japanese castles

The gateway of Pusan castle. The reconstructed gateway, in classic Korean style of a wooden pavilion on top of a solid stone gate-house with a curved tunnel entrance, stands at the foot of the hill that formed the focal point for the city's defence.

with which the samurai were familiar, most of which were purely military buildings, Pusan castle formed part of a walled town on the Chinese model and contained many civilians.

The day before the attack began the governor of Pusan, Chŏng Pal, had been out hunting on Chŏryŏng island, the very place the Japanese had chosen to drop anchor. Some Korean accounts state unkindly that he immediately fled on seeing them, others that he hurried back to Pusan to take charge of the defence and died heroically. This is the accepted version, his defiance being captured perfectly on the statue of him in the centre of Pusan, which is to be found, appropriately enough, next to the Japanese Consulate.

Early in the morning of 4m 13d Sō Yoshitomo attacked Chŏng Pal within the main city walls of Pusan, while Konishi Yukinaga led the assault on the harbour fort of Tadaejin. Rocks and lumber were flung into the moats and ditches, and bamboo scaling ladders raised for an assault under the cover of volleys of gunfire. Tadaejin was defended bravely by Yun Hŭng-sin, but the castle soon fell, and every member of the garrison was put to the sword.

With the attack on Pusan we encounter for the first time the voluminous Japanese literature that exists about the Korean campaign, and can compare the different styles of reportage that are to be found, ranging from the bombastic and the glorifying, through the matter-of-fact acceptance of Japanese superiority, to the occasional rare and moving accounts that somehow seem to appreciate the suffering that this vicious and unprovoked attack inflicted upon a guiltless people. The account in the *Taikōki* falls into the 'matter of fact' category:

The defence of the harbour fortress of Tadaejin. While one detachment of the Japanese army assaulted Pusan itself, another attacked Tadaejin. In this painting from the Ch'ungyŏlsa at Tongnae a group of Koreans under Yun Hŭng-sin, who is standing on top of the gateway, lead a counterattack.

We made those who attacked us flinch with our firearms and drove them back into the second and then the third bailey of Pusan castle. At about 9.00 a.m. we captured the main castle, and made a wholesale slaughter of more than 8,500 men. We took 200 prisoners, and questioned these men through interpreters about the local situation.[12]

It is in a very different style that the samurai chronicler Yoshino Jingoza'emon uses the Pusan battle to open his dramatic account of the Korean War. After a brief introduction where he reminds his readers that 'Japan is the Land of the Gods' (an expression we will encounter again), and an honourable mention of the precedent set by Empress Jingū's invasion of yore, he tells how the men of the First Division ignored the Korean arrows 'that fell like rain' and replied with fire of their own from massed volleys of arquebuses. Yoshino describes their effect:

The noise echoed between heaven and earth, and as the attack continued shields and towers alike were destroyed, and not one of the enemy stuck his head up. Immediately our vanguard climbed up the fourteen-foot-high walls and raised the war cry.[13]

At this point Yoshino slips in some details of the effect the attack was having on the ordinary people of Pusan, and in its easy acceptance of horror the resulting paragraph sums up what would be the future pattern of the terrible war that would devastate Korea for the next six years. For a work of literature intended for the edification of his samurai readers the inclusion of such scenes of savagery is perhaps surprising, but his words would not have shocked his clients, and were no more than a foretaste of what was to come:

> We found people running all over the place and trying to hide in the gaps between the houses. Those who could not conceal themselves went off towards the East Gate, where they clasped their hands together, and there came to our ears the Chinese expression, 'Manō! Manō!', which was probably them asking for mercy. Taking no notice of what they heard our troops rushed forward and cut them down, slaughtering them as a blood sacrifice to the god of war. Both men, women, and even dogs and cats were beheaded, and 30,000 heads were to be seen.[14]

The contempt and ignorance which led Yoshino to think that the people of Korea spoke Chinese provides a clue towards understanding the attitude held about their victims, from the lowliest foot soldier to Hideyoshi himself, but an attack that led to the frenzied decapitation of even stray animals indicates the unleashing of a fury that had no precedent, even in the darkest pages of Japan's civil wars. A Korean account, which refers to the Japanese only as 'the robbers', relates how Pusan held out as long as it could, its garrison killing many Japanese before being overwhelmed. 'In one day,' it notes, 'the bodies of the robbers had piled up like a mountain. However, at length the arrows were exhausted and all they could do was just wait for reinforcements.' At that moment Chŏng Pal was suddenly hit by a bullet and died. Morale collapsed with his death, and the castle soon fell.

The heroism of Chŏng Pal at Pusan. This detail from a painting in the Ch'ungyŏlsa at Tongnae shows the governor of Pusan in black armour fighting a single combat with a samurai during the first battle of the Korean War.

> Chŏng Pal's concubine Ae-hyang wept when she heard of his death and came running up, and committed suicide next to his dead body. Even Chŏng Pal's servant attacked the robber's lines and was killed as he left. Afterwards the Japanese generals said, 'Among the generals of your country, the general of Pusan dressed in black must have been the most feared general of all.'[15]

With the death of the brave general 'dressed in black' the Japanese army completed its first objective, but there was one more thing to do to secure their bridgehead, because a few miles to the north of Pusan lay the fortress of Tongnae. Unlike Pusan Tongnae was a sansŏng (mountain castle) that dominated the main road north towards Seoul. After resting overnight at Pusan, the First Division left at 6.00 a.m. the following morning and began the attack on Tongnae two hours later.

Tongnae was to provide Korea with its second heroic martyr of the war. Its governor was called Song Sang-hyŏn, and it was to this brave young man

The defiance of Song Sang-hyŏn at Tongnae. In this painting in the Ch'ungyŏlsa at Tongnae the brave young governor is shown maintaining his cool dignity as the samurai advance upon him to kill him.

that Konishi Yukinaga presented anew the Japanese demands for a clear road through to China. It was again rejected with the words, 'It is easy for me to die, but difficult to let you pass.'[16] For a second time the ramparts of a Korean castle were swept with bullets. An assault was made and 3,000 killed, but only after a fight lasting twelve hours. The cool defiance of Song Sang-hyŏn has become a legend in Korea, and in the Ch'ungnyŏlsa shrine at the foot of the castle hill in Tongnae, where he is honoured beside Chŏng Pal and Yun Hŭng-sin, there is a dramatic painting of him sitting impassively in his chair as the fierce Japanese approach. A popular legend about the siege tells us:

> A Japanese warrior cut off Song's right arm with his long sword and his commanding sceptre fell to the floor, but Song picked it up with his left hand. The Japanese warrior cut off his left arm and the commanding sceptre fell to the floor again. But this time Song picked it up with his mouth and held it between his teeth. The third sword thrust killed the unyielding keeper of the fallen city.[17]

The legend finishes by telling us that Konishi Yukinaga was so impressed by Song's bravery that he executed the samurai who killed him, but it is possible to contradict this by reference to the chronicles of the Matsuura family, which credit his head to the Christian samurai Don Jeronimo Koteda of Ikitsuki.[18] Other Japanese accounts confirm that the invaders were indeed impressed by Song's bravery, and note that his body was buried with respect.[19]

In one of Admiral Yi Sun-sin's Memorials to Court there is a moving account of the human cost of the Tongnae battle. A Korean prisoner who had been rescued from a Japanese ship after the battle of Tanghangp'o told

Yi how he had fled from Pusan with his parents and entered Tongnae, at which 'the Japanese gathered in countless numbers and surrounded the city wall in five lines', with other troops crowding into the nearby fields. 'The vanguard, consisting of about one hundred men, wearing helmets and armour and each holding a tall ladder, dashed to the city wall together with others and placed bamboo ladders and climbed over the ramparts in many places.' The man added that after the fall of Tongnae many people were killed, which implies a massacre similar to that which had happened at Pusan. 'During the confusion I lost my parents and elder brother, and did not know where to go. I looked up to heaven and cried, when a Japanese took me by the hand and led me off to Pusan.'[20]

With the fall of Tongnae on 4m 15d the Japanese bridgehead was secured and the road to the north was open. Pusan and Tongnae castles were quickly garrisoned, and the harbour of Pusan began to provide a safe and almost unchallenged landing stage to disembark more than 100,000 Japanese soldiers with their equipment, horses and supplies over the next month.

THE ROAD TO SEOUL

Having failed to prevent the Japanese from landing, the Korean government was genuinely determined not to allow them to proceed any further. When news of the Japanese invasion reached Seoul the government followed the established practice of despatching a sunbyŏnsa (mobile border commander) to the scene. The man chosen was the well-respected Yi Il, whom we encountered earlier in connection with his campaign against the Jurchens in 1583 and his subsequent reform of the Hamgyŏng garrison. Yi Il was now 54 years old, and in spite of any personal misgivings he may have had about the task required of him, he was greatly heartened when the court granted to him the use of 300 crack troops from the capital as his personal contingent. Unfortunately this changed to despair when he discovered that the so-called crack troops consisted of a motley crew of new recruits, lowly government administrators and yangban students for the civil examinations who turned up with their books in their hands. Leaving nearly all of them behind he took along only 60 horsemen and headed for the agreed rendezvous point of Mun'gyŏng, which lay near the southern end of the strategic Choryŏng pass.

Kyŏngsang province, which included Pusan and was the nearest Korean territory to Japan, was now in complete turmoil. Its two naval commanders, Wŏn Kyun and Pak Hong, had both evacuated their posts, the former by sea to the west, the latter overland to the north to Kyŏngju. Pak Hong's announcement there of the fall of Pusan and Tongnae caused panic, and Yi Kak, Left Commander of Kyŏngsang's provincial army, immediately withdrew from Kyŏngju, leaving word with Kim Su, the governor of Kyŏngsang, that he was regrouping his forces at Taegu. As a result, when Yi Il arrived from Seoul at Mun'gyŏng there were no troops there to meet him because all had been called south to assemble at Taegu. However, on making contact with Kim Su, Yi Il was urged to abandon Taegu and to make a stand at Sangju. The survivors of the slaughter at Tongnae clearly needed a respite, so before heading for Sangju Yi Il pulled them out of the Taegu garrison and sent them further back as a rearguard at the Choryŏng pass under General Sŏng Ung-gil, who had followed Yi Il from the capital.

The Japanese forces had been far from idle while the Koreans manoeuvred into position. The Second Division had not yet landed, and although Konishi Yukinaga had been given orders to wait at Pusan to advance north with them this was not the course of action which he adopted. Historians have speculated that this was because of the rivalry that existed between Konishi and Katō Kiyomasa, but Konishi had already succeeded in the common samurai obsession to be the first into battle, so perhaps his move was dictated by a simple unwillingness to be caught by a counterattack within Pusan. He was not to know of the disarray in the Korean defence forces, so it is not unreasonable to expect him to head north to strengthen his position, but to some extent circumstances forced his hand. On the night of 4m 15d Sō Yoshitomo sent out a small group of samurai with ten ashigaru to scout the position of Yangsan castle, the next strongpoint on the road towards Seoul. On drawing near the ten ashigaru fired a volley from their arquebuses, which so terrified the defenders of Yangsan that they immediately abandoned the castle and fled. Yangsan was occupied at dawn the following morning, so the front line of the Japanese bridgehead was moved further north almost by default.

That afternoon Konishi's main body left Tongnae, passed Yangsan, and headed for the next castle on the road, which was Miryang. There was a minor skirmish en route, and Miryang was occupied. Over the next few days the Japanese army took the minor fortress of Ch'ŏngdo and then destroyed Taegu, a place already denuded of troops because of the Korean decision to make a stand at Sangju. On 4m 24d Konishi Yukinaga led his army in a crossing of the Naktong river and took up a position at Sŏnsan, where his scouts brought him news that a Korean army was waiting for him at the fortress of Sangju. By now the First Division had been on Korean soil for eleven days. They had met virtually no opposition since leaving Tongnae, and had advanced beyond what would have been reasonable limits of safety had it not been for the fact that both the Second and Third Divisions had now landed and were covering his flanks to right and left.

As noted earlier, the Second Division of the Japanese army were commanded by Katō Kiyomasa, daimyō of Kumamoto, the fief that lay immediately to the north of Konishi's. There can be no greater contrast in

Katō Kiyomasa at the battle of Shizugatake. This print by Yoshitoshi shows Kiyomasa in a classic warlike pose prior to the battle in 1583 that first secured his reputation. His two mon (badge) appears on his jinbaori (surcoat), and he carries his famous cross-bladed spear.

Katō Kiyomasa led the Second Division, and is shown here as his fleet sails towards Pusan to make the second landfall of the invasion.

how posterity remembers its heroes than that between the disgraced Konishi Yukinaga, who was to have his face erased from the pages of history, and the larger-than-life figure of Katō Kiyomasa. In contrast to Konishi's Catholicism, Kiyomasa was an adherent of the Nichiren sect of Buddhism, and flew as his battle standard a long white pennant which bore, in characters said to have been written by Nichiren himself, the slogan 'Namu Myōho Renge Kyō' (Hail to the Lotus of the Divine Law), the motto and battle cry of his followers. Statues, prints and painted scrolls of Katō Kiyomasa abound, and usually depict him bewhiskered and carrying a long cross-bladed spear, his suit of armour invariably graced by a helmet with an enormous crown built up on a wooden framework into the shape of an extravagant courtier's cap. One extant specimen is silver with a red rising sun lacquered on to each side, while others are black with Kiyomasa's 'snake's eye' mon (badge) in gold. Katō Kiyomasa was greatly respected and valued by Hideyoshi, by whom he had been brought up in childhood. He had been one of the valiant 'Seven Spears' at Hideyoshi's victory at Shizugatake in 1583, and was to make his reputation in Korea.

Marching with Katō was Nabeshima Naoshige (1537–1619), who hailed from an old Kyushu family with wakō interests in China, and who had submitted to Hideyoshi early in the campaign of 1587. He owned the fief of Saga in Hizen province. The Second Division was completed with the contribution of 800 men from Sagara Nagatsune, the daimyō of Hitoyoshi in Higo.

The bloody struggles which Konishi and Sō had fought at Pusan ensured that the Second Division landed unopposed on 4m 17d, by which time Konishi was already at Miryang. On being told of this Katō led the Second Division as far as Yangsan, and then swung to the right towards the east coast of Kyŏngsang, taking T'ongdo on 4m 18d, the garrison having fled to Kyŏngju, the capital of

Katō Kiyomasa captures Kyŏngju in Kyŏngsang province. Kyŏngju was the former capital of the old Silla Kingdom, and both food and loot have been found in plenty. (ETK detail)

Korea's ancient Silla Kingdom. Here the Second Division saw its first taste of action, capturing Kyŏngju on 4m 20d. Once again it was a case of bullets against arrows, and by the following morning the Second Division were in Yŏngchŏn as they began a wide and rapid sweep to the north via Andong, which would ultimately allow them to approach their primary objective, the vital strategic fortress of Ch'ungju, from the east.

The western flank protection for Konishi's forward position at Sŏnsan was provided by the Third Division under Kuroda Nagamasa (1568–1623). Nagamasa was the son of a famous father called Kuroda Yoshitaka (1546–1604), a noted scholar samurai whose capabilities had aroused the jealousy of Hideyoshi, forcing Yoshitaka to relinquish his domains in favour of his son in 1589, whereupon Yoshitaka retired and took the name of Jōsui by which he is usually known. It was therefore the Christian daimyō Damian Nagamasa who took the Kuroda samurai to Korea. A son from another great Kirishitan daimyō family supplied the other half of the Third Division. This was Ōtomo Yoshimune (1558–1605) of Bungo, son of the late Ōtomo Sōrin Yoshishige, whose defeat by the Shimazu of Satsuma had provided Hideyoshi's excuse for the Kyushu campaign in 1587.

Unlike the Second Division, the Third did not simply disembark at Pusan, but fought their way ashore on 4m 18d to the west of the Naktong to attack Kimhae castle. The chronicle of the Kuroda family states that this was to obtain glory denied to them at peaceful Pusan, which may well be true, and goes on to give a fascinating account of their disembarkation at Angolp'o, including a rare glimpse of ashigaru (foot soldiers) in action:

Kuroda Nagamasa, the leader of the Third Division of the Japanese army, as shown just prior to the battle of Pyŏkje in 1593. (ETK detail)

> having seen that all was well from on board, half the ashigaru landed, led by the kashira [captain]. This first unit quickly ran up to a low piece of raised ground, and when they saw that they had taken up a position with their arquebuses, the remaining ashigaru under Nagatori and Shinza'emon also disembarked.

> They [the commanders] landed the horses and mounted them, and galloped off to nearby high ground, while in addition positions were taken with arquebuses among the bamboo and wooded areas. After this the five

ranks of the whole army successively disembarked without difficulty. Subsequently the 100 arquebus ashigaru divided into two. The advance unit reformed their original ranks and turned against the enemy, and attacked the left flank of the enemy who were withdrawing from the second unit, firing arquebuses. Seeing the signs that the Korean soldiers were shaken by this, those who remained advanced as one, and many arquebuses were fired. Because the enemy were arranged in close ranks no bullets were wasted, and they fell in rapid succession.[21]

Waving his war fan Kuroda Nagamasa led his men towards Kimhae, which was defended by high walls. Seeing this he ordered his men into the nearby fields to reap any crops that were growing, bind them into bundles, and pile them up at the ramparts. As the defenders' heads were kept down by gunfire a pile was soon amassed which allowed the attackers to scale it and enter the castle, at which Kimhae's commanders opened the west gate and fled for their lives. The Third Division took 1,000 heads, and followed up their victory by capturing Ch'angwŏn. On 4m 24d, as Konishi was crossing the Naktong, the Third Division captured Sŏngju, having already taken possession of Unsan, Ch'angnyŏng and Hyŏnp'ung en route.

THE BATTLES OF SANGJU AND CH'UNGJU

We left the Korean General Yi Il at Sangju. He had managed to recruit an army of less than 1,000 men, and when a villager from Kaenyŏng risked his life to come and inform him that the Japanese were approaching he had the

man beheaded on the grounds that the information would be harmful to morale. It was soon officially confirmed that Taegu had been destroyed by the Japanese, and that the army that had done the destroying were in position just a few miles to the south. He may also have been told that another Japanese army lay almost due east of him, and that a third was moving up behind the first. It was now Yi Il, not Konishi, who felt

General Yi Il nervously observes the rapid approach of the Japanese at Sangju. Although an experienced general, Yi Il was hopelessly outclassed in this first field battle of the war. (ETK)

isolated. Not wishing to be caught inside Sangju he left the castle the next morning and drew up his little army on two small hills, where he took his position at its head, mounted on his horse to await Konishi's attack.

The Japanese had moved up from Sŏnsan the previous night in a single formation. They were now approaching a mountainous area with valleys to the right and the left, both of which led to Sangju. While still out of sight of the Korean position Konishi and Matsuura continued forward by the shortest direction, which brought them face on to Yi Il on his hill, while Sō, Arima and Gotō swept round to the right to approach from the side. Yu Sŏng-nyong, who received a report of the battle of Sangju from Yi Il himself, wrote a concise account in *Chingbirok* of how the disaster began to unfold:

> Before long, several figures appeared from the forest. They loitered about for a few minutes before they returned. The officers and men wondered if they might be a scouting party of the enemy. However, they did not dare say so because of their knowledge of the beheaded villager.[22]

> The next thing to be observed was smoke arising from burning buildings. Realising that the Japanese must be very close, Yi Il sent one of his officers to ascertain the truth.

> When the officer mounted his horse, two foot soldiers took the bridle and went off very slowly. A Japanese soldier below a bridge then shot at the officer with a musket. When he fell off his horse, the soldier beheaded him and ran away. The friendly soldiers were all greatly shocked at the incident.[23]

A Korean officer, sent on a scouting mission by Yi Il, is shot off his horse by a Japanese arquebusier just prior to the battle of Sangju. The death of the scout confirmed the approach of the Japanese. (ETK detail)

The death of the scout confirmed the presence of the Japanese. Fierce arquebus fire then followed, which began to cut into the Korean front line. At this Yi Il ordered his men to return fire with their bows, but the arrows fell short of their targets. Konishi Yukinaga and Matsuura Shigenobu then led their forces forward to attack the two hills just as the rest of the Japanese army approached from the right. Ōmura, Gotō and Arima moved in for an attack on the right-hand hill, while Sō went further round from the flank. Realising that the situation was hopeless, Yi turned his horse round to escape, which became a signal for his entire army to follow suit, but few of them managed to flee before the Japanese were upon them. Three hundred were killed.

As Yi Il retreated northwards the one thread of comfort he possessed was the thought that the rearguard he had sensibly sent back from Taegu were waiting for him at the impregnable Choryŏng pass, the only crossing point from south to north over the western end of the mighty Sobaek mountain range. Here the Japanese advance could be easily checked until massive reinforcements arrived from Seoul. It was unfortunate for Yi Il, and also for Korea, that there had already arrived from Seoul another eminent general in the person of Sin Rip, whom we last encountered executing people during his tour of inspection, and making the immortal statement to Yu Sŏng-nyong that even though the Japanese possessed arquebuses they couldn't hit anyone with them. Sin Rip had left Seoul with 80 men, an army that had grown to 8,000 on his arrival at Ch'ungju, where he took command. Ch'ungju, a large castle which lay in the middle of a flat plain to the north of the mountains, was of major strategic importance, as a captured Korean told Konishi Yukinaga:

> in order to defend Seoul there is an exceedingly superior and famous castle called Ch'ungju. There are many generals of valour, 6 or 7,000 troops, and many archery experts have gone in, and it is a fact that they have stocked up with enough provisions. In the capital they rely upon this castle, and therefore have an easy heart.[24]

Yi Il soon arrived at the Choryŏng pass on his retreat from Sangju and discovered to his horror that its defences had been abandoned. Sin Rip had panicked on hearing of the battle at Sangju and had left the Choryŏng pass for the fortress of Ch'ungju. The two Korean generals met there, and Yi Il forwarded a report on his defeat to King Sŏnjo. 'The enemy today were like warriors from heaven, and no one can match them,' he wrote. ' To your loyal subjects all that remains is the highway of death.'[25] As Ch'ungju was the last fortress between the Japanese and Seoul this can hardly have been encouraging.

The Japanese cross the undefended Choryŏng pass and head north towards Ch'ungju. The failure to halt the invasion at this strategic point was a major blunder. (ETK detail)

Worse was to come, because while the Japanese were moving towards the undefended Choryŏng pass in some elation Sin Rip decided to abandon Ch'ungju and meet the Japanese in battle. 'The other side are on foot,' he had explained to the Ch'ungch'ŏng commanders, 'while we are mounted. This ground (i.e. the pass) does not suit cavalry. I have planned that we will engage them on the flat plain.'[26]

The hill of T'angumdae overlooking the plain to the north of Ch'ungju, where Sin Rip set up his head-quarters, hoping that his cavalrymen would have an easy victory on the flat land.

Sin Rip decided to make his stand on and in front of a hill two and a half miles to the north of Ch'ungju, called T'angumdae. From there, he reasoned, the Korean cavalry could swoop down on the slow-moving Japanese with their flails and halberds. Sin Rip, of course, had not yet experienced the Japanese arquebuses, and a more disastrous position for an army to adopt can hardly be imagined. T'angumdae is a modest wooded bluff, named picturesquely because in ancient times a famous musician used to practise his gum (zither) there. To the south stretched a flat plain allowing a distant view of the walls of Ch'ungju, which could now be successfully cut off from supporting the army by an advancing enemy. The plain was indeed level, but was totally unsuitable for a cavalry action because of the numerous flooded rice fields. Its scenic beauty was completed by the vast expanse of water at its rear, because at T'angumdae the Talch'on river joins the Han in the shape of an inverted letter 'Y'. On the hill, which fitted neatly within the fork of the 'Y', Sin Rip set up his command post, utterly and completely trapped, with no room for manoeuvre and certainly no scope for retreat. In vain did Yi Il protest, and was sharply reminded by Sin Rip that he was 'the general of a defeated army'.[27]

The confluence of the Talch'on and the Han rivers at the rear of T'angumdae, which made the Korean position into a death trap. Thousands were drowned as they were driven into the rivers.

A Buddhist monk called Tenkei accompanied the Japanese army and wrote an account of the subsequent battle of Ch'ungju. He recorded how Konishi's forces left Sangju at 6.00 a.m. on 4m 26d, passed Hamch'ang at 2.00 p.m. and reached Mun'gyŏng at 10.00 p.m. to find the castle burning, having been abandoned by its defenders. The following day they left Mun'gyŏng at 4.00 a.m. and crossed the Choryŏng pass in high spirits to reach the environs of Ch'ungju at 2.00 p.m. where 'a Korean general, who had come down from the capital, deployed his forces'.[28]

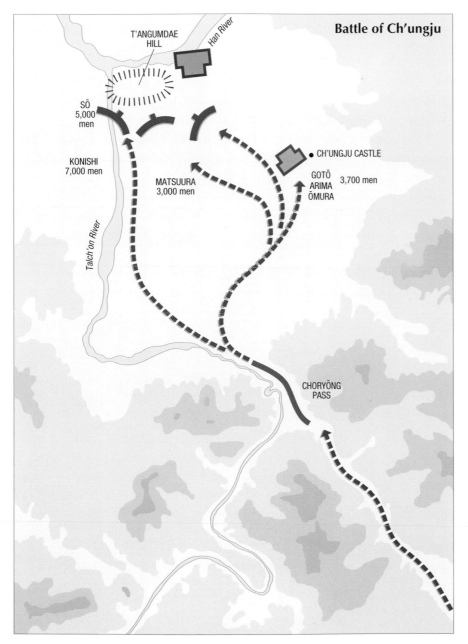

Map of the battle of Ch'ungju, showing the advance of the Japanese army over the Choryŏng pass and their attack on the Korean position on T'angumdae.

Sin Rip had set up his lines at T'angumdae at noon. Using the tactic that had worked for them at Sangju, Konishi divided his army. There was almost no need to mask Ch'ungju, because its terrified garrison fastened the gates and stayed inside. Matsuura Shigenobu led a frontal attack, while Konishi and Sō took the left wing, hugging the right bank of the Talch'on river, and Ōmura, Arima and Gotō followed the road out of Ch'ungju on the right. When all were in position, devastating arquebus fire began from the flanks and Matsuura advanced against the hill. Once again the Korean arrows fell short, and as the Korean army began to give way the flanking armies charged forward, driving the defenders into the rivers. Whipping his horse, the brave Sin Rip tried twice to lead a charge against the Japanese army and was hit by arrows, whereupon he rode his horse into the river and killed himself. Thousands of the Korean army tried to escape across the rivers, but were dragged out and decapitated, producing for the Japanese army a head count of 3,000.

Thus ended the most disastrous field battle of the Korean campaign. The failure to hold Choryǒng must rank as a classic blunder of military history, but it is possible that even a stand there would have been nullified by the approach of the Second Division, who were presently on a wide sweep round to the east. As it was, the following day, 4m 28d, Katō Kiyomasa's men arrived at Ch'ungju from the east to find Konishi's and Sō's banners flying from its ramparts, and the victorious First Division looting and celebrating within. They had much with which to be satisfied. The battle honours of Pusan, Tongnae, Sangju and Ch'ungju, together with several minor skirmishes, had

Katō Kiyomasa (on the right) and Konishi Yukinaga (on the left) are prevented by their comrades from coming to blows over who should advance first on the final stage of the march on the Korean capital of Seoul, a prospect that promised great personal glory. (ETK detail)

all been earned by the armies of Augustin Konishi, Dario Sō, Protasio Arima, Sanche Ōmura and the infidels Matsuura and Gotō. The Second Division, for whom the First had supposed to have waited at Pusan, had little to show for their long march but a few fortresses of little strategic importance and a handful of Korean heads.

THE RACE FOR SEOUL

In a warrior culture where achievement was all, it is not surprising that resentment was expressed at Ch'ungju, where Konishi and Katō are depicted as almost literally coming to blows. Nabeshima Naoshige separated them. Realising that their mistrust of each other hinged on Katō's belief that Konishi had pressed on and made a name for himself for reasons other than those of strict military necessity, Nabeshima proposed a compromise for the next move, which would result in huge prestige for someone by being the one who captured Seoul, the Korean capital:

> . . . as for the vanguard against Seoul, should it not be that we divide and attack from two sides?' Konishi too recognised the truth of this, and said, 'There are two roads to Seoul. The road to the Southern Great Gate is about 100 ri, but there is a large river on the way. The road to the Eastern Great Gate is more than 100 ri, not less than it, but in addition there is no river. As to which road is taken let it be as Lord Kiyomasa likes.'[29]

By now the Third Division were also very near to Ch'ungju, having crossed the Ch'up'ungnyŏng pass and captured Yŏngdong and Ch'ŏngju. If Katō did not move soon he would have another rival on his heels, and great glory was to be gained. Katō Kiyomasa therefore agreed to the proposal, which would keep him separate from Konishi if nothing else, and chose the southern route. The final advance on the Korean capital therefore became less of a planned tactical operation involving two wings of an army supported by a rearguard, than a fierce personal competition for samurai honour carried out as a race to be first.

In fact the journey to Seoul, which began on 4m 29d, proved highly uneventful for both armies, although Katō Kiyomasa must have cursed his decision to take the shorter route across the Han when he discovered that there were no boats readily available to transport his troops across. Instead Konishi Yukinaga, who crossed much further upstream, arrived at the East Gate of Seoul on 5m 1d (10 June) before his rival was anywhere near the South Gate. To everyone's surprise, the city seemed strangely quiet:

> The Eastern Great Gate was tightly closed, so there was no entering to take it. There was no sign of generals or soldiers defending, but it was

Konishi Yukinaga arrives at the East Gate to find it strangely quiet. In fact the city had been abandoned by King Sŏnjo the day before, and no soldiers were on duty behind the tightly locked city gates. (ETK detail)

Kido Saku'emonnojō uses a number of gun barrels tied together as a massive lever to force open the iron floodgate in the wall of Seoul next to the East Gate. (Photograph by courtesy of Yuri Varshavsky)

enclosed on four sides by high stone walls, and the gate itself was even 10 ken high, so they could not easily get in.[30]

A discussion developed over what should be done, at which point someone noticed a small floodgate in the wall.

> However, the floodgate was five shaku square and made of strong iron and could by no means be entered. Thereupon Kido Saku'emonnonjō, saying, 'This is how to do it,' disconnected the wooden stock from an arquebus, and using the barrel as a lever forced it open, and from inside they opened the castle gate.

To the attackers' amazement Seoul was deserted, and Konishi's men simply walked in. Here and there were wrecked buildings, and fires were still smouldering in many places. Even the palaces were unguarded, because, unknown to Konishi, King Sŏnjo had fled the day before. The loyal citizens of Seoul had already taken the opportunity to do some looting, and a thorough arson attack had been mounted on the offices that held the slave records. Unfortunately for the Korean war effort the King's entourage had not taken their stocks of weapons with them, but they did not fall into Japanese hands either, because a gang of looters helpfully burned the weapons bureau to the ground. Yet to Konishi the honour of being first to the Korean capital far outweighed any disappointment at the sight of the destruction all around him. Once more he had stolen a march on Katō Kiyomasa, and in some style, as the chronicler records in amazement:

In the year period of Eiroku [1558–69] there were many who attained the honour of ichiban yari (first spear, i.e. first into battle), but an occasion like this, where one keeps to the criteria and enters a castle in silence in a foreign country is a rare occurrence.[31]

Konishi Yukinaga, of course, took sensible precautions against a Korean counterattack, including mounting a guard over the city gates. The bizarre incident which followed was then almost inevitable. Katō Kiyomasa, who had travelled via Chuksan and Yong'in, arrived at Seoul's Namdaemun (Southern Great Gate) and:

Katō Kiyomasa's vanguard soldiers showed up and ordered that the gate be opened. From inside the castle came the reply, 'We are Konishi's troops. We form the vanguard and are now defending the great gates. If you are on an errand we have the right to let about three or five men enter.'[32]

Katō Kiyomasa's reaction to this may be guessed at!

It was 5m 2d. On the following day Kuroda's Third Division also arrived in Seoul. They had followed a completely separate route via Suwŏn, and were joined shortly by Mōri Yoshinari with most of the Fourth Division, who had landed at Pusan in the middle of the previous month and had followed Konishi's victorious footsteps. The Fifth, Sixth, Seventh and Eighth Armies had also landed at Pusan, and the Ninth Army was deployed on Iki. Seoul had fallen within twenty days of Konishi's landing at Pusan, and although King Sŏnjo and his family had unfortunately escaped they would not get far. Korea was at Japan's mercy.

The Namdaemun at Seoul. The Great South Gate, through which Katō Kiyomasa entered the capital, is one of Seoul's most historic landmarks, and now stands on an almost inaccessible traffic island!

chapter 4

A SLOW MARCH TO CHINA

As Konishi and Katō stood in the middle of the enemy capital, captured almost intact within three weeks of landing, neither can have envisaged that the furious blitzkrieg pace of the first days of the invasion was never to be repeated. Both were naturally keen to pursue the fleeing King as quickly as possible, but the Japanese army was about to reach its first real obstacle of the campaign in an encounter that would expose serious weaknesses in Hideyoshi's invasion plans.

King Sŏnjo and his entourage had left Seoul on 4m 29d. The following day they reached Kaesŏng, thirty miles to the north, just as Konishi Yukinaga was wondering how to open the capital's Eastern Great Gate. It was not the sort of journey to which the Korean monarch was accustomed, but the decision to flee had been made hurriedly when the dreadful news of the fall of Ch'ungju

In heavy rain King Sŏnjo and his entourage flee from Seoul through Kaesŏng and on to the safety of P'yŏngyang in the north. (ETK detail)

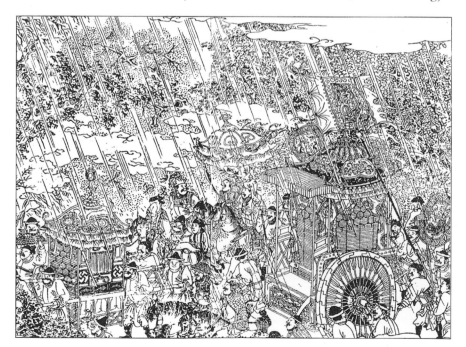

reached the capital. With that mighty fortress gone nothing stood in the way of disaster except for the natural moat of the Han river and Seoul's city walls. Both had enormous potential to provide secure defences, but such was the panic that these barriers were abandoned, and the court headed for the distant security of northern Korea.

The Han was but the first of five wide rivers that drained the Korean mountains into the Yellow Sea, and each had the potential to seriously hamper the Japanese advance into China. Not far to the north flowed the second natural moat of the Imjin. For much of its length nowadays the Imjin provides the southern border of the Demilitarised Zone and, being virtually undeveloped, its appearance today cannot be very different from the sight that met the eyes of King Sŏnjo on his miserable journey north in 1592. Its high banks hung out over mud flats that dotted the long, wide, deep and sluggish river, which the King crossed on a poor train of farm horses and pack animals, because the animals in the royal stables had all been stolen by those of his majesty's loyal subjects who had fled before he did. The rain poured down, and the royal party had no food, so hasty had been their departure. In every village through which the wretched royals passed they were greeted by lines of people standing beside the road, not paying homage to their King, but weeping bitterly that they were being abandoned to their fate.

The Japanese army faces a long stalemate at the Imjin river. The Koreans have pulled all the available boats to the northern shore. (ETK detail)

The fording of the Imjin was carried out after dark, the way illuminated by the fires from the barracks and defence lines on its southern shore, burned to deprive the pursuing Japanese of materials with which to effect a crossing of their own. Every boat within sight was either destroyed or ferried across the river, and as they proceeded north King Sŏnjo ordered all the troops he could find to take up positions on the Imjin's northern bank under the command of Kim Myŏng-wŏn, the same general who had abandoned the line of the Han a few days earlier. General Kim gathered 12,000 troops in all, including Yi Il, late of Sangju, and deployed them at five places along the Imjin to cover the most likely places where the Japanese might try to cross.

After spending two days in Kaesŏng the royal party set off again and arrived at P'yŏngyang on 5m 7d. This location provided a further level of security from the Japanese threat, because in front of P'yŏngyang (which is now the capital of North Korea) flowed the third of the country's natural moats. This was the mighty Taedong, which was made all the more formidable by the presence of P'yŏngyang's city walls and towers on its northern bank. Yet if even the Imjin was crossed and P'yŏngyang should fall there were two other river barriers left, the Ch'ŏngch'ŏn near Anju and the Yalu, which formed the border with China. The Korean position was by no means as hopeless as it may have looked.

For the Japanese army, revelling in the capture of Seoul, the decision now had to be made as to which of the commanders should move the invasion forward again and earn for himself the accolade of 'First Spear of the Imjin'. It was not a difficult choice to make, and while the First Division recuperated briefly in Seoul, Katō Kiyomasa set off north with an understandable eagerness to engage the Koreans and even capture the fleeing King, but within less than a day's march from Seoul his enthusiasm turned to frustration as he gazed across the wide and deep Imjin, devoid of boats and with a huge Korean army lined up on its northern bank. Not knowing what to do, he sat there in high dudgeon, glaring across the river at his Korean enemies who stayed out of range and defiant.

Nothing illustrates the lack of real strategic planning that had gone into Hideyoshi's invasion of Korea than the farce that was enacted upon the south bank of the Imjin while the King of Korea rode further and further away. In dramatic contrast to the rapid advance on Seoul, the Japanese army now did effectively nothing for almost an entire month, and had no plans to do anything else. Should they outflank them? If so, did anyone know where the roads led? Could a fleet sail round the coast in a sixteenth-century version of the Inch'on landings? If any of these possibilities were considered they remain unrecorded, but by 5m 15d, two weeks into the vigil, the stalemate had become so infuriating that it was decided to employ the negotiating skills of Sō Yoshitomo. Messages were therefore sent to General Kim Myŏng-wŏn reiterating the by now familiar Japanese demands for a safe passage to China. Secure behind his watery barrier, Kim refused.

Leaving the negotiators to their business a disappointed Katō Kiyomasa eventually pulled his main body of troops back from the Imjin to rest them within the security of nearby P'aju castle. Something was desperately needed if the deadlock was to be broken, and unwittingly or otherwise, Katō's withdrawal provided just that incentive. Some young hotheads on the Korean side perceived Katō's move as a retreat. Abandoning the safety of the northern bank they clambered into the boats and launched a fierce dawn attack on the troops of the Second Division vanguard who had been left guarding the southern shore, crossing somewhere near to the modern road bridge. The news quickly reached Katō, who responded with a crushing advance against the isolated Korean force who were now fighting, like Sin Rip at Ch'ungju, with the river to their backs. The force of the Japanese advance drove them into the river with the loss of their commanders. General Kim Myŏng-wŏn could only watch helplessly as his vanguard were slaughtered, yielding their precious boats to Katō's troops. When the Japanese looked as if they were about to cross Kim whipped his horse and fled back to Kaesŏng, at which his entire army followed suit. It may not have been the most glorious of victories for Katō Kiyomasa, but the battle of the Imjin, fought on 5m 27d (6 July), had served its purpose. Being desperate to make up for the lost time, Konishi rapidly led his First Division out of Seoul to join Katō. Crossing by the captured boats and via other fords downstream that had been revealed by panic-stricken Koreans, the Japanese soon occupied Kaesŏng.

PLANS OF CONQUEST

During the month-long stalemate at the Imjin the Japanese commanders had taken the opportunity for a brief moment of reflection and reorganisation, a matter made more acute by the arrival of a new supreme commander from Japan. In his original plans Toyotomi Hideyoshi had intended to lead his army in person once the bridgehead had been secured, but this became the first of his war aims to be abandoned when he received earnest entreaties against going abroad both from the Emperor of Japan and his own mother. Their misgivings at Hideyoshi exposing his august person, and the fate of Japan, to the risks of a long overseas campaign were shared by the three most senior daimyō to have remained in Japan: Tokugawa Ieyasu, Asano Nagamasa and Maeda Toshiie. As a result the new commanding officer, who arrived in Pusan on the same day that Seoul fell to the First Division, was not Toyotomi Hideyoshi but his adopted son Ukita Hideie, the daimyō of Okayama. Hideie had been an infant when his father Ukita Naoie had died in 1582 and, along with being confirmed in his inheritance by Hideyoshi, the child Hideie was actually adopted by the future Taikō, a matter that no doubt greatly helped his future career development.

When the news of the taking of Seoul had reached Hideyoshi it had thrown him into ecstasies of joy. His immediate reaction was to draft the famous letter to his nephew the Kampaku Toyotomi Hidetsugu, in which he set out his plans whereby the rapid conquest of Korea would be consolidated. No document reveals more about Hideyoshi's grandiose plans for an Asian empire than this remarkable letter, and his boundless self-confidence permeates every item. After a warning to Hidetsugu to be ready to move at short notice, he continues:

> The capital of Korea fell on the second day of this month. Thus, the time has come to make the sea crossing and to bring the length and breadth of the Great Ming under our control. My desire is that Your Lordship make the crossing to become Kampaku of Great China.[1]

According to Hideyoshi's grand plan, on becoming Regent of China, Hidetsugu's current position of Kampaku of Japan would then pass either to Hideyoshi's half-brother Hidenaga or to his adopted son Ukita Hideie. Hidetsugu was to proceed to China accompanied by 30,000 men, and 'although no hostility is expected in the "Three Kingdoms" (echoes of Empress Jingū, when Korea was three separate states!), these men would allow the maintenance of Hideyoshi's reputation and would also be useful "in case of an emergency"'. The most glorious progress to China would however occur after a year had passed, when His Majesty the Emperor of Japan would go to Beijing and be installed as Emperor of China. His place in Japan would be taken by either of two imperial princes, one of whom was another adopted son of Hideyoshi. The remaining official position of Kampaku of Korea would be allotted to one of three suitable candidates, all of whom had also been adopted by Hideyoshi.

The establishment of the Toyotomi Dynasty of the Empire of East Asia was thus succinctly mapped out, and from Hideyoshi's point of view, would be a straightforward operation, because 'Korea and China are within easy reach, and no inconvenience is expected'.[2] As for Toyotomi Hideyoshi himself, his future role was both vague and all-encompassing. He seems to have seen himself as something of a universal monarch, because in letters that followed the missive to Hidetsugu he writes of taking up temporary residence in China prior to moving on to conquer India.

Back in the real world the young Ukita Hideie took up his new job as supreme commander of the Japanese army in Korea. He was assisted in this role by seven other appointees sent to Seoul with him. These were the 'three bugyō' (commissioners) Mashita Nagamori, Ishida Mitsunari and Ōtani Yoshitsugu, together with the 'four generals' Hasegawa Hidekazu, Kimura Shigekore, Katō Mitsuyasu and Maeno Nagayasu, who were to form the equivalent of Chiefs of Staff. Prior to his unexpected promotion Ukita Hideie had been commander of the Eighth Division of the invading army, who were originally ordered to stay on Tsushima as a rearguard, and it is indicative both of the Japanese belief in the lack of any reprisals from Korea, together with a new appreciation of the manpower needs for a Chinese conquest, that the former rearguard should be moved up to a forward position.

The first decision made by Ukita and his colleagues concerned the division of labour for the further conquest and pacification of Korea. In summary, each of the eight divisions was to be allocated one of the eight Korean provinces as its theatre of operations, as listed in Table 2 under the name of the principal commander. Perhaps mindful of the undoubted rivalry that existed between Konishi and Katō, Ukita sent them on separate operations which would keep

Table 2: Allocations of Korean provinces 1592

P'yŏngan	1st Division	Konishi Yukinaga
Hamgyŏng	2nd Division	Katō Kiyomasa
Hwanghae	3rd Division	Kuroda Nagamasa
Kangwŏn	4th Division	Mōri Yoshinari
Ch'ungch'ŏng	5th Division	Fukushima Masanori
Chŏlla	6th Division	Kobayakawa Takakage
Kyŏngsang	7th Division	Mōri Terumoto
Kyŏnggi	8th Division	Ukita Hideie

them as far apart as possible. Konishi Yukinaga was to continue into P'yŏngan province in pursuit of the King, while Katō's Second Division were allotted the north-eastern fastnesses of Hamgyŏng province where the Koreans shared a border with the fierce Jurchens. This would cover Konishi's eastern flank, and also allow the pursuit of the two Korean princes, who were reported to have split up from the royal party and headed somewhere to the east. Kuroda's Third Division was allotted the job of pacifying Hwanghae province through which Konishi had to pass en route for P'yŏngyang, making him again the First Division's rearguard. The Fourth Division under Mōri Yoshinari were to provide a similar service to Katō by pacifying Kangwŏn province, which covered the central east coast area. Chŏlla, which covered the whole of the south-west, was the main area of southern Korea that had so far escaped conquest, and this demanding role fell to the veteran Kobayakawa Takakage. The duties of the two divisions allotted to Kyŏngsang and Ch'ungch'ŏng provinces was largely that of ensuring the continued pacification of these territories through which the armies had already swept, and of maintaining the communication links between Pusan and Seoul. The final province, Kyŏnggi, covered Seoul itself and extended beyond the Imjin river to Kaesŏng. This fell to Ukita Hideie, who was based in the capital.

Each commander accepted his orders willingly, and the fact that no protest was raised by Katō at Konishi Yukinaga's allocation of the shortest road to China shows very clearly that none of the Japanese generals underestimated the enormity of the task that now awaited them. The stalemate at the Imjin had taught them a valuable lesson, and they all knew that Konishi Yukinaga was not simply going to march into Beijing at the head of only 20,000 men. One general, Mōri Terumoto of the Seventh Division, expressed similar misgivings in a letter home when he wondered if they had enough troops to conquer the huge country of China. He also added in a somewhat bemused tone that the Koreans whom his men were busily looting 'regard us in the same light as pirates'.[3]

At the same time other troops began to appear in Korea to swell the numbers. The transfer of Ukita's Eighth Division from Tsushima has already been mentioned, and in addition to them came the Ninth Division of Hashiba Hidekatsu (8,000) and Hosokawa Tadaoki (3,500), who were moved across from Iki, together with 10,800 men from the Tenth Division stationed in Nagoya. Orders were also given for the establishment of a line of castles to secure communications between Pusan and the Chinese border. To compensate for the arduous task of garrisoning an occupied country, the generals placed in charge of these forts (all of which were captured Korean castles) were permitted to have concubines with them. The women were given a stipend of rice for their troubles, a small indication that the Japanese were expecting a long stay. The initial distribution of commands was as listed in Table 3, reading from north to south.[4]

Concubines or not, these garrison duties were no sinecures, as was soon proved when Wakizaka Yasuharu came under attack at Yong'in on 6m 5d. The fort was being held by a small force, under Wakizaka's retainers Wakizaka Sabei and Watanabe Shichiemon, when a huge Korean army attacked by night, one group besieging the fort, the other taking up a position on a nearby hill. A message was sent to Yasuharu, who hurried to the scene. 'They displayed their flags, and his family member Yamaoka Ukon charged ahead of the others so that he could engage in single combat. When the enemy ranks saw this, they were afraid,' wrote the chronicler of the Wakizaka family. Following the example of this lone warrior the rest of the relieving army charged forward, and scattered the besiegers, so that, 'In the space of half an hour several tens of thousands of the enemy were destroyed by our little force.' Wakizaka's main body then dislodged the other group.[5]

Table 3: Communications forts and their commanders 1592.

Kaesŏng	Toda Katsutaka	3,900
Seoul	Ukita Hideie plus staff	20,000
Yong'in	Wakizaka Yasuharu	1,500
Chuksan	Fukushima Masanori	4,800
Ŭmsŏng	Ikoma Chikamasa	5,500
Ch'ungju & Ch'ŏngju	Hachisuka Iemasa	7,200
Mun'gyŏng & Hamch'ang	Chōsokabe Motochika	3,000
Sangju	Inaba Sadamichi	4,000
Sŏnsan	Miyabe Nagahiro	1,000
	Kakiya Tsunefusa	400
Kaenyŏng	Mōri Terumoto	30,000
Kimsan	Tachibana Muneshige	2,500
	Takahashi Munemasu	800
	Chikushi Hirokado	900
	Mōri Hidekane	1,500
Indong	Kinoshita Shigekata	850
	Nanjō Motokiyo	1,500
Kŭmsan	Kobayakawa Takakage	10,000
Taegu	Saimura Hirohide	800
	Akashi Norizane	800
Pusan	Hashiba Hidekatsu	8,000

THE FALL OF P'YŎNGYANG

Meanwhile Konishi's First Division continued their steady progress northwards, crossing into Hwanghae province just north of Kaesŏng and occupying Pyongsan, Sŏhŭng, P'ungsan, Hwangju and Chunghwa, arriving in the last named on 6m

6d. Here Konishi was joined by Kuroda, and from Chunghwa a short scouting ride gave the Japanese their first glimpse of the Taedong river and the city of P'yŏngyang. Once again the Korean defence preparations had ensured the removal of every boat within miles, and the location of the fords was also unknown to the Japanese. Hoping to persuade the Koreans to repeat their helpful action at the Imjin, a few rafts were cobbled together from timber and a detachment of arquebusiers discharged a few volleys against the guards of the Korean river boats moored beneath P'yŏngyang's walls. The Korean generals, who included Yi Il among their number together with several others who had retreated from the Imjin, did not look as if they were willing to oblige the Japanese by making the same mistake twice, but they cannot have

inspired much confidence in King Sŏnjo, who immediately left P'yŏngyang and fled northwards for Ŭiju, the town that lay at the very limits of his kingdom. It stood on the southern shore of the Yalu, while across the river lay China. The Korean monarch was now as secure as he could be without actually going into exile.

P'yŏngyang was the last major obstacle between Konishi's army and the Chinese border. Frustrated again by a river, Sō Yoshitomo's negotiating team were once more summoned into action, and parleyed with the Korean commanders between two boats anchored in the middle of the Taedong. Kim Myŏng-wŏn could afford to be more contemptuous than usual about the demand for safe passage. He was no longer merely standing on the banks of a river, but safely ensconced with 10,000 men inside one of the strongest castles in Korea. Yet here lay the seeds of their weakness. So strong was the Korean army, so firm was their base, and so far north were the Japanese, that the Korean generals felt that the time was right to hit back and make P'yŏngyang

A view from the river of the Taedong Gate of P'yŏngyang, which was built in 1406. The sight facing the advancing Japanese in 1592 would have been little different from this photograph.

the beginning of an ignominious Japanese retreat. They therefore planned an audacious night attack on Sō Yoshitomo's camp, to be launched with a silent river crossing at 10.00 p.m. on 6m 15d and followed by a full-scale dawn attack on the Japanese lines.

The attack on Sō's camp worked perfectly, and by sunrise hundreds of Japanese lay dead, but the commotion had inevitably stirred the other Japanese contingents, so both Konishi's and Kuroda's armies quickly prepared

The crossing points having been revealed by the abortive Korean night attack, Konishi Yukinaga gleefully pursues the Koreans across the Taedong to take P'yŏngyang. (ETK detail)

themselves and hurried to the scene. They easily managed to take the Korean force in the rear, which bad coordination had left unguarded. A further aspect of the botched operation was that more Koreans were still crossing the river. In *Kuroda Kafu* the chronicler of the Kuroda family eagerly recounted the reaction to this by Nagamasa's troops:

> As the night at last began to end, and with the eastern sky turning white, they looked out over the banks of the river as about 3,000 Korean soldiers, all dressed alike in their white costumes, came out of the castle and swarmed into the shallows.[6]

It was an ideal opportunity for samurai glory, and in a passage worthy of the ancient warrior tales, battle was joined:

> At their head were Gotō Mototsugu, Yoshida Rokurōdaifu and Toda Heiza'emon who crashed into the enemy. Mototsugu wore a helmet which had a crest of two golden irises, and couched his long-shafted spear from his horse. Rokurōdaifu wore a sashimono [flag worn on the back] of a crane within a circle and a crest of a polar bear on a shaft. The two men vied with each other over the lead position, then plunged into the midst of the enemy, wielding their spears in every direction.[7]

At P'yŏngyang one young warrior called Yoshida Matanosuke took the first head of his military career, and finding himself near to his leader Gotō Mototsugu, proudly brandished it before his commander with the comment (somewhat freely translated!) of: 'I said I would do well! How's this for a young warrior?'[8]

Deliberately holding back from slaughtering the entire Korean vanguard who were now at their mercy, the Japanese commanders calmly stood and watched as the survivors fled back across the river, thus revealing the precious information about the location of the fords. By the evening the Japanese were standing ready on the southern banks of the Taedong at the newly discovered crossing points, and cautiously beginning to send detachments across for a major push forward against the city walls. Incredibly, the Korean generals, some of whom had already evacuated strong positions on three occasions, concluded that they had little chance of holding P'yŏngyang, and began to dump their weapons into the pond that provided the garrison's water supply. In *Chingbirok* Yu Sŏng-nyong summed up the events of the ignominious surrender:

The enemy, who had already crossed the river, did not make any further advance, out of suspicion that there might be a trap within the walls. That night Yun Tu-su and Kim Myŏng-wŏn opened the gates of the castle in order to mobilise the citizens for the task of sinking the arms and guns into the pond near the Pungwŏllu Pavilion. Yun Tu-su and his party escaped to Sunan through the Botongnum gate. No enemy pursued them. [9]

The following day, 6m 16d (24 July), the Japanese walked into the deserted city in a curious rerun of their silent triumph in Seoul. Not a single person was to be seen, and a huge grain store was still intact. It was Konishi's greatest triumph, because the last major defence line before the Chinese border had now collapsed. It was only 80 miles to Ŭiju, his right flank was secure, and his rear communications from P'yŏngyang through Seoul to Pusan were safely covered by a string of defended castles. All he needed were massive reinforcements, and then nothing could stop his magnificent First Division from leading the way once again towards the final realisation of Hideyoshi's grandest dreams.

To the great surprise of the Japanese, the Koreans evacuate P'yŏngyang without a fight. (ETK detail)

KATŌ KIYOMASA'S INVASION OF MANCHURIA

While Konishi Yukinaga was advancing towards P'yŏngyang the other Japanese generals were making their own contributions to the conquest of Korea and the preparations for an invasion of China. The eastern province of Kangwŏn had been allocated to the Fourth Division of Mōri Yoshinari, an obscure daimyō of whom few details are known. Together with Akizuki Tanenaga, Itō Yūbei and Takahashi Mototane he set out from Seoul in July and marched across the peninsula towards Anbyŏn, which lies just south of modern Wŏnsan. He then turned south to capture a line of fortresses down the east coast as far as Samch'ŏk, then turned inland, taking Ch'ŏngsŏn, Yŏngwŏl and P'yŏngch'ang. Mōri Yoshinari finally set up his base in the provincial capital Wŏnju, where he busied himself with the thoroughly respectable business of land surveys, civil administration and squeezing the peasants in the classic Hideyoshi style. His colleague Shimazu Yoshihiro had been delayed because of the Umekita rebellion, and on landing went via Ch'ŏrwon to the coast as far as Kansŏng, then turned inland via Yanggu and set up base at Ch'unch'ŏn. The whole of Kangwŏn province was thereby secured.

With Mōri's Fourth Division providing his rearguard, Katō Kiyomasa began to make slow but steady progress towards Korea's north-eastern tip in a campaign that was to take him the best part of the next four months. His Second Division army of more than 20,000 men crossed the peninsula over a precipitous road through Koksan, and dropped down to the Sea of Japan coast at Anbyŏn after a ten-day march guided by captured Koreans. He then followed the coast northwards via Yŏnghŭng, taking the important castle of

Map of Katō Kiyomasa's campaign in Hamgyŏng province in the north-east, including his fight with the Orangai in Manchuria.

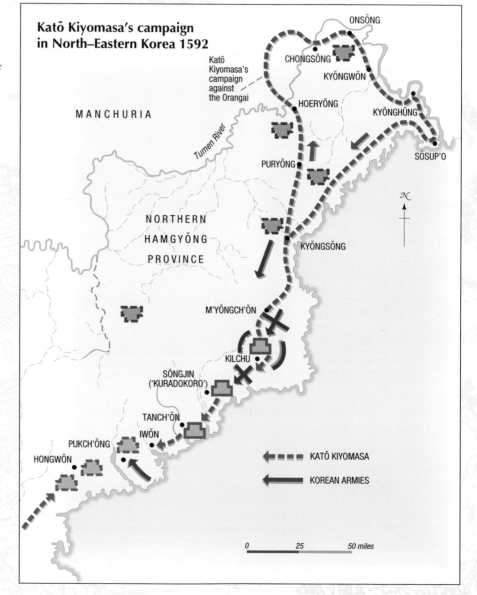

Katō Kiyomasa's campaign in North–Eastern Korea 1592

Hamhŭng (called Kankō in the Japanese chronicles), which was Hamgyŏng's
provincial capital. Here it was decided that Katō would press on along the
coast with his own army, while his comrades Nabeshima Naoshige and Sagara
Nagatsune stayed in Hamhŭng to provide a rearguard and also to set in motion
Hideyoshi's plans for the civil administration of the captured territories.

Much marching lay ahead. Northern Hamgyŏng province was an area so
wild and remote that even Korean troops hesitated to enter its mountains,
but Katō Kiyomasa battled on. Tanch'ŏn, where Katō took possession of an
extensive silver mine, was reached about a month later, but not far to the
north he received his first real challenge of the campaign. This happened at
Sŏngjin (present day Kimch'aek) where there was a large grain storehouse
by the sea ('Haejŏngch'ang'), so that the ensuing battle is referred to in the
Japanese chronicles as the 'battle of Kuradokoro (the grain store location)'.
Opposing Katō were Yi Yŏng, commander of the southern Hamgyŏng army,
and Han Kŭk-ham of the northern Hamgyŏng force. The flat plains of Sŏngjin
allowed the Korean cavalry an opportunity to perform at their best, and they
succeeded in driving the Japanese into the storehouse itself. Believing that he
had Katō at his mercy, Han ordered a mass formation attack, to which the
Japanese responded with volleys of arquebus fire from behind makeshift

*The battle of Sŏngjin
(Haejŏngch'ang), where
Katō Kiyomasa's men
barricaded themselves
inside a rice warehouse
using rice bales as defences.
(ETK)*

barricades erected from bales of rice. In this way the Korean army was not only held off, but forced to retreat to the safety of a nearby hill as night fell. Han planned a fresh attack in the morning of 7m17d (24 August) but Katō anticipated this by a night raid of his own before dawn broke. Under the cover of darkness and fog his army left the storehouse and surrounded the Korean position almost completely. One very obvious gap was left. It led to a swamp, and as the massed arquebus fire began the Koreans naturally made for the only visible escape route, and were cut down in the mire. Han Kŭk-ham fled north to Kyŏngsŏng.

The fact that the 'battle of the storehouse' at Sŏngjin happened a full month after Konishi captured P'yŏngyang illustrates how much longer the campaigning distance was been for Katō's division. However, Han Kŭk-ham's precipitate retreat from Sŏngjin speeded Katō's subsequent progress considerably, because the fleeing Korean general caused alarm in every garrison through which he passed, making the capture of Kilchu and M'yŏngch'ŏn an easy matter. When Katō arrived at Han's home base of Kyŏngsŏng he found that it, too, had been abandoned.

The two Korean princes are brought as captives to Katō Kiyomasa in the frontier town of Hoeryŏng by renegade Koreans. (ETK detail)

Here Katō left the coast and headed inland via Puryŏng for Hoeryŏng where, he had been reliably informed, the two Korean princes had taken refuge. 'Refuge', however, was perhaps an inappropriate term to use, because Hoeryŏng, which lay on the Tumen river, was actually a penal colony used by the Korean court for political exiles, none of whom had a great deal of sympathy for the Korean royal family. The ordinary population of northern Hamgyŏng also bore many a grudge against the policies of the remote and grasping Seoul government. As a result, when Katō marched into Hoeryŏng on 7m 23d he found the two princes already captured by their own subjects! The prisoners were willingly handed over to the Japanese along with a further captive in the person of the provincial governor Yu Yŏng-nip. Soon after this another welcome presentation was made to Katō when a local warrior band brought him the fugitive Han Kŭk-ham tied in ropes, and the severed head of another Korean general. At this Katō Kiyomasa drew the not unreasonable conclusion that Hamgyŏng province had been pacified, and despatched the good news back to Hideyoshi in Kyoto together with thirty pieces of silver from the plundered mines of Tanch'ŏn, a gift which had an ironical side that may not have been entirely lost on any Christian daimyō who got to hear of it.

It was now early September, and after sending the two princes down to Kyŏngsŏng with an armed escort of 1,000 men, Katō Kiyomasa prepared for a short but symbolic military operation. Across the Tumen river from Hoeryŏng lay Manchuria, the land of the ancient Jurchens, whom the Japanese referred to as Orangai (from the Korean word *oranke*, which means barbarian). The Koreans of Hamgyŏng had no more love for the Jurchens, who periodically raided them, than they had for the distant government in Seoul who taxed them, and eagerly offered to become Katō's guides, and even his vanguard, for a punitive raid.

According to the compiler of the *Kiyomasa Kōrai no jin oboegaki*, the chronicle of Katō's Korean exploits, the motivation for the attack was simply to test the mettle of his troops against the Orangai, and his 3,000 Korean allies proved to be a great help in this.[10] Their presence raised the numbers of Katō's army to 11,000, and with the men of Hoeryŏng leading the way Katō Kiyomasa became the first Japanese general to cross into China. The fact that he was destined to be the only one who would ever do so could not have been entertained as the slightest possibility at this stage in the triumphant Korean campaign. With a mind set only on glory the Japanese advanced, the chronicler noting with satisfaction the Nichiren slogan 'Namu Myōhō Renge Kyō' carried forward proudly on the breastplates of Katō's foot soldiers.[11] The first objective was an Orangai fortress.

A group of samurai attempt to dislodge an enormous rock. Beyond is a fanciful view of eastern Manchuria, the home of the Jurchens, called the Orangai by the Japanese. (ETK detail)

> As dawn was breaking we arrived . . . and drew up our ranks. As is the usual way in this strange country they are not only enclosed securely in front, but at the rear they have recourse to high stone walls in mountain recesses. When we saw that it did not appear to be very well defended, the men from Hoeryŏng went forward, while the Japanese went round to the mountain at the rear, and with 50 men or 30 men working together prised out the stones using crowbars, and the wall collapsed.[12]

Fierce arquebus volleys followed, and the Orangai castle fell. At the end of a day's fighting in the vicinity the Japanese pulled back in the direction of the border and set up their lines on a hill for the night.

The following morning the Koreans headed back across the Tumen, leaving Katō's men to face a counterattack from perhaps as many as 10,000 Jurchens. This was a bitter contest, and at one stage Katō Kiyomasa took his cherished Nichiren standard into his own hands when his standard bearer was killed beside him. 'For every Japanese slain,' wrote the chronicler proudly, 'there were twenty or thirty Orangai',[13] but the situation was so desperate

The hero Saitō Toshimitsu grapples with a Chinese soldier in this print by Kuniyoshi. Saitō's opponent is described on the print as 'a foe man more than eight shaku in height, his bristly moustache like growing thorn'. The ferocity of their struggle caused both to fall into the river, where the combat continued in the Japanese warrior's favour.

that Katō gave orders that the heads cut off were not to be collected as trophies but to be discarded after being counted. Over 8,000 Orangai heads were tallied, but still the fighting continued. However, as the chronicler noted with some relief, 'Japan is the Land of the Gods, consequently on that day an exceptionally heavy rain fell on our behalf, and blew on the faces of the Orangai, so they withdrew.'[14] 'Thus,' added an enthusiastic nationalist historian many years later, 'Katō Kiyomasa showed those savages the bravery of the Japanese.'[15]

This brief but bloody engagement had in fact provided the beginning and the end of the Japanese invasion of China. Oblivious of this, and no doubt vowing to return, a well-satisfied Katō Kiyomasa returned to Korean territory across the Tumen a short way downstream from Hoeryŏng, and then began to plod slowly eastwards towards the sea, capturing the fortresses of Chongsŏng, Onsŏng, Kyŏngwŏn and Kyŏnghŭng, which together with Hoeryŏng and Puryŏng made up the so-called 'Six Garrisons'. The Japanese finally reached the Japan Sea coast at Sŏsup'o on the Tumen river estuary, where these fierce invaders allowed themselves a brief moment of poetical whimsy. As Katō's chronicler notes, 'From Sŏsup'o, when the weather was clear, there was the illusion that Mount Fuji was somewhere near, and although Mount Fuji could not actually be seen from there, one could believe that it lay due north of the pine-clad beach.'[16]

So Katō Kiyomasa set up his camp stool on this remote beach where nowadays North Korea, China and Russia come together, and gazed across at the shape of the nearby volcanic island that reminded everyone of home.

Katō Kiyomasa's men do battle with the Orangai during the only time in the whole campaign when a Japanese army actually crossed into China. (ETK)

It provided a short but welcome rest from marching and slaughter, and was carried out in the classic samurai style of the tranquil detachment that allowed a ruthless warrior to contemplate cherry blossoms and tea bowls while death lay all around him. All too soon Katō managed to tear himself away from the aesthetic spectacle, rose from his seat, and began to follow the coast back to Kyŏngsŏng and reality.

Resting on the beach at Sŏsup'o, Katō Kiyomasa's men are entranced by what appears to be a view of Mount Fuji. (ETK detail)

While Katō Kiyomasa had been off on his adventures his colleague Nabeshima Naoshige had busied himself with converting Hamgyŏng province into a Japanese colony, treating it as if it were to all intents and purposes one more Japanese province to be conquered in the name of Toyotomi Hideyoshi. Tax rolls, land surveys and sword hunts all went ahead with the same methodical ruthlessness by which Japan had been made to submit, and with the same penalty for non-compliance – that of having your head cut off.

By contrast, Katō's gestures towards the occupation of northern Hamgyŏng proved to be somewhat rudimentary. There was a limit to which his communications could be stretched, and the rebellious spirit shown by the locals against the Korean government encouraged Katō to put the fortresses of Hoeryŏng and Kyŏngsŏng into Korean hands in return for a pledge of allegiance on the well-tried Hideyoshi model. As M'yŏngch'ŏn was regularly subject to Jurchen attacks from the Musan area near the Chinese border, this too was placed in local hands. Japanese garrisons only began at Kilchu, where 1,500 men were stationed, together with 500 in Sŏngjin, 500 in Tanch'ŏn, 550 in Iwŏn, and Pukch'ŏng, which was held by 1,300 troops. Here Katō's men gave way to Nabeshima's chain of coastal garrisons at Hongwŏn, Hamhŭng, Chŏngp'yŏng, Yŏnghŭng, Kowŏn, Munch'ŏn, Tŏkwŏn and Anbyŏn.[17]

Katō Kiyomasa eventually rejoined Nabeshima at Hamhŭng on 9m 7d (12 October), proud of his achievement in pacifying Korea's wildest province. Exactly four months had passed since he had stared in frustration across the Imjin river. He had probably been informed of Konishi's success in taking P'yŏngyang, but how much else did Katō know of what had happened subsequently? Had anyone dared tell him that during the intervening period the Japanese forces had been overtaken by a series of military disasters, and that the invasion of China was now effectively cancelled?

chapter five

THE DEFEAT OF
THE JAPANESE ARMADA

Konishi Yukinaga's First Division had secured P'yŏngyang within two months of landing in Korea. His communications were covered by a chain of forts that stretched right back to the port of disembarkation, and any threat to his eastern flank was being slowly taken care of by Katō Kiyomasa's Hamgyŏng campaign. The plan now was that the troops who would cross the Yalu into China, together with their food and equipment, would be ferried round the south-western coast of Korea, up the Yellow Sea coast, and disembarked on the Taedong river at P'yŏngyang.

The reason why the reinforcements never arrived is the subject of this chapter, because in spite of the initial disasters suffered at Pusan and Ch'ungju, Korea rallied, and within days of the loss of Seoul there were three separate developments whose influence continued until all the Japanese invaders had been driven away. These factors were the naval campaign, the actions by volunteer guerrilla armies, and the intervention of Ming China. All were of the utmost importance, but of the three the naval campaign is probably the most remarkable because its success was due almost entirely to one man: Admiral Yi Sun-sin.[1]

Yi Sun-sin is Korea's greatest hero, and is one of the outstanding naval commanders in the entire history of the world. He was born in 1545, and received the thorough Confucian education that was so necessary for men of his social station. Yi passed the military service examinations in 1576, after which he was appointed to his first command in Hamgyŏng province. After a brief spell in a naval command in Chŏlla in 1580, he was moved back to the army and saw action against the Jurchens in Hamgyŏng in 1583, distinguishing himself in one particular battle beside the Tumen river where he enticed the Jurchens forward with a false retreat. In 1587 he fell foul of the political and factional rivalry that plagued Korean society, and found himself back in the ranks as a common soldier after annoying General Yi Il. Fortunately for Korea,

Yu Sŏng-nyong, the future prime minister of Korea, was a rising star at court and had been Yi's boyhood friend, so through Yu's influence Yi was reinstated and new responsibilities soon followed. In 1591, following Yu's recommendation, Yi Sun-sin was appointed to the post of Left Naval Commander of Chŏlla province, where he threw himself enthusiastically into his duties as the Japanese threat loomed ever nearer.

The eventual destruction of the Japanese fleet by Admiral Yi Sun-sin is a story so familiar and so splendid that it completely overshadows the fact that, had circumstances been only slightly different during the early months of 1592, the Japanese should never have landed at all. It will be recalled from an earlier chapter that in 1588, the same year that Sir Francis Drake was defeating an Armada of his own, a certain Cho Hŏn had advocated the despatch of an armed force to Japan and was exiled for his presumption. Such an act may indeed have been audacious in 1588, but once Hideyoshi's war aims had been made clear following the failure of Sō's embassies, and the invasion fleet was assembling, it would have been opportune for a Korean fleet to sail to Tsushima and 'singe the King of Japan's beard'. History might then have recorded a subsequent interception off Pusan as Korea's 'Spanish Armada', with the prospect of hundreds of Japanese transports being harried along the southern coast of Korea and up through the Yellow Sea, their survivors cast adrift or slaughtered on the beaches. The reality, however, was to be very different.

In 1592 the responsibility for the maritime defence of Korea was divided between four men who covered the two southern provinces of Kyŏngsang and Chŏlla. The Right Naval Commander of Chŏlla was Yi Ŏk-ki, who was based on Korea's south-western tip and therefore covered the passage up to the Yellow Sea. The Left Naval Commander of Chŏlla was Yi Sun-sin, who was based at Yŏsu, but his authority only extended as far as the provincial border, which in maritime terms meant the strait between the Yŏsu peninsula and Namhae island. Here the Chŏlla command gave way to Kyŏngsang's Right Naval Commander, Wŏn Kyun, whose base lay on the western shores of Kŏje island. He shared this crucial sea area with Left Naval Commander Pak Hong, who was stationed on an island near to Pusan harbour.

According to Yi Sun-sin's Memorial to Court dated 4m 15d, the Japanese invasion fleet, which was 'sailing towards Pusan in a long line of battle' was first spotted by the lighthouse keeper who relayed the news to the commander of a fort on Kadŏk island at the mouth of the Naktong. This commander quickly sent the message on to Wŏn Kyun, while he himself sent out patrol boats to monitor the Japanese movements.[2]

History does not record whether or not Wŏn Kyun was playing a Korean equivalent of bowls when the alarming message arrived at about 10.00 a.m. but his demeanour was as relaxed as that attributed to Sir Francis Drake, although Wŏn Kyun's conclusion was somewhat different, as he believed that the Japanese fleet was on a trade mission. By 4.00 p.m. a further report from Kadŏk island that hundreds more Japanese ships were approaching, confirmed by similar reports from his colleague Left Naval Commander Pak Hong, seems finally to have convinced him that something very serious was happening.

That night the Japanese fleet carrying the First Division under Konishi Yukinaga lay packed together and vulnerable in Pusan harbour, but neither Pak Hong nor Wŏn Kyun did anything about it. By 6.00 a.m. the following morning it was too late to act, because about that time the keeper of a lookout beacon in the Sŏmyŏn area of Pusan reported to them that the attack on Pusan had begun, and that the road to Tadaejin, the coastal fort attacked by Konishi, had been cut. At this point Left Commander Pak Hong took decisive action. He descended from the mountain where he had been observing the Japanese attack, scuttled his fleet and destroyed all the armaments and provisions. He then deserted his garrison and escaped overland to Kyŏngju, where he created panic. Wŏn Kyun responded somewhat less drastically, merely scuttling part of his fleet and, abandoning his station on Kŏje island, fleeing with four ships to Konyang. As a result of their disgraceful actions there were no Korean ships left in the waters of Kyŏngsang province within hours of the Japanese attack.

Being based many miles to the west at Yŏsu, and also having no jurisdiction over Kyŏngsang, Yi Sun-sin of Chŏlla province could only listen, wait and prepare as best he could, and every day a note in his diary records some new

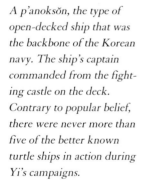

A p'anoksŏn, the type of open-decked ship that was the backbone of the Korean navy. The ship's captain commanded from the fighting castle on the deck. Contrary to popular belief, there were never more than five of the better known turtle ships in action during Yi's campaigns.

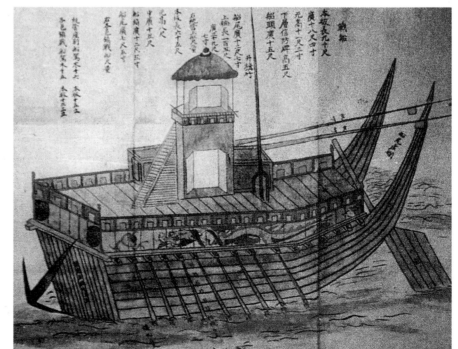

disaster. In his entry for 4m 15d the Japanese have arrived in Pusan harbour. On 4m 16d we read of the capture of Pusan castle. The entry for the 17th day notes the occupation of the city, and for the 18th the fall of Tongnae. Meanwhile he is preparing his own defences, and is eager to go into action, his emotions spilling over from his private diary into the reports he is sending to King Sŏnjo. In a Memorial to Court dated 4m 16d he expresses his 'astonishment and indignation',[3] while in a later report we read that 'the enemy's attack is raging with such ferocious speed that Pusan, Tongnae and Yangsan have already fallen into his hands, and his spearhead is now penetrating the interior regions', making Yi's heart 'rent with anger and grief'. However, he assures the king, the time is now right to hit back. 'We must make surprise attacks on them, displaying our martial spirit and shooting power.'[4]

On 4m 29d Yi Sun-sin received a report from Wŏn Kyun, written in his refuge at Konyang. He was somewhat economical with the truth over the reasons for his sudden presence there, claiming that he had engaged the enemy but that overwhelming numbers had driven him back. At least Wŏn Kyun was still around, unlike the cowardly Pak Hong, and was willing to join in the fight with Yi Sun-sin at his side.[5] Yi therefore sent a messenger on ahead to the nearby island of Namhae to ensure that ships and troops were ready to join them for an attack. The messenger returned with the disturbing news that Namhae had been looted and deserted by its own inhabitants, with 'not a human soul in the government buildings or private houses, no smoke in the chimneys, warehouses and armoury doors flung open, with food grain scattered and weapons stolen'.[6] The result was that Yi Sun-sin found himself commanding a vastly reduced force that was rapidly haemorrhaging:

Even veterans, on hearing of the enemy coming, escape at night with their families, carrying bundles of household goods on their heads and backs . . . I sent troops to arrest escapees and had two of the fugitives brought back, beheaded them and had their heads exposed . . .[7]

The above quotation is from Yi's Memorial to Court for 4m 30d, by which time Yi had been told of the battle at Sangju and the crossing of the Choryŏng pass. 'It may be a foolish thought,' he muses and, without mentioning any names, continues:

. . . but in my opinion the enemy attacks fiercely, trampling our fair land under iron feet, because we allowed him to set foot on our shores instead of fighting him at sea . . . Had our captains of war stationed along the coast of Pusan and Tongnae maintained their warships in formation at sea, menacing the enemy's flank with surprise attack and feigned retreat . . . the catastrophic national disgrace would not have reached to this depth.[8]

As Yi's military intelligence was very good the information he was receiving allowed him to work out accurately what was actually going on, and in the same report he writes that 'the cruel Japanese are divided into two groups – one marching north through our heartland and another entering our coastal towns to perpetrate outrages'.[9] He is also wise enough to realise that he can do little about the land invasion marching north, but that his naval forces could make a significant contribution against the second group.

The reality that lay behind Yi's conclusion was that while Konishi Yukinaga and Katō Kiyomasa were forging roads through northern Korea by sieges and pitched battles, a lesser known, but no means less savage, campaign was being launched along the southern coast of Kyŏngsang province, and to its inhabitants it was as if the Japanese pirates had returned. There were no major battles in this war, just the securing of land and sea communications to the west by using the weapon of terror, and it is perhaps for this reason that the Japanese movements are largely anonymous. In most cases it is impossible to identify the units engaged, and even the identity of the high-ranking Japanese commanders remains a mystery. No heroic chronicles record their movements in this war of rape, raiding and pillage which so resembled the wakō depredations of yore, and it is only from the Korean records of the victories achieved against them that we know anything of their activities. Mōri Terumoto had been given overall command of Kyŏngsang by Ukita Hideie, but the coastal raids appear to have been carried out by the minor daimyō held originally in reserve and shipped over to Korea after Pusan had fallen. A definite impression is given that these men, who were clearly not in the first rank of samurai heroes, were left very much to their own devices like the pirate raiders of old. The only prominent daimyō known to have taken part in the depredations were the Kurushima brothers and Kamei Korenori, whose gold fan, presented to him by Hideyoshi, was among the booty of the battle of Tanghangp'o. Apart from them, the generals and captains whom Yi was to defeat so decisively are conveniently lost in the annals of samurai disgrace.

Yi's next Memorial to Court is dated 5m 4d. It is short, and in it he announces his plans to join forces with Wŏn Kyun and attack the enemy, 'at this time when the enemy spearheads, which marched north through our heartland, will soon invade Seoul'.[10] Had he known then that his country's capital had already fallen and that King Sŏnjo was on the way through the rain to P'yŏngyang he might have hesitated from the action he was about to take. Happily ignorant of these developments, Yi Sun-sin set out to give Korea its first victory of the war.

THE RIVAL NAVIES

Before describing the first clash between the naval forces of Korea and Japan it is worth spending some time assessing their rival capacities, because among all the meticulous planning that went into the recruitment and assembly of troops for the invasion of Korea, naval support did not figure highly. The presence of thirty miles of sea between Tsushima and Pusan was perceived merely as a problem of transport, not as a matter that might pose any potential military hazard. It will be recalled that in 1585 Hideyoshi had tried to obtain the services of Portuguese ships to escort his fleet, but the refusal to cooperate does not seem to have caused him any concern over the next few years. The requisition of ships and sailors for the invasion followed a similar pattern to the muster of troops. Each daimyō with a coastline to his province was required to supply two large ships for every 100,000 koku of assessed revenue, and ten boatmen for every 100 households. The result was a naval force of about 9,200 men.

In the previous chapter reference was made to the attack on the communications fort of Yong'in by a Korean army, the first counter offensive by a Korean army on land. This minor action had added significance in that the commander of Yong'in was a certain Wakizaka Yasuharu, whose name does not appear in the muster roll of the invading army. This was because Hideyoshi had given him a job as an admiral, and it says a great deal about the lack of concern Hideyoshi had for naval matters that as soon as an admiral landed in Korea he could be put in charge of a communications fort a few miles south of Seoul!

But Wakizaka was not the only naval commander to find that his primary duties were not needed when Wŏn Kyun's navy failed to intercept, harass or in any way hinder the invasion fleet before it landed. Together with Horibe Hirotada and Kuki Yoshitaka, Wakizaka had been responsible for naval operations in the Tsushima area after the departure of the invading armies. Three others, Hitotsuyanagi Naomori, Katō Yoshiaki and Tōdō Takatora had a similar, but even lighter responsibility for Iki. Even the four admirals appointed to Korean waters were only required to supervise the safe transportation of the various divisions, and all had been completely untroubled in the pursuance of their duties. Kurushima Michiyuki, an ex-pirate who supplied 700 men to the Fifth Division, had so little to do that he was switched to the arduous task of finding a suitable palace for Hideyoshi in Seoul to be used when he made his grand entrance.

As no seaborne challenge had been expected the Japanese ships that crossed the straits of Tsushima were little more than transport vessels, their only armaments being the weapons carried by the soldiers. This was a decision based on long experience, because few battles had been fought at sea during

Japan's century of civil wars. In 1578 there had been one major clash between ships of the Mōri daimyō, who were supplying the Ikkō-ikki sectarians of the Ishiyama Honganji, and the fleet of Oda Nobunaga who had sworn to destroy them. Nobunaga had built several large warships reinforced in places with iron plates, and a fierce battle ensued at the mouth of the Kizu river with rival boarding parties attempting first to sweep their opponents off their decks with arquebus fire, and then engaging in hand-to-hand combat. This pattern of naval warfare, involving close combat rather than long-range artillery, regarded sea fights as nothing more than land battles conducted from floating platforms. It was a tradition going back to the time of the Mongol invasions, and had sufficed for the very limited number of encounters seen during Hideyoshi's wars.

The Korean tradition was very different. At the beginning of the eleventh century Koryŏ shipbuilders had produced the kwasŏn (spear vessel), a ship built specifically for ramming marauding Jurchen vessels. Strength and size were the characteristics of Koryŏ ships. Their largest carried a crew of between 100 and 200 sailors, and one was said to be so large that it was possible to race a horse round the deck. The ships were quite simply designed, but were much stronger compared with contemporary Yuan (Mongol) Chinese vessels, as is shown by the fact that whereas nearly all the Yuan ships that took part in the Mongol invasion of Japan in 1281 were destroyed by the kami-kaze, the 'divine wind' that saved Japan, little damage was suffered by some 900 Korean ships that accompanied them.[11]

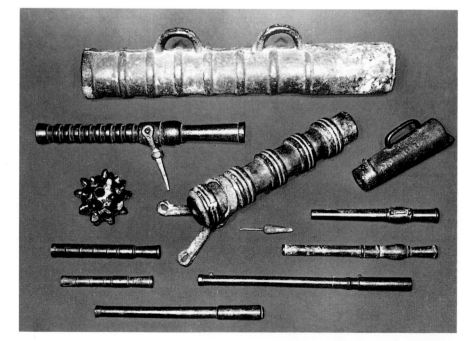

Types of gunpowder weapons used during the Korean War. At top, a chŏnja (heaven) mark cannon. Below it, at left, a hwangja (yellow) mark cannon fitted with a swivel at its trunnions. The spike of the swivel would be sunk into a wooden carriage. Centre is a Chinese 'crouching tiger' cannon, which has a loose collar with two legs to enable it to be laid on to a target. The six small guns are all varieties of sŭngja (victory guns), the hand-held Chinese-style firearms. At the end of the barrel is a hollow stock which would be fitted on to a wooden handle. Also shown is a gunpowder spoon, a breech container for a Chinese breech-loading folang zhi cannon, and a variety of hand grenade, probably of pottery.

The ships of the Chosŏn dynasty continued to emphasise solidity and strength rather than speed, but with a change in design that came about as a reaction to the Japanese pirates, whose favourite way of capturing a vessel was by using a boarding party. The traditional Chinese style of a ship with a flat freeboard, known in Korea as the maengsŏn type, unfortunately provided an ideal fighting ground for this. The first response was to build ships with simple raised gunwales behind which defenders could shelter. The Koreans then developed the p'anoksŏn ('board-roofed' or 'superstructured' ships), which added an extra deck, so that the oarsmen below were separated from the fighting sailors above. A rudimentary castle on the deck provided a command post for the captain. Like their predecessors, the p'anoksŏn were very solidly built, and the sizes of different p'anoksŏn are usually noted as either 50, 60 or 70 feet long at the bottom plates, with the largest on record being 110 feet long. All had a complement of 125 men and both sail and oar propulsion. Sturdy p'anoksŏn such as these made up the vast majority of the ships in the Korean navy of 1592.[12]

A Korean 'black' naval cannon mounted on a reproduction carriage at the Chesungdang on Hansan island. Ropes would be passed through the hoops on top of the barrel and secured to the rings on the carriage.

The p'anoksŏn were also well armed, a strange reversal of the situation on land, where the greatest discrepancy between the Korean and Japanese armies lay in their personal firearms. The Koreans only had the primitive sŭngja hand guns of a Chinese model, and were faced by Japanese troops armed with literally thousands of sophisticated arquebuses. In contrast, the Koreans who fought at sea had access to a wide range of effective artillery weapons denied to the Japanese. The lack of cannon on Japanese ships no doubt derived from their confidence in the power of concentrated arquebus volley fire to clear an enemy's decks, together with a long tradition of naval warfare by boarding parties who fought as if they were on land. Nonetheless, it is perhaps surprising that the Japanese should have expected no resistance from Korean ships armed with cannon, because vessels equipped in this way were by no means a new idea. The first Korean ships to carry cannon dated from the mid-fourteenth century, and were introduced specifically to tackle the menace of Japanese pirates. The cannon came originally from China at the end of the Yuan dynasty, but there are records of them being cast in Korea as early as 1377, and two successful battles against Japanese pirate fleets in 1380 and 1383 were won with the aid of cannon.[13]

The heavy cannon used on board Korean ships were of four types called ch'ŏnja (heaven), chija (earth), hyŏnja (black) and hwangja (yellow), in order of decreasing size and weight. The names have no particular significance, and refer simply to the first four characters of a classic Chinese text used for learning the alphabet, making them effectively 'cannon types A, B, C and D'. The 'black' and 'earth' mark cannon are the most frequently reported in battle accounts. They were mounted on simple box-like gun carriages, the barrels being tied on and secured with ropes that also enabled them to be laid on to a target. The heavy cannon could shoot cannonballs of iron or polished stone, but the favourite missile was the wooden arrow, winged with leather and tipped with iron. An early trial of an arrow firing cannon carried out in Seoul records the arrows being fired with such force that they entered the ground on impact, burying themselves beyond their feathers. The massive 10-foot-long arrows fired from the 'heaven' cannon were able to cause immense destruction when they struck the planking of a Japanese vessel. Fire arrows loosed from ordinary bows were also important, and some of the larger cannon-based arrows could also be converted into fire arrows. We may also add the use of exploding iron-cased bombs fired from mortars, such as were used in Korean siege work, although most accounts speak ambiguously of 'firebombs' or 'fire bullets' being used from ships.[14]

THE BATTLE OF OKP'O

Yi Sun-sin therefore prepared to do battle against this new variation on the theme of Japanese pirates, but the first requirement was to find out where his enemy was. The coast of Kyŏngsang province is a maze of beautiful islands, straits and inlets which provided many places for the Japanese to raid and also to hide. Yi Sun-sin was based at Yŏsu, which was just inside Chŏlla province, and west of the large island of Namhae. Beyond Namhae was the bay of Sach'ŏn which lay on the western side of the Kosŏng peninsula. Beyond Kosŏng was another large island called Kŏje, followed by a few small islands at the mouth of the Naktong including Kadŏk, which was close to Pusan. Yi's strategy was to send scouting boats on ahead through this archipelago, and also to receive intelligence from local fishermen about the Japanese movements.

As with so many of Yi Sun-sin's operations, we have a full and detailed account of the subsequent battle of Okp'o in his own words written in a Memorial to Court. 'Yi, Your Majesty's humble subject, Commander of Chŏlla Left Naval Station,' he begins, 'memorialises the throne on the slaughter of the enemy.'[15] Having sent a message to Right Commander Yi Ŏk-ki to follow him, Yi set sail under cover of darkness at 2.00 a.m. on 5m 4d at the head of 24 p'anoksŏn, 15 smaller fighting vessels, and 46 other boats. The fleet travelled for the whole of that day, entering Kyŏngsang waters at sunset, where he anchored for the night. At dawn he left for the agreed rendezvous point of Tangp'o, but Wŏn Kyun was nowhere to be seen. Wŏn eventually appeared

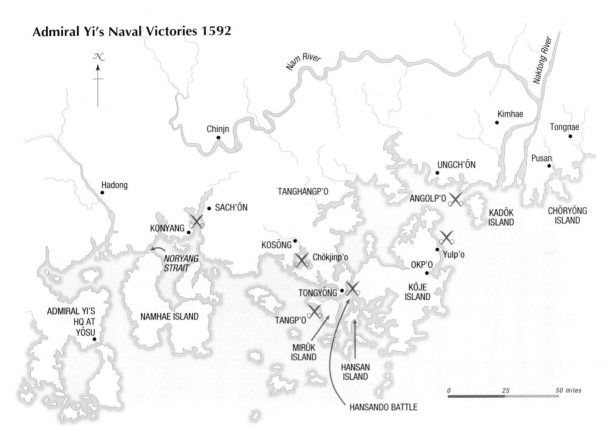

Admiral Yi's Naval Victories 1592

Map of the coastal area of Korea that saw Admiral Yi's great naval victories at Okp'o, Sach'ŏn, Tangp'o, Tanghangp'o and Hansando.

on 5m 6d, together with other captains who had been separately summoned. The augmented flotilla sailed on, and spent another night at sea. At dawn on 5m 7d the fleet rounded the south coast of Kŏje island and headed towards Kadŏk, where enemy ships had been seen gathering, but while they were on their way Yi's scouting vessels announced the discovery of fifty Japanese ships lying off the harbour of Okp'o, on the eastern coast of Kŏje. As with most of these encounters, it is by no means clear who the Japanese units actually were, but their purpose was clear. Having no opposing armies to fight they were carrying out their mission to pacify Kyŏngsang by looting and burning the nearby port like their wakō ancestors:

> At that point the Japanese, who had been plundering the port, burning and killing, saw our warships through the smoke that rose above the mountain crests, and ran about in great confusion, shouting, trying to regain their boats and man their oars but being afraid to come out to the open sea, they fled along the shores. Six vanguard vessels led the way.[16]

Yi's ships encircled the fleeing Japanese, and bombarded them with cannon balls, wooden arrows and fire arrows. The Japanese returned their fire with arquebuses and bows, but the Korean tactic of attacking from a distance did not allow them any opportunity to board. 'They threw their stores overboard and jumped into the water to swim to the shore, dying in blood, while the survivors scattered over the rocky cliffs.'[17] Resisting the temptation to send parties ashore to mop up survivors, Yi pulled his fleet back to the open sea, and preparations were being made to spend the night when five more Japanese ships were spotted.

The Korean fleet gave chase and caught up with them near the mainland at Ungch'ŏn. Deserting their ships the Japanese hurried ashore, at which the Korean ships moved in and destroyed four out of the five with cannon and fire arrows. When it grew dark Yi pulled away and spent the night at sea. Twenty-six Japanese vessels had been sunk on that first day. The following morning reports were received that more Japanese ships had been sighted to the west so, completing the circuit of Kŏje island, Yi's fleet set off and eventually encountered thirteen ships at Chŏkjinp'o near Kosŏng. Once again a raid was being carried out on land, and as before the Koreans destroyed eleven out of the thirteen ships.[18]

The two-day fight around Kŏje island is known as the battle of Okp'o. It was fought without the loss of a single Korean ship, and caused consternation among the Japanese command when the news spread to newly conquered Seoul. At the time the stand-off at the Imjin river was still continuing, and a defeat in their rear was not what the Japanese generals wanted to hear. The rest of Yi's report to the King contains fascinating details of the plunder that fell to the Korean victors, and some moving tales were related to Yi by local people and released prisoners of war. One villager from near Kosŏng was distraught because he could not find his wife and his mother from whom he had been separated when the Japanese attacked. One young girl told of her father who was a Korean sailor, and how she did not know if he was alive or dead. As a captive of the Japanese she had become an eyewitness to the battle of Okp'o:

> Cannonballs and long arrows poured down like hail on the Japanese vessels from our ships. Those who were struck by the missiles fell dead, bathed in blood, while others rolled on deck with wild shrieks or jumped into the water to climb up to the hills. At that time I remained motionless with fear in the bottom of the boat for long hours, so I did not know what was happening in the outside world.[19]

In the midst of his triumph two things distressed Yi. One was the news just brought to him of the flight of the King. The other was the sight of the hundreds of refugees he kept meeting who were fleeing from the Japanese sack of Kyŏngsang province. They pleaded to be taken somewhere on his ships, but there were too many of them. Some of the gloom was happily lifted by the revelations provided by the booty from the Japanese ships. Certain articles quite amused him, and Yi was particularly intrigued by the Japanese habit of wearing elaborately ornamented helmets:

> The red-black Japanese armour, iron helmets, horse manes, gold crowns, gold fleece, gold armour, feather dress, feather brooms, shell trumpets and many other curious things in strange shapes with rich ornaments strike onlookers with awe, like weird ghosts or strange beasts.[20]

Not wishing to exclude King Sŏnjo from such wonders, Yi forwarded with his report 'one armoured gun barrel and one left ear cut from a Japanese beheaded by Sin Ho, Magistrate of Nagan'.[21]

Not surprisingly, Wŏn Kyun comes in for some criticism in Yi's report. The complaint was not, however, about his tardiness in arriving, but about Wŏn's extraordinary lack of discipline that allowed his men to shoot arrows at fellow Koreans who had captured Japanese vessels, so that Wŏn Kyun's men could claim them as their own prizes. With that stinging rebuke, the Memorial closes.[22]

THE BATTLE OF SACH'ŎN AND THE TURTLE SHIP

The people Yi had interviewed during the Okp'o actions provided ample proof of the savagery of Japan's pacification process along the coast of Kyŏngsang, and following his initial victory, Yi was naturally determined to take the fight to the enemy again. His original intention was to mount a major sea offensive in conjunction with Right Commander Yi Ŏk-ki, but on receiving a report from Wŏn Kyun that Japanese vessels had been sighted as far west as Sach'ŏn and Konyang, which lay very near the border with Chŏlla, Yi realised that he had to act swiftly, because it was very likely that ground troops were advancing along the coast as well. Wŏn Kyun moved his squadron to Noryang, at the northern end of Namhae island where the narrow straits divide Namhae from the mainland, and briefed Yi on the situation.

It appeared that many Japanese ships were moored in the bay of Sach'ŏn, and when Yi sailed there to confirm the report with 23 of his own ships and three of Wŏn Kyun's he observed much activity on land. Beyond the wharf at Sach'ŏn stood a prominent rocky crest. It was a naturally strong position, and would be the site of a bloody siege before the war was over, but for now a Japanese commander had merely set up his maku (the field curtains favoured as a command post) on the heights, and appeared to be supervising a small army. The hill was covered in red and white flags:

The bow of the 1:2.5 scale replica of the turtle ship in the War Memorial, Seoul. This reconstruction is based on the best available evidence and is regarded as the most accurate ever made. The dragon's head and the lower 'face' for ramming is clearly shown.

Below the mountain twelve large Japanese pavilion vessels were alongside the wharf. The Japanese standing on the heights of their position brandished their swords as if to strike at us at any moment.[23]

Yi was in a very difficult situation. He knew his arrows would not reach the Japanese on the hill, and the ebbing tide made it most unwise for the p'anoksŏn to sail in for close-range artillery fire. It was also getting dark, but the one encouraging sign was the extreme arrogance being shown by the Japanese. If they could be goaded into chasing the Korean fleet out on to the open sea then the situation could be very different. The Korean navy therefore turned tail and appeared to flee. As if on cue hundreds of Japanese poured down from the Sach'ŏn heights and leapt into their ships for a hot pursuit. By the time they caught up with the Koreans the tide had turned, and it is at this crucial point that we first read of the use in battle of Yi Sun-sin's secret weapon. 'Previously, foreseeing the Japanese invasion,' he writes modestly in his report to King Sŏnjo about the battle of Sach'ŏn, 'I had a turtle ship made . . .'[24]

The customarily self-effacing Yi Sun-sin would have been the last to claim that the famous kŏbuksŏn (turtle ship) was his own invention, although that is what many historians assume. Its creation actually went back centuries to the conversion of the single-decked maengsŏn into the double-decked p'anoksŏn with its high raised gunwales. The next logical step was to remove the p'anoksŏn's fighting castle and cover the upper deck area completely with a curving boarded roof stretching across from the gunwales, which had now become side walls. The original idea was that the turtle ship would function primarily as a ramming instrument, as was clearly outlined in an appeal that a certain T'ak Sin sent to the King of Korea in 1415:

> The turtle ship is capable of ramming the enemy fleet and causing damage to enemy vessels without incurring any itself. It is therefore a decisive tactical instrument. I suggest Your Majesty build more of such solid and cleverly designed vessels as instruments of victory.[25]

It seems likely that the long years of peace that Korea enjoyed for the subsequent century and a half allowed the idea of the turtle ship to fall out

of favour. It is therefore to the eternal credit of Yi Sun-sin that once danger
threatened he was able to revisit the idea and put it into practice. A note in
his diary for 2m 8d (21 March 1592) includes the sentence: 'Received at the
Headquarters 29 p'il of canvas to be used in the turtle ship'.[26] On 3m 27d his
diary notes that he has been watching the test firing of cannons 'from the
deck of the turtle ship',[27] while on 4m 12d there is a similar entry which reads:
'Tested shooting cannons of type "earth" and "black" on the deck of the turtle
ship.'[28]   Remarkably, this second session of testing took place the day before
the Japanese invaded. The turtle ship was not a moment too soon in being
produced!

The account of the appearance of the turtle ship in his Memorial on the
battle of Sach'ŏn is in fact the longest description Yi gives of his famous vessel
anywhere in his writings. It was fitted:

> . . . with a dragon's head, from whose mouth we could fire our cannons,
> and with iron spikes on its back to pierce the enemy's feet when they tried
> to board. Because it is in the shape of a turtle, our men can look out from
> inside, but the enemy cannot look in from outside. It moves so swiftly
> that it can plunge into the midst of even many hundreds of enemy vessels
> in any weather to attack them with cannon balls and fire throwers.[29]

*A view of the replica
turtle ship in the War
Memorial looking from
above. The authenticity
of the hexagonal metal
plates is still subject to
dispute, but the spikes
are confirmed by several
contemporary observers.
The scale of the ship is
1:2.5.*

A particularly brave captain was chosen to command the turtle ship on its first outing, and he led it as the Korean navy's vanguard when they counterattacked, firing 'heaven', 'earth', 'black' and 'yellow' mark cannon, and pouring a selection of cannon balls, wooden arrows and fire arrows into the Japanese fleet. All the Japanese ships that had followed them out of the bay were sunk or burned, in spite of fierce resistance, but when the fighting was at its height a lone Japanese arquebusier nearly changed the course of Asian history by putting a bullet through Yi's left shoulder. 'It was not serious,' wrote Yi with characteristic modesty, and with the coming of night the Korean fleet calmly withdrew.[30]

The battle of Sach'ŏn took place on 5m 29d (8 July). On the following day Yi's troops rested while Wŏn Kyun busied himself cutting the heads off dead Japanese, a choice of pastime which Yi allowed him on the grounds that 'having lost his ships and his sailors he has nothing to command'.[31]

THE BATTLES OF TANGP'O AND TANGHANGP'O

The second day of the sixth lunar month was to see the turtle ship in action once again at the battle of Tangp'o, off the southern coast of Mirŭk island. Once again it was the same pattern of a Japanese squadron lying at anchor to cover the looting and burning of a town. There were 21 Japanese ships in all, and their formation was dominated by a large vessel with:

> a tall pavilion of about three body lengths, soaring high into the sky, surrounded by a red brocade curtain, painted on the outside and embroidered with a large Chinese character 'yellow' on the four directions. Inside the pavilion was seen a Japanese Commander with a red parasol planted in front. He showed no expression of fear, like a man resigned to death.[32]

It is by no means clear who this impassive commander actually was. He is usually identified as Kurushima Michiyuki, who was descended from Kōno Michiari, one of the greatest heroes of the repulse of the Mongols in 1281. It was this same Kurushima who had been given the task of locating a residence for Hideyoshi in Seoul, but now we find him back on military duties. Whatever his identity, the interviews which Yi conducted after the victory with released Korean prisoners leave no doubt over how the man died, and include a remarkable eyewitness account by a Korean girl who had been captured by the Japanese and forced to be the commander's mistress. 'On the day of the battle,' she related, 'arrows and bullets rained on the pavilion vessel where he sat. First he was hit on the brow but was unshaken, but when an arrow pierced his chest he fell down with a loud cry.'[33]

The hail of arrows and bullets came chiefly from the turtle ship, which 'dashed close to this pavilion vessel and broke it by shooting cannon balls "black" from the dragon mouth, and by pouring down arrows and "heaven" and "earth" cannon balls from other cannon'.[34] It was an archer on a p'anoksŏn who put an arrow into the Japanese commander, at which a Korean naval officer cut off the prestigious victim's head with a stroke of his sword. The loss of Kurushima was a decisive blow to Japanese morale, and nearly all the Japanese ships were subsequently sunk or burned.

Although the booty may not have been as curious as that obtained at Okp'o, it was nonetheless very interesting, as on searching the captured flagship the Koreans found a golden fan on which was written the name of Toyotomi Hideyoshi. It turned out that the fan had been presented to Kamei Korenori in 1582, and provided a small symbolic link with the distant Taikō whose enterprise had brought the invasion into being.

For the next two days Yi's fleet, now augmented by the ships of his comrade Yi Ŏk-ki, searched the islands, beaches and straits of the complex sea lanes of Korea's southern coast for signs of the enemy. The morning of 6m 5d was foggy, and as it cleared some boatmen approached with news that a Japanese squadron, including some ships that had escaped from Tangp'o, were anchored in the bay of Tanghangp'o. Tanghangp'o was a wide bay across the peninsula from Kosŏng that was entered to the north-west by a narrow gulf. Twenty-six Japanese ships lay at anchor. Most were large, black painted warships of the size of p'anoksŏn, but one was a three-storeyed pavilion vessel like the flagship at Tangp'o. At the sight of the Korean ships the Japanese opened a

This modern painting hangs in the shrine to Admiral Yi at Noryang on Namhae island, the site of his final battle. In the middle ground a turtle ship acts as the vanguard for the Korean fleet as it races into action against the Japanese. In the foreground Admiral Yi commands from the deck of his p'anoksŏn flagship, while small boats add to the mayhem.

heavy fire, so Yi's fleet held back in a circle spearheaded by the turtle ship, which penetrated the enemy line and rammed the pavilioned flagship. The other Korean ships then joined in with cannon and arrow fire, but Yi realised that if the Japanese were driven back they might escape to land, so he again tried a false retreat to draw them on. Once again the ruse worked:

> Then our ships suddenly enveloped the enemy craft from the four directions, attacking them from both flanks at full speed. The turtle with the Flying Squadron Chief on board rammed the enemy's pavilion vessel once again, while wrecking it with cannon fire, and our other ships hit its brocade curtains and sails with fire arrows. Furious flames burst out and the enemy commander fell dead from an arrow hit.[35]

Pursuit began of the escaping ships and continued until nightfall with the destruction of all the Japanese vessels except one and the taking of 43 heads. The one ship to escape was apprehended by a Korean warship the following morning and a fierce fight ensued. The Japanese captain 'stood alone holding a long sword in his hand and fought to the last without fear', and it was only when ten arrows had been shot into him that 'he shouted loudly and fell, and his head was cut off'.[36]   Next to arrive on the scene was Wŏn Kyun, whose men proceeded to pull the dead bodies of the Japanese out of the water and cut off their heads, as he was wont to do. The battle trophies from Tanghangp'o produced more revelations about Japanese warfare when Yi discovered a military muster list of names of men with a blood seal next to each name, together with numerous suits of armour, weapons, tiger skins and saddles.

There was one more round to play of the furious campaign of the past few days. On 6m 7d Yi led his squadron further east again towards Kadŏk, and was rounding Kŏje towards Okp'o once again when they saw seven Japanese ships beat out of Yulp'o and escape towards Pusan. Yi immediately gave chase with his men rowing furiously, so that the ships were intercepted and all destroyed. With this battle of Yulp'o the successful episode came to a temporary halt, and for the next few days Yi searched the inlets and bays, but no enemy was to be found. As his fleet was not strong enough for him to contemplate a raid against Pusan harbour Yi sailed back to his base at Yŏsu on 6m 10d while Yi Ŏk-ki and Wŏn Kyun went their separate ways.

The Japanese raids appeared to have been severely curtailed thanks to Yi's defeat of his largely anonymous enemies. He notes in his Memorial that the flags at Okp'o were red, at Sach'ŏn white, at Tangp'o yellow and at Tanhangp'o black, but apart from suggesting that these were separate units no further information can be gleaned. As for the Korean victims of the Japanese raids, 'they danced for joy as if they had found new life'.[37]

Yi then had an unsavoury incident to deal with when a patrol-boat captain reported to him that his crew had cut off three Japanese heads from an escaping vessel, but that 'an unknown naval officer of the Kyŏngsang Right Naval Station Commander [Wŏn Kyun] came riding on a fast boat and robbed us of one of the heads by threats'.[38] Yi had in fact ordered his men not to collect heads as it was too time-consuming in the heat of battle, saying: 'I promise to recommend those who fight best by killing the living enemy or by shooting as expert marksmen even though they cut off no heads of the enemy dead.' As a result Yi's actual head count was far less than that of Wŏn Kyun, but when the above comments were made to him Yi sent as proof to King Sŏnjo the ears his men had cut off from 88 heads, 'salted and packed in a box for shipment to the court'.[39] By now Konishi Yukinaga had reached the southern bank of the Taedong at P'yŏngyang and was about to gain his most devastating victory, but on the seas the position of the two contending forces was totally reversed.

THE BATTLE OF HANSANDO

By strange coincidence, the victory at Tanghangp'o happened on the same day that a Korean attack was being launched on another Japanese admiral. This was carried out at Yong'in, near Seoul, on the landlocked admiral Wakizaka Yasuharu. Born in 1554, Yasuharu had served Hideyoshi loyally at the battle of Shizugatake in 1583, where he had become one of the 'Seven Spears', the bravest warriors who fought that day. In 1585 he had received in fief the island of Awaji in the Inland Sea, and the notorious whirlpools that are created there under certain tidal conditions must have acquainted him very rapidly with the dangers of seafaring. When the Korean campaign began Wakizaka was one of three commanders placed in charge of naval matters for the Tsushima theatre but, as noted earlier, he was transferred to land-based duties at Yong'in as soon as the army had landed.

The *Wakizaka ki* contains the text of the order given by Hideyoshi on 6m 23d recalling Wakizaka and his fellow admirals Katō Yoshiaki and Kuki Yoshitaka from their landlubberly duties following the débâcle at Tanghangp'o.[40] The account goes on to say that they actually arrived in Pusan nine days before Hideyoshi's order was actually issued, implying that the urgency of the situation on the south coast had been rapidly conveyed to them, and that a local decision was made before Hideyoshi had time to issue a formal command. Their mission was clear. Instead of expecting the raiding parties of the Kyŏngsang coast to resist the Korean navy, the three admirals would assemble a fleet and seek out Yi Sun-sin to destroy him.

Katō Yoshiaki (1563–1631), who was no relation to the other Katō presently

Wakizaka Yasuharu, identifiable from the double circle mon on the sails of his ship, pursues Admiral Yi into an ambush. As on so many occasions the desire by a Japanese general to be first into battle led to his undoing. (ETK detail)

tramping through Hamgyŏng province, had also been one of the illustrious 'Seven Spears of Shizugatake', and at the start of the Korean campaign he had been one of the naval commanders for the Iki area. The third member of the trio, Kuki Yoshitaka (1542–1600), was the only one who had real naval experience. He had once been a pirate operating on the Pacific coast from Ise and Shima, had served Oda Nobunaga in the amphibious attacks on the Ikkō-ikki sectarians of Nagashima, and had commanded Oda Nobunaga's fleet of 'iron ships' at the battle of Kizogawaguchi in 1578.

During the early days of the Korean invasion Kuki had shared the Tsushima command with Wakizaka, but now that there was the prospect of real action such willingness to share responsibilities rapidly disappeared. Wakizaka's fleet was ready, but neither Katō nor Kuki had enough time to assemble the number of ships they felt they needed for the operation. Being eager for personal glory, Wakizaka decided to act alone instead of waiting until they were all ready. The *Wakizaka ki* implies that the challenge from Admiral Yi was too pressing to consider any delay in responding, but it is more than likely that Wakizaka merely seized the opportunity to gain the personal honour of being the commander who single-handedly destroyed the Korean fleet. He therefore gleefully set sail from Angolp'o without his colleagues on 7m 7d with a fleet of 73 ships, including 36 large vessels, 24 medium-sized ships and three small boats.

We are fortunate in that detailed accounts of the ensuing battle are available from both Korean and Japanese sources. Admiral Yi wrote a lengthy Memorial to Court, while a briefer account from the Japanese side is found in the *Wakizaka ki*. The ensuing struggle takes its name from the island of Hansan near to which it was fought, so the battle, which was both the Salamis and the Trafalgar of Korea, is usually called the battle of Hansando, although Japanese sources usually refer to it by another local geographical feature and call it the battle of Kyŏnnaeryang. Like Okp'o, the overall action included a follow-up operation which is called by both sides the battle of Angolp'o. The later engagement was fought against the joint commands of Katō and Kuki, who had by then sailed to join Wakizaka.

Yi begins his report to King Sŏnjo with his assessment of the situation prior to the battle. Japanese ships still controlled the sea area between Pusan and the islands of Kadŏk and Kŏje, but had not ventured any further west since the Tanghangp'o operation. But there was a worrying development on land. Yi had heard that Japanese troops had captured Kŭmsan. This meant that

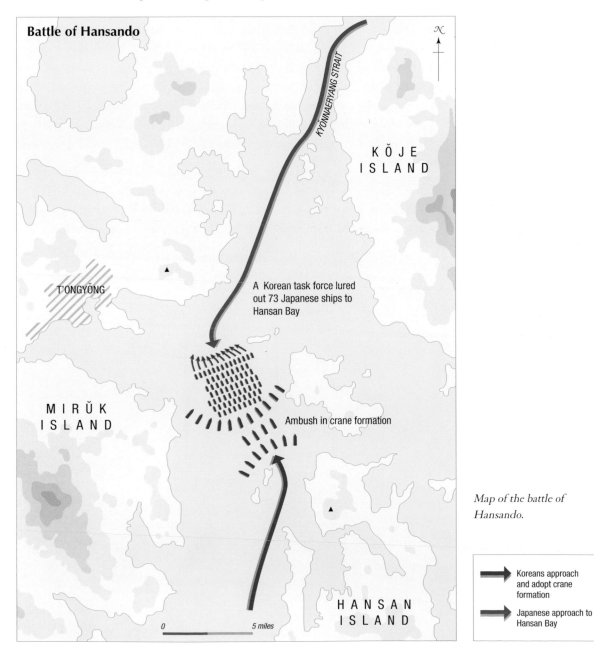

Battle of Hansando

KYOMNAERYANG STRAIT

KŎJE
ISLAND

T'ONGYŎNG

A Korean task force lured
out 73 Japanese ships to
Hansan Bay

Ambush in crane formation

MIRŬK
ISLAND

*Map of the battle of
Hansando.*

0   5 miles

HANSAN
ISLAND

Koreans approach
and adopt crane
formation

Japanese approach to
Hansan Bay

they were poised to make their first inroads into Chŏlla province from the north, and up to that time Yi's homeland of Chŏlla had been the only province still free of invaders. As naval support along the coast of Chŏlla would be vital to the Japanese advance, Yi decided to join Yi Ŏk-ki and Wŏn Kyun in a large-scale search and destroy operation against the Japanese fleet that he confidently expected to find.[41]

On 7m 6d the combined fleets of the Chŏlla stations made rendezvous with Wŏn Kyun in the straits of Noryang. The following day they continued eastwards in the face of a hostile gale, and anchored off the southern edge of Mirŭk island at Tangp'o, the site of the previous victory, where they took on water. On seeing them a local man came running down to the beach with the news that a large Japanese fleet had been spotted nearby. The Japanese ships had sailed south-west into the narrow straits of Kyŏnnaeryang which divided Kŏje from the mainland, and had anchored there for the night. Contact was made early the following morning when Yi's fleet headed for the straits and counted 82 enemy vessels:

> but the channel of Kyŏnnaeryang was narrow and strewn with sunken rocks, so it was not only difficult to fight in the bay for fear our p'anoksŏn might collide with one another but also the enemy might escape to land.[42]

The full-size replica turtle ship which lies at anchor in Yŏsu, the site of Yi's naval headquarters.

Yi therefore decided to try his well-rehearsed manoeuvre of a false retreat to lure the Japanese out into Hansan Bay to the south-west, where a wide expanse

of sea fringed by several uninhabited islands would provide an ideal location for a sea battle. Nowadays one can stand next to the statue of Admiral Yi on top of the hill that overlooks the port of T'ongyŏng and look out across this bay, where the whole of the battle of Hansando took place. To the south lies the island of Mirŭk, and to the south-east, framing the horizon of the bay, is Hansan island itself, with several islets dotted about before it.

The bait was taken, and from the north-east came Yi's vanguard of six p'anoksŏn, beating down the straits of Kyŏnnaeryang with Wakizaka's entire fleet in hot pursuit. When the Japanese were well clear of the rocky strait and out into the bay before Hansan island they found Yi's main body waiting for them near the place marked today by a lighthouse designed to look like a turtle ship. Here the Korean ships had spread out into a semi-circular formation which Yi's report calls a 'crane's wing'. The *Wakizaka ki* tells this part of the story as follows:

> The guard ships passed through the middle of the strait and out into a wide area. We took to our oars, at which they spread out their ships like a winnowing fan, drew our ships on and enveloped them.[43]

By the time of the battle of Hansando the number of turtle ships appears to have grown to at least three, because references to them in Yi's account clearly indicate a plural, and the Japanese account noted below counts three. With the turtles acting as the vanguard once again, the Korean fleet rowed towards the focal point of their crane's wing formation.

'Then I roared "Charge!",' writes Yi. 'Our ships dashed forward with the roar of cannon "earth", "black" and "victory" (the latter being the sŭngja hand-held firearms) breaking two or three of the enemy vessels into pieces.'[44] The fight now became a bloody free-for-all, the Korean ships trying initially to keep their chosen victims at a distance so as to bombard the Japanese without the risk of a boarding party being sent against them. Much hand-to-hand fighting took place, but Yi only allowed this if the Japanese vessel was already crippled. Thus we read that 'Left Flying Squadron Chief (a turtle boat captain) Yi Ki-nam captured one enemy vessel and cut off seven Japanese heads', and a certain Chŏng Un, captain from Nokto, 'holed and destroyed two large enemy pavilion vessels with cannon fire and burned them completely by attacks in cooperation with other ships, cut off three Japanese heads, and rescued two Korean prisoners of war'.[45] The greatest glory, however, fell to two individuals:

> Sunch'ŏn Magistrate Kwŏn Chun, forgetting all about himself, penetrated the enemy position first, breaking and capturing one large enemy pavilion vessel, and beheading ten Japanese warriors including the Commander, and bringing back a Korean prisoner of war. Kwangyang Magistrate Ŏ

Yŏng-tam also dashed forward, breaking and capturing one large pavilion vessel. He hit the enemy Commander with an arrow, and brought him back to my ship, but before interrogation he fell dead without speaking, so I ordered his head to be cut off.[46]

The expression 'Commander' in the above paragraph probably indicates the captains of the individual ships concerned, but it is known that two people very close to the overall commander Wakizaka Yasuharu were killed at Hansando, and the *Wakizaka ki* gives their names as Wakizaka Sabei and Watanabe Shichi'emon.[47] Yasuharu himself had a very narrow escape:

However, as Yasuharu was on board a fast ship with many oars he attacked and withdrew freely to safety. Arrows struck against his armour but he was unafraid even though there were ten dead for every one living and the enemy ships were attacking all the more fiercely. As it was being repeatedly attacked by fire arrows, Yasuharu's fast ship was finally made to withdraw to Kimhae.[48]

Unlike Wakizaka, one ship's captain could not face the dishonour of withdrawal:

A man called Manabe Samanosuke was a ship's captain that day, and the ship he was on was set on fire. This tormented him, and saying that he could not face meeting the other samurai in the army again, committed suicide and died.[49]

The *Wakizaka ki* also adds some detail about the Korean attacks, mentioning that the Japanese fleet was bombarded with metal-cased fire bombs shot from mortars similar to those used in Korean sieges. These weapons would probably have been fired from the open p'anoksŏn rather than from the confined space of a turtle ship.

The destruction of Wakizaka's fleet was almost total. Hardly a single ship escaped, and 'countless numbers of Japanese were hit by arrows and fell dead into the water', but not all were killed, because '... about four hundred exhausted Japanese, finding no way to escape, deserted their boats and fled ashore'.[50] The victorious Koreans, similarly exhausted, withdrew for the night.

Thus ended the first phase of the most severe defeat to be suffered by a Japanese force in the entire Korean campaign, but the battle of Hansando had a sequel, because the two colleagues whom Wakizaka had left behind had hurried after him to secure their share of the glory. Leaving Pusan on the day of the battle of Hansando, they were apprised of the disaster that same evening. One chronicle tells it rather differently, and reads: 'The two men Kuki Yoshitaka and Katō Yoshiaki heard tell of the distinguished service

Gunners roll out a cannon on the replica turtle ship at Yŏsu.

performed by Wakizaka Yasuharu',[51] but whatever their motivation, their fleet only got as far as the port of Angolp'o to which Wakizaka had withdrawn in defeat.

Hindered by an unfavourable wind, Yi Sun-sin had to wait one full day before pursuing Wakizaka and coming to grips with Kuki and Katō at the battle of Angolp'o. Yi Ŏk-ki remained off Kadŏk while Yi Sun-sin headed for the harbour to make a reconnaissance in force. Sailing forward in the crane's wing formation, with Wŏn Kyun's ships following closely behind, Yi found 42 Japanese ships lying at anchor with the protection of nearby land and shallow waters around. An attempt at a false retreat produced no response – the experience of Hansando had been enough to kill that trick stone dead – so Yi changed tactics and arranged for a relay of ships to row in, fire at the Japanese, and then withdraw, so that a rolling bombardment was kept up. Yi's report notes that this was indeed successful, and that almost all the Japanese 'pirates', as he perceptively calls them, on the larger vessels were killed or wounded, while many were seen escaping to land. This indicated further danger, because there was every likelihood that the Japanese would take their revenge on the Korean villagers living nearby, so when only a few Japanese ships were left undamaged, Yi called his fleet off and pulled out to sea to rest for the night. On returning the following morning the surviving Japanese had escaped by ship, leaving the local inhabitants untouched. The report continues:

We looked over the battle ground of the day before, and found that the escaped Japanese had cremated their dead in twelve heaps. There were charred bones and severed hands and legs scattered on the ground, and blood was spattered everywhere, turning the land and sea red . . .[52]

From the Japanese side the chronicle *Kōrai Funa Senki* gives a concise account of what happened at Angolp'o which tallies with Yi's report on most points of detail, and includes in its description the only specific mention in a Japanese chronicle of the turtle ships:

However, on the ninth day from the Hour of the Dragon [8.00 a.m.], 58 large enemy ships and about 50 small ships came and attacked. Among the large ships were three mekura-bune [blind ships, i.e. turtle ships], covered in iron, firing cannons, fire arrows, large (wooden) arrows and so on until the Hour of the Cock [6.00 p.m.].[53]

Oarsmen and an archer in action on the replica turtle ship at Yŏsu.

The same account also adds the interesting information that Kuki Yoshitaka was commanding the fleet from the huge warship, built originally for Hideyoshi, that had become the flagship of the Japanese navy on the outbreak of the Korean War. It was called the Nihon-maru (the equivalent of 'HMS *Japan*'), of which more details appear in the *Shima gunki*:

A three-storey castle was raised up, with a brocade curtain arranged in three layers, and on top was a 'Mount Hōrai', and on top of the mountain was a prayer offered to the Ise Shrine.[54]

The decorative 'Mount Hōrai' (Hōrai is the treasure mountain of Chinese mythology), was a Shintō device with rice heaped up on three sides, and adorned with various sacred objects, so that when 'they blew the conch and advanced upon the Chinamen the sight gave the impression that the Mount Hōrai was floating'.[55] The Koreans were clearly unintimidated by this mystical addition to the Japanese armoury and opened up on the Nihon-maru with everything they possessed:

However, when the fire arrows came flying, we were ready and pulled the charred embers into the sea with ropes, and the ship was not touched. They fired from near at hand with half-bows too, which went through the threefold curtain as far as the second fold, but ended up being stopped at the final layer. They then moved in at close range and when they fired the cannons they destroyed the central side of the Nihon-maru for three feet in each direction, but the carpenters had been ordered to prepare for this in advance, and promptly made repairs to keep out the sea water.[56]

The battle of Angolp'o was fought on 7m 9d (16 August), and it was noon of 7m 12d when Yi's fleet sailed back into the bay in front of Hansan island, which had been the scene of his most complete triumph. There they saw 'the Japanese who had escaped to that island sitting dazed on the shore, lame and having gone hungry for many days'.[57] There were 400 of them, although the Japanese records claim only half this number. By now Yi was receiving reports of Japanese ground troops advancing into Chŏlla province from the Kŭmsan area, so he withdrew to his base at Yŏsu, leaving Wŏn Kyun to his favourite pastime of beheading surrendered prisoners. 'As for the 90 enemy heads which my officers and men had cut off,' writes Yi, ' I had the left ears cut off and preserved with salt in a box to be sent up to the royal headquarters.'[58]

Fortunately for the marooned Japanese, Wŏn Kyun's natural cowardice outweighed his pleasure at the gory task, and when false reports reached him that another Japanese fleet was on its way to rescue them he sailed away. The fugitives then escaped by making rafts out of broken ships' timbers and trees, so that 'the fish in the cooking pot jumped out, to our great indignation', as Yi put it in a later Memorial to Court, which was written specifically as a complaint about Wŏn Kyun,[59] but the escape of the Japanese prisoners was only a minor blot on an otherwise complete victory. The Korean prime minister Yu Sŏng-nyong, heartened by a further piece of good news on the naval front, pondered on the significance of Hansando in *Chingbirok*:

> Japan's original strategy was to combine her ground and naval forces and advance into the western provinces. However, one of her arms was cut off by this single operation. Although Konishi Yukinaga has occupied P'yŏngyang, he can hardly dare to advance because he is isolated.[60]

News of the disaster at Hansando also travelled very rapidly up the Japanese chain of command, reaching Hideyoshi at Nagoya only seven days after the battle took place. Like his counterpart Yu Sŏng-nyong, Hideyoshi immediately realised the significance that Hansando had for the whole of the Korean operation, and on 7m 16d addressed an order to Tōdō Takatora, another of his naval commanders, who up to that point had remained in the safe haven of Iki island. While sending Tōdō to the assistance of his battered colleagues, Hideyoshi also instructed that all active naval operations should cease forthwith, and that the unfortunate Wakizaka Yasuharu should bend his immediate energies towards fortifying Kŏje island. The construction work soon began with alacrity, producing the first of the purpose-built castles that, together with the commandeered Korean fortresses, were to play such an important role in the long months of bitter fighting that were still to come.

chapter six

SOUTH TO THE NAKTONG – NORTH TO THE YALU

THE Korean province of Chŏlla was more fortunate than most in the quality of its leaders. The long coastline was defended by the redoubtable duo of Yi Sun-sin and Yi Ŏk-ki, while on land its commanders included Kwŏn Yul, who was one of Korea's few generals of real talent. Chŏlla had also been fortunate in that the Japanese dash to reach Seoul by the shortest possible route, which devastated Kyŏngsang and Ch'ungch'ŏng provinces in its wake, had left Chŏlla's borders unscathed. As a result, when Yi Sun-sin received reports in mid-August of a Japanese drive into Chŏlla, it was matter to be taken very seriously indeed.

The means by which the invasion of Chŏlla was to be resisted as successfully on land as it had been at sea illustrates the second of the three factors that eventually led to Japan's defeat – the war on land conducted by volunteers and guerrilla armies. These campaigns, piecemeal and sporadic though they may have been, made a lasting and valuable contribution to Korea's fight back against the invader. As this chapter will reveal, they would probably have done much more had it not been for a destructive mistrust and lack of cooperation between the different military units and social groups that made up the coalition of resistance.

In broad outline, the counterattacks on land against the Japanese, which began within a few days of the fall of Seoul, were conducted by three main types of soldier. The first were those members of the Korean regular army who had seen their generals flee or be killed, and who were then reorganised under a new commander. Some of these new leaders were serving officers who had received rapid promotion following the death of a general. Others were opportunistic yangban patriots, but most leaders who fell into this second category led the various citizens' brigades or peoples' volunteer units that went under the general heading of the Ŭibyŏng or 'Righteous Armies'. The final

group were the monk soldiers, armies of whom were established in every province very soon into the campaign. The activities carried out by the reorganised armies and resistance forces ranged from straightforward battles and sieges through guerrilla raids, to the support functions of transporting supplies and building walls. Their operations covered every area where Japanese forces might be challenged, from the Naktong delta in the south to the Yalu in the north. For the seven months prior to the arrival of Ming forces in January 1593, an estimated 22,200 irregulars shouldered the burden of resistance together with 84,500 regular soldiers, and made a considerable contribution to the war effort.

Within days of the Japanese landing the Koreans began to fight back, either as regular soldiers, civilian volunteers, guerrillas or warrior monks. In this painting in the Ch'ungyŏlsa at Tongnae the civilians of Tongnae join the Korean soldiers against the Japanese, and in the right background tiles are pulled from a roof and hurled down on to the invaders.

THE KYŎNGSANG VOLUNTEERS AND THE NAKTONG RIVER

Admiral Yi's first victory at Okp'o was achieved on 5m 7d (16 June), only five days after the fall of Seoul. Korea's first victory on land happened only a short time afterwards but is little known by comparison, even though it was won by Kwak Chae-u, one of the most celebrated and flamboyant characters in the Korean resistance movement.[1]

Kwak Chae-u was a landowner of Ŭiryŏng, a town on the Nam river in the south-west of Kyŏngsang province. Ŭiryŏng had been abandoned by the Korean regular army in the face of the advance by Kuroda's Third Division,

The line of the Naktong and Japanese-held Fortresses 1592–93

MUN'GYŎNG
HAMCHANG
SANGJU
SŎNSAN
KAENYŎNG
KIMSAN

ANDONG

KYŎNGSANG PROVINCE

Naktong River

■ **CHINJU** Korean Fort

Ankokuji Eke's advance to Ŭiryŏng

CH'UNG CH'ŎNG PROVINCE

CHŎLLA PROVINCE

INDONG

SŎNGJU

Kumho River

MUGYE
TAEGU

HYŎNP'UNG

■ **HAPCH'ON**
CH'ANGNYŎNG

■ **SAMGA**
UNSAN

ŬIRYŎNG
HAMAN

CHINJU
KIMHAE
TONGNAE

CH'ANGWŎN

Nam River
UNGCH'ŎN
PUSAN

KADŎK ISLAND

KŎJE ISLAND

0   25   50 miles

Map of the line of the Naktong, showing how the river was utilised by the occupying forces as an additional line of defence for their line of communications castles, which crossed the Naktong at Mugye.

its commander fleeing as soon as he heard the news of the invasion, but four days later Kwak Chae-u gathered a force of fifty villagers to resist the expected Japanese attack. None came, as Kuroda's men turned north after taking nearby Ch'angwŏn, and then kept on a straight course towards Sŏngju, which fell on 4m 24d. Nevertheless, Kwak Chae-u had achieved the distinction of being the first person in Korea to raise troops to fight the invaders, and this was only nine days after Konishi had taken Pusan. Kwak's army was assembled in great haste, so that he was forced to supply the men with food and equipment scavenged from abandoned government stores and arsenals.

This very necessary act of plunder proved too much for certain local officials, who reported Kwak's conduct to Kim Su, the governor of Kyŏngsang province, which was now a land in turmoil. Left Naval Commander Pak Hong had fled to Kyŏngju, and the Japanese First Division had taken Sangju and were converging on the undefended Choryŏng pass. As Kim Su had already ordered the population of Kyŏngsang to avoid all contact with the invaders and leave the business of fighting to skilled professionals like Yi Il and Sin Rip, he sent a message to Kwak branding him a rebel and ordering him to disband his tiny army. Kwak responded by asking for help from other landowners and sending an appeal directly to the King. Unbelievably, Kim Su then found both the opportunity and the resources to send troops against Kwak Chae-u! Fortunately an official had just been sent from Seoul to help raise troops in Kyŏngsang. He was a local man and knew Kwak's abilities, so he tried to mollify Kim Su, but relations deteriorated to such a point that when Kwak went recruiting he had to take a letter from the government fixed to his banner as proof of his legitimacy.

Kwak Chae-u, Korea's most celebrated guerrilla leader, from the portrait of him in Uiryŏng. Although always depicted as a flamboyant character dressed in a red coat and mounted on a white horse, Kwak's campaigns were invariably cautious and restrained, unlike those of many of his fellow countrymen.

Kwak Chae-u is remembered today as a romantic and mysterious patriotic hero, appearing from nowhere to defeat the Japanese, and then disappearing again into the mountains like a Korean Hereward the Wake. On his statue in Taegu and on the paintings of him in the Ch'ung Iksa shrine in Ŭiryŏng, he is depicted riding a white horse and wearing a scarlet coat, of which legend has produced the most outrageous hyperbole, saying that the coat was dyed red from the blood of the first menses of Korean maidens, the 'yin' of which overcame the 'yang' of Japanese bullets![2] Curiously, his flamboyant appearance contrasts sharply with his military activities, which were always careful and prudent.

Kwak's first military operations were directed against the western flank of the Japanese advance on Seoul, and made use of a powerful natural feature: the mighty Naktong river, which rises in the mountains near Andong and flows west before making a right-angled turn east of Hamch'ang. From here it flows south until its confluence with the Nam river, where its broadened flow continues eastwards towards Yangsan and then turns south to empty

Kwak Chae-u's followers harry the Japanese supply boats on the Naktong river at Kigang. This section of the river was ideal for guerrilla operations.

into the sea just west of Pusan. Kwak's base at Ŭiryŏng lay on the Nam river, which flows eastwards to join the Naktong in the area called Kigang. Here the river was wide and its flow was complex, and tall reeds could easily hide an ambush, so Kwak's guerrillas began to prey on the Japanese river boats ferrying newly landed supplies upstream. As well as disrupting the Japanese advance, attacks on the line of the Naktong also provided a similar defence by land to that which Admiral Yi was providing at sea against an incursion westwards into Chŏlla.

In the allocation of provinces made by Ukita Hideie, Chŏlla had fallen to the Sixth Division under Kobayakawa Takakage (1532–96), who had landed in Pusan on 4m 19d, having travelled across with his nephew Mōri Terumoto's Seventh Division. Both men belonged to the prestigious Mōri family who had ruled over much of the area of the Inland Sea from the mid-1550s. Mōri Terumoto (1553–1625) had been fighting Hideyoshi at the time of Nobunaga's murder in 1582, and had retained the Mōri territories after peace was negotiated in the usual Hideyoshi fashion. Kobayakawa Takakage was now 60 years old and one of the veterans of the Japanese army, a man who brought to Korea an immense amount of military experience on both land and sea.

The duties assigned to the two generals were very different. Mōri Terumoto's role was one of consolidation and pacification of the already-conquered province of Kyŏngsang, so his armies advanced slowly via Hyŏnp'ung on 5m 10d and Sŏngju on 5m 18d, eventually arriving on 6m 12d at Kaenyŏng, where he set up his headquarters. By contrast, Kobayakawa's role was one of new conquest. He therefore followed the existing invasion route as far as Sŏngju, then headed due west to Kŭmsan in Ch'ungch'ŏng, which he captured on 5m 11d to provide a jumping-off point for him to take possession of his own allocation: the neighbouring province of Chŏlla.

Back in Kaenyŏng, Mōri Terumoto's careful observation of the scene, and his long military experience had led him to draw a similar conclusion to Kwak Chae-u about the strategic importance of the Naktong basin, although he regarded the river as a line of defence for Kyŏngsang against a possible Korean attack. This was the feature of the Naktong that was to be used almost four centuries later by the United Nations in Korea when they were driven back towards Pusan by the North Korean advance in 1950. The line of the Naktong therefore became Mōri Terumoto's 'Pusan Perimeter', the river providing a rear line of defence to which the garrisons of the communications chain anchored on Sangju, Sŏnsan, Kaenyŏng, Kŭmsan and Sŏngju could fall back if necessary. For the forts downstream from Taegu – Hyŏnp'ung, Ch'angnyŏng and Unsan – the Naktong was their forward moat.

THE BATTLE OF ŬIRYŎNG

Meanwhile Kobayakawa Takakage was preparing to head south from Kŭmsan to invade Chŏlla, but the first we hear of an attack on that province comes in the form of an assault by another army from the south. Just as in the case of Admiral Yi's earliest campaigns against the anonymous bands of latter-day wakō, this attack on Chŏlla, which proved to be as much of a disaster for them as the naval campaign, is shrouded in obscurity. Even the date of its launch is unknown. Some authorities state that it happened in the middle of the fifth lunar month, others that it took place early in the sixth lunar month. It was planned as the southern arm of a two-pronged attack from the north and the south, and as the northern action was to be led by Kobayakawa Takakage from Kŭmsan, it is not unreasonable to assume that the southern advance was also carried out by men of the Sixth Division. However, the name of its leader, Ankokuji Ekei, does not appear in the muster lists of any division in the Japanese army! [3]

Ankokuji Ekei had originally been a Buddhist priest who had entered the service of Mōri Terumoto and played an important role in the negotiations between the Mōri and Hideyoshi. Hideyoshi had then taken Ankokuji into his own service, where the erstwhile priest discovered a hidden military talent. He was rewarded after the Shikoku campaign with a fief of 23,000 koku in Iyo province, which would have required him to supply a tiny force of about 150 men for the Korean campaign. Ankokuji appears to have been one of those generals retained by Hideyoshi for vague administrative duties, and we read of him crossing to Korea originally to identify suitable accommodation and transport for Hideyoshi's triumphant progress from Pusan to Seoul. A

Kobayakawa Takakage, commander of the Sixth Division and one of the veterans of the Japanese army, as depicted just before his great victory at Pyŏkje in 1593. Kobayakawa successfully defended Kŭmsan three times, but ultimately failed to capture Chŏlla province. His banner bears the mon of the Mōri family to which he belonged. (ETK detail)

The battle of Uiryŏng. This little known action was Korea's first victory on land of the war, and saw the guerrilla army of Kwak Chae-u thwart an attempt by Ankokuji Ekei to cross the Nam river and launch an invasion into Chŏlla province.

letter sent home by Ankokuji describes the condition of the capital and the Korean countryside in some detail, but like Kurushima Michiyuki, who was originally given the job of finding a mansion for Hideyoshi in Seoul and ended up being shot dead at Tangp'o, Ankokuji appears to have been suddenly switched to military duties, and at the end of June we find him leading the advance into Chŏlla, which we must assume consisted of more than 150 troops.

Whichever units of the Sixth Division Ankokuji was leading, the southern route into Chŏlla would take him and his men from Japanese-held Ch'angwŏn, which lay south of and outside the Naktong line, through Haman, Ŭiryŏng and Samga. To reach Ŭiryŏng from Haman Ankokuji's men had to cross the Nam near Ŭiryŏng, and this was inside Kwak Chae-u's guerrilla territory. Finding the river apparently undefended, Ankokuji's scouts tested the depth of the water at various places and selected a shallow fordable section which they marked with stakes. That night Kwak's men uprooted the markers and moved them to a deeper part of the river. When the crossing began the Japanese troops quickly began to founder, and Kwak's army attacked, causing heavy losses. In spite of repeated attempts to cross, Ankokuji was forced to pull his army back and eventually abandoned the Ŭiryŏng route to try a wider sweep to the north, where the line of communications forts promised some security on his right flank. This little known battle of Ŭiryŏng, which is sometimes referred to as the battle of Chŏngjin, was Korea's first victory on land of the war, and was fought while Konishi and Katō were still sitting on the south bank of the Imjin river. Kwak's success also gave the Korean government a new respect for his abilities, and he was placed in command of all Korean forces in the Ŭiryŏng and Samga region.

At about the same time as the battle of Ŭiryŏng, Mōri Terumoto had begun looking to his communications further up the line of the Naktong. The most important crossing point for the road between Pusan and Seoul lay at Mugye, just south of the point where the Kumho river joined the Naktong west of Taegu. This was also the place where the Naktong divided the line of Japanese communications forts into two, so on 5m 18d Mōri ordered his subordinate general Murakami Kagechika to build a fort at Mugye to cover this vital area. On 6m 5d the new fort came under surprise attack from a Korean volunteer army under Chŏng In-hong, Son In-gap and Kim Myŏn. The defenders rallied and beat the assailants off, killing several hundred of them, but the fortress commander Murakami Kagechika was wounded. That same day, further north on the Naktong, Mōri's cousin Kikkawa Hiroie advanced against a Korean detachment near Andong, and took many heads.

Meanwhile the unfortunate Ankokuji Ekei, defeated at Ŭiryŏng, was heading north to try to attack Chŏlla from a different route, and the armies who had previously attacked Mugye hastened to meet this new challenge. Ankokuji was therefore confronted by Son In-gap somewhere between Unsan and Hyŏnp'ung. 'We arrived at Unsan on the eighteenth day of the sixth month,' wrote Ankokuji, 'and stayed there for two days. The Koreans hid in the mountains of Hyŏnp'ung and attacked us firing bows and arrows. There were about 3,000 of them, but we beat them all off that day.'[4]

Ankokuji then continued north and eventually arrived safely at the security of Mōri Terumoto's castle at Kaenyŏng, where his attack plan was changed yet again, and early in the seventh lunar month Ankokuji headed south towards Kŏch'ang. Here he planned to launch a coordinated attack on Chŏlla along with Kobayakawa Takakage, who had finally been assured that some progress was being made by his colleague and had moved south to attack Chŏnju. However, Kŏch'ang was the heartland of the other guerrilla leader Kim Myŏn, who led Ankokuji's men into an ambush in the mountains, shooting arrows at them from hidden locations against which the Japanese were unable to return fire. With this final hindrance to his advance the defeated Ankokuji Ekei gave up all hope of invading Chŏlla and withdrew his troops back to Mōri's line of castles. Almost nothing further was to be heard from him for the entire duration of the war.

THE CHŎLLA VOLUNTEERS AND THE FIRST KŬMSAN CAMPAIGN

While the guerrilla and volunteer armies of Kyŏngsang were saving Chŏlla province from being invaded from the south, Chŏlla's own armies had not been sitting idly by, and – unlike most of the armies of southern Korea – their forces were still largely intact. The leaders of the regular forces, none of whom was directly affected by the Japanese blitzkrieg that passed them by, had reacted bravely, if a little unwisely, to the Japanese surge northwards. Provincial Governor Yi Kwang had even regarded the fact that Chŏlla had been spared as a marvellous opportunity for them to attack the Japanese army before it reached Seoul. He accordingly led an army north early in July, but on the way received the dismal news that Seoul had already fallen, so he resolved to return. However, there were many in his army who objected to this. As they were being continually joined by other enthusiastic contingents the result was that a large Korean army of at least 50,000 men under various commanders, including Yi Kwang, Kwŏn Yul and Kwak Yŏng, assembled at Suwŏn to attempt the Herculean task of recapturing the capital.

Near Suwŏn lay the Japanese communications fort of Yong'in, then held by 600 men under the landlocked admiral Wakizaka Yasuharu. A Korean vanguard of 1,900 men was sent on to secure it on 6m 5d with the disastrous results that were recorded in a previous chapter. Wakizaka counterattacked, and after saving Yong'in proceeded to assault the Korean main body, taking many of its high-ranking officers prisoner. Abandoning arms and equipment, the men of Chŏlla hurriedly withdrew to fight another day.

Chŏlla also saw the early creation of irregular forces, and within days of Kwak Chae-u raising his volunteer army in Kyŏngsang province, we read of a similar force being created over in Chŏlla by a certain Ko Kyŏng-myŏng (1533–92). Ko was 60 years old and a yangban scholar who succeeded in forming an army of 6,000 men on 6m 13d, but the brevity of his career, which ended with his death in battle, has prevented him from attaining the legendary status of Kwak Chae-u. His military skills were considerable, but he lacked Kwak's appreciation of the need for caution in the face of the Japanese war machine. Kwak's style of making guerrilla raids and withdrawing was not to Ko Kyŏng-myŏng's liking, as we shall see.[5]

At the beginning of August Ko Kyŏng-myŏng sent a message to Cho Hŏn, the leader of the Righteous Army of Ch'ungch'ŏng province, suggesting that they should combine forces to march north for another attempt to liberate Seoul. Cho Hŏn immediately set about the task, gathered his forces, and waited for Ko Kyŏng-myŏng to join him, but when Ko crossed the provincial border he heard that Kobayakawa Takakage had set off to attack Chŏnju from Kŭmsan. As his own province was now under threat Ko changed his mind about joining Cho Hŏn and took a detour back to Chŏlla, where he joined up with regular troops under Kwak Yŏng and set out to attack Kŭmsan.

Kŭmsan, which today is one of the main centres in Korea for the growing of ginseng, had been occupied by Kobayakawa Takakage's Sixth Division on

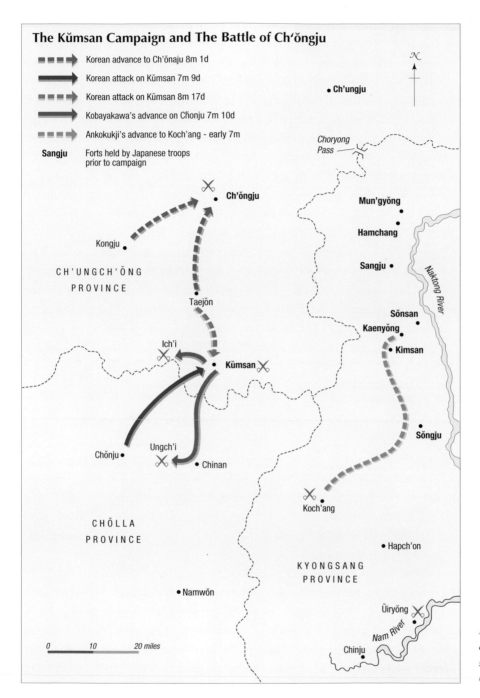

The Kŭmsan Campaign and The Battle of Ch'ŏngju

▪▪▪▪➤ Korean advance to Ch'ŏnaju 8m 1d

━━━➤ Korean attack on Kŭmsan 7m 9d

▪▪▪▪➤ Korean attack on Kŭmsan 8m 17d

━━━➤ Kobayakawa's advance on Chonju 7m 10d

▪▪▪▪➤ Ankokukji's advance to Koch'ang - early 7m

Sangju   Forts held by Japanese troops prior to campaign

𝒩

• Ch'ungju

Choryong Pass

✕ Ch'ŏngju

Kongju •

Mun'gyŏng

Hamchang

CH'UNGCH'ŎNG PROVINCE

Taejŏn •

Sangju •

Naktong River

Sŏnsan •

Kaenyŏng •

Ich'i ✕

Kŭmsan ✕

• **Kimsan**

Chŏnju •

Ungch'i ✕   • Chinan

• **Sŏngju**

CHŎLLA PROVINCE

✕ Koch'ang

• Hapch'on

KYONGSANG PROVINCE

• Namwŏn

Ŭiryŏng ✕

Nam River

Chinju •

0   10   20 miles

Map showing the campaigns of the Kŭmsan salient and the Battle of Ch'ŏngju.

5m 11d. It was somewhat isolated, as it lay to the west of the string of communications forts between Pusan and Seoul, but by means of this 'Kŭmsan salient' a Japanese army had been brought quite close to Chŏlla's provincial capital of Chŏnju, which was Kobayakawa's primary objective in his mission to conquer Chŏlla.

The first battle of Kŭmsan proved to be but one action among several in an exceedingly complex operation by both sides, and is an excellent illustration of how the slowness, or even the absence of, communication between two allied armies could result in a victory by one unit and a defeat of another cancelling each other out. The overall aim of the Japanese action was to attack Chŏnju; the Korean aim was to stop them. In the event neither side managed to coordinate the movements and attacks of its various units, so several battles took place, the first of which was the defeat of Ankokuji at Kŏch'ang described above, with the second being an attack by the Chŏlla army on Kŭmsan.

With Ko at their head the united Chŏlla army moved in to attack Kŭmsan on 7m 9d (16 August). Ko led 100 picked troops against the Japanese line. Resistance was fierce, and the regular troops under Kwak Yŏng on the flank of the Chŏlla army began to waver, so Ko pulled the whole army back. The following day they attacked again, led by 800 men from the Righteous Army, but the Japanese recalled the effect their tactics had produced the previous day, and concentrated their attacks on the regular troops. The pressure had the desired effect, and a furious Ko Kyŏng-myŏng saw Kwak Yŏng's troops falling back all round his own gallant band. With a shout to the fleeing Kwak Yŏng of 'To a defeated general death is the only choice!' he plunged into the enemy and was killed along with his two sons.[6]

As part of the Korean threat was now eliminated, Kobayakawa Takakage reckoned that his attack on Chŏlla could be pressed home without further hindrance, so his army advanced on Chŏnju by an indirect route through Chinan. Yi Kwang had sent two separate armies against the Japanese incursion. Kwŏn Yul advanced to a defensive position with his regular troops at Ich'i, to the west of Kŭmsan, while other units of Righteous Armies combined at Ungch'i, between Chŏnju and Chinan, where the terrain provided good natural defence. Wooden palisades were erected on top of a hill, and it was covered by many archers.

On 7m 10d one section of Kobayakawa's army, who were still fresh from their triumph earlier that same day against Ko at Kŭmsan, began a fierce assault on Ungch'i, choosing to attack each of the three Righteous Armies in turn. When one unit retreated it unsettled the next, until the mountain was swept clear of defenders, leaving hundreds dead. Under cover of darkness the surviving Koreans withdrew towards Chŏnju. To provide a rear line of defence Yi Kwang had set up a position on a hill two miles to the north of the town, where he had cleverly rigged up an array of flags and banners to give the impression that a sizeable rearguard was in attendance. This was reported back to Kobayakawa Takakage by the Japanese scouts. As the Japanese had no rear support and their troops were exhausted from three days of fighting and marching they decided to make a prudent withdrawal. The Koreans showed no inclination to pursue them, so after a brief stop at Ungch'i to raise a burial mound over the Korean dead, the Japanese pulled back to Kŭmsan.

Meanwhile another unit of the Sixth Division was attacking Kwŏn Yul at Ich'i. Kwŏn Yul was a skilled general, and placed a detached unit in a mountainous area as an ambush. The attack was successful, although the leader was hit by a bullet, at which Kwŏn Yul took over to rout the Japanese. This was a rare and very welcome Korean victory by regular troops, for which Kwŏn was later promoted. This section of the Japanese army also pulled back to Kŭmsan, so through a strange combination of two victories (over Ankokuji at Kŏch'ang and Kobayakawa at Ich'i) and two defeats (at Kŭmsan and Ungch'i), Chŏlla province was saved from invasion by land. By curious coincidence, the battle of Ungch'i took place on the same day that Admiral Yi saved Chŏlla by sea with his victory at Hansando. It was an auspicious time for the Korean resistance, but could they exploit it further?

THE CH'UNGCH'ŎNG VOLUNTEERS AND THE KOREAN WARRIOR MONKS

Reference was made above to the Righteous Army of Ch'ungch'ŏng province and their leader Cho Hŏn. We will now return to Cho Hŏn, who was to carry out the next phase of the war in company with the third component of the Korean army: the warrior monks.

The initiative for inviting Korea's monastic community to join in the struggle against the Japanese seems to have come originally from King Sŏnjo himself. While in exile in Ŭiju the King summoned the monk Hyujŏng and asked for his cooperation. Hyujŏng was based in P'yongan province, and had been falsely implicated in a rebellion of 1589 when the ringleader had used his name in an attempt to rouse the monks to join the cause. The matter had been settled amicably, but realising the potential of the monks as a fighting force, and no doubt hoping that Hyujŏng felt under some obligation to him, King Sŏnjo appointed him national leader of all the monk soldiers in Korea.[7]

On 5m 6d Hyujŏng despatched a manifesto calling upon monks throughout the land to take arms against the Japanese. 'Alas, the way of heaven is no more,' it began. 'The destiny of the land is on the decline. In defiance of heaven and reason the cruel foe had the temerity to cross the sea aboard 1,000 ships.'[8] The samurai were 'poisonous devils', and 'as virulent as snakes or fierce animals'. He reminded his listeners that one of the Five Secular Precepts, a series of teachings combining Confucianism and Buddhism that had been brought to Korea by Master Wŏn'gwang (d. 640), had been to face battle without retreating. This principle was the inspiration for true patriotism, and if somewhat foreign to traditional views of Buddhism, it was very similar to the single-minded attitude of the Japanese Ikkō-ikki sectarians, who were also very warlike. The precepts also neatly blended Buddhism with Confucianism, which was the underlying doctrine of the Chosŏn dynasty. Hyujŏng then called on the monks to 'put on the armour of mercy of Bodhisattvas, hold in hand the treasured sword to fell the devil, wield the lightning bolt of the Eight Deities, and come forward'.[9]

The result of the manifesto was the recruitment of 8,000 monks over the next few months. Some were undoubtedly motivated by patriotism, but others saw it as an opportunity to raise the social status of Buddhist monks, who had suffered from the Chosŏn kings' obsessive Confucianism. Although their numbers were small compared to the civilian volunteers their units were cohesive and clearly associated with a particular leader and a particular province. Monk units, therefore, were largely spared from the in-fighting that plagued the Righteous Armies, nor did they tend to find themselves in conflict with the regular army forces, who usually ignored them. Unfortunately, however, they were not immune from jealousy towards the Righteous Armies, which was to lead to trouble on more than one occasion when a joint operation was being planned.

The response to Hyujŏng's call varied from province to province. Many of the monasteries in Kyŏngsang had been destroyed by the advancing Japanese, leaving few monks to be recruited there. Chŏlla saw an active response, with the unique feature of the creation of sailor monks, who joined Admiral Yi's navy. In Ch'ungch'ŏng, the province with which this chapter will be chiefly concerned, recruitment had begun even before Hyujŏng's manifesto was issued. The driving force here was the monk Yŏnggyu, who enthusiastically promoted an anti-Japanese movement among his clerical brothers. The first operations in which the monks engaged were guerrilla activities similar to those of their volunteer colleagues, until a major action in September against the Japanese garrison of Ch'ŏngju thrust them into the limelight.

Ch'ŏngju had been captured by the Third Division under Kuroda Nagamasa on 4m 25d during the first days of the war. In the allocation of provincial responsibilities Ch'ungch'ŏng had fallen to Fukushima Masanori (1561–1624), who was yet another of the 'Seven Spears of Shizugatake'. Ch'ŏngju was one of the most important bases in the province, and Fukushima had placed both Ch'ŏngju and Ch'ungju under the care of Hachisuka Iemasa (1558–1638). Ch'ŏngu was an important transport centre for the Japanese army as it lay

In Ch'ungch'ŏng province Yŏnggyu goes recruiting for warrior monks and civilian volunteers to fight against the Japanese.

directly on the main route to Seoul, and also housed an important granary. It was, however, lightly garrisoned, and the Korean volunteers knew it.

The recapture of Ch'ŏngju would cut the Japanese line of communications, and could also provide the base for an attack to recapture Kŭmsan and stop forever any prospect of an invasion of Chŏlla being tried again. It is therefore not surprising to hear that the provincial governor of Ch'ungch'ŏng, Yun Sŏn-gak, and the provincial commander, Yi Ok, had already been recruiting stragglers from Korean forces for an attack on Ch'ŏngju long before the monks came on the scene. The local Righteous Army too, under its leader Cho Hŏn, had also been active, and this force was on its way to attack Ch'ŏngju when they met Yun Sŏn-gak and his regulars near Taejŏn. Yun naturally proposed taking Cho Hŏn's men under his command, but as Yun had been the commander who had lost Ch'ŏngju in the first place Cho Hŏn was understandably reluctant to hand his troops over. So great was the mistrust between them, however, that they could not even agree on a joint operation, and parted with no arrangement being made.

Cho Hŏn then contacted Yŏnggyu and his monks, who agreed to cooperate in retaking Ch'ŏngju. As their forces were small Yŏnggyu asked Yun for help from his regulars, but the governor, still in high dudgeon, sent only a token force as a rearguard. Thus it was that on 8m 1d (6 September), Cho Hŏn's Righteous Army of 1,100, together with 1,500 warrior monks and a rearguard of 500, advanced on Ch'ŏngju. The monks attacked the north and east gates, while the volunteers assaulted the west gate. Hachisuka's men quickly drove them off, so Cho Hŏn took up a position on a hill to the west for a second attempt. During the night they lit fires and set up many flags to give the impression of a large host. Fooled completely, the small Japanese garrison planned an immediate evacuation, and the next day Cho Hŏn and his men walked into the castle in triumph.

Unfortunately, within days of this considerable Korean victory an argument developed among the three leaders over who was to take the credit for it. Different reports were submitted from different viewpoints, all of which

The fall of Ch'ŏngju to the Righteous Army of Cho Hŏn and the warrior monks under Yŏnggyu. Ch'ŏngju was one of the most important gains for the Korean volunteers, but was squandered by their failure to cooperate in the operation against Kŭmsan which followed.

served only to increase the mistrust between the three contingents, and relationships deteriorated even further. The tragic result was that a Korean army was at last in a position to take the fight to the enemy, but internal squabbles were threatening to destroy any chance of success.

Thus it was that when a Korean army marched south from Ch'ŏngju to attack Kŭmsan and cut off a further arm of the Japanese occupation of Ch'ungch'ŏng, it was a force already doomed by division. The regulars under Yun Sŏn-gak had again refused to participate, so the monks and volunteers decided to go ahead without them, but even they were determined to mount two operations independent of each other. The haughty Cho Hŏn planned to launch his attack before the monks, in spite of the fact that the monastic army had now been greatly strengthened by the welcome arrival of another contingent under the monk Ch'ŏyong from Chŏlla. Cho's incredible plans faced opposition even from within his own depleted ranks, because Kŭmsan was not a lightly garrisoned fort like Ch'ŏngju, but a well-defended salient held by 10,000 battle-hardened men under Kobayakawa Takakage. Governor Yun Sŏn-gak was so opposed to the idea, albeit for selfish reasons, that he went to the lengths of imprisoning close relatives of the volunteers to dissuade them from fighting, and even the well-respected Kwŏn Yul lent his weight to the arguments against Cho Hŏn's foolhardy plans.

The second battle of Kŭmsan, where Cho Hŏn's Righteous Army of 700 men were annihilated by Kobayakawa Takakage's Sixth Division. Shortly after this a monk army also attacked Kŭmsan, and although they too were defeated, the ultimate result was that the Japanese abandoned the Kŭmsan salient.

The day before the planned attack Yŏnggyu met Cho Hŏn and urged him to abandon the suicidal assault on mighty Kŭmsan, but Cho Hŏn rejected his advice, saying it was no time to be 'pondering victory or defeat, sharpness or dullness of weapons' while the Japanese were putting people to the sword.[10] Thus it was that on 8m 17d (22 September) Cho Hŏn led an army of only 700 volunteer soldiers against 10,000 of the toughest samurai in Korea at the second battle of Kŭmsan. Kobayakawa Takakage soon realised that this isolated force were all that were being sent against him. As night fell the Japanese encircled them and exterminated the entire army including the reckless Cho Hŏn. Seeing the destruction of his comrade's army, the monk Yŏnggyu felt that he had to follow where Cho Hŏn had led, so over the next three days the monk armies took part in a third battle of Kŭmsan. The result was the same as at the second battle – total annihilation.

A lavish yet very moving memorial shrine called the 'Shrine of the Seven Hundred' now stands on the site of the battles of Kŭmsan. It honours both monk and volunteer alike, and inside one of the halls two dramatic paintings recall the glory of Ch'ŏngju and the disaster of Kŭmsan. Everywhere there is the memory of self-sacrifice and the exhortation for patriotic Koreans to emulate these heroes of old, but nowhere is there any account of the rivalry, pride and selfishness that snatched defeat out of the hands of victory.

FROM THE NAKTONG TO THE SEA

Although Cho Hŏn's recklessness lost the battle, it had certainly helped to win the campaign. The fact that Kŭmsan had now suffered three attacks made the Japanese command question whether the Kŭmsan salient was worth retaining. An invasion of Chŏlla had already become unthinkable following the sea battles of Hansando and Angolp'o, so Kobayakawa's Sixth Division were pulled back to Kaenyŏng. The scandal was that while sensible campaigns at Ch'ŏngju and Hansando had saved Chŏlla by land and sea only a month before, petty rivalries had destroyed the best hope the resistance had of driving the Japanese not only out of Chŏlla, but out of Korea itself.

Yet to the guerrillas of Kyŏngsang the withdrawal of Kobayakawa was all that mattered, not the wasteful way in which it had been obtained, and the example of what could be achieved encouraged them to carry on with their own campaigns. Even before the second battle of Kŭmsan, Ukita Hideie in Seoul had become very concerned by reports he was receiving of guerrilla attacks in northern Kyŏngsang. The most serious development was the loss of Sŏnsan, which had been defended by 1,400 men. Massive reinforcements were needed, so Ukita took the unprecedented step of sending three of his headquarters generals, Hosokawa Tadaoki, Hasegawa Hidekazu and Kimura Shigekore, with an army of 12,000 men to retake Sŏnsan and strengthen the line. On 8m 7d they cleared the guerrillas out of Sŏnsan, and joined forces with Nanjō Motokiyo in Indong to mop up other local resistance. The three generals and their forces then moved down to Kimhae, which they made into their new base.

The battles at Kŭmsan also provided the inspiration for the Kyŏngsang armies to make renewed attempts against the Naktong river line. Kobayakawa Takakage had withdrawn to Mōri Terumoto's headquarters at Kaenyŏng, and was to share in his nephew's surprise when news came to them on 8m 20d of an attack on Sŏngju by Kyŏngsang irregulars. A relieving army was sent and the guerrillas withdrew, but instead of being discouraged their numbers grew to a possible 15,000 men over the next few weeks. On 9m 10d Chŏng In-hon advanced once more against Sŏngju, and Mōri again sent out a relieving force, but events had moved on in other nearby places. From Ŭiryŏng the redoubtable Kwak Chae-u marched to the Hyŏnp'ung area and threatened the castle so severely that on 9m 11d the defenders abandoned the fort and pulled back to Ch'angnyŏng. On the same day Mugye, which covered Mōri's important crossing point on the Naktong, received the attentions of Kim Chun-min, and the commander was forced to abandon the castle and join the forces at Sŏngju. Ch'angnyŏng castle too had to be abandoned following a guerrilla attack. Within the space of one month the Naktong line had acquired several large holes in it .[11]

An attack is launched by Korean guerrillas on a Japanese army column. The greatest contribution made by the guerrillas was to harass the Japanese lines of communication. (ETK detail)

Everywhere in Kyŏngsang the volunteers were on the march. Over towards the east coast on an unknown date in September a volunteer army enticed the Japanese garrison out of Yŏngch'ŏn and ambushed them, then attacked the castle and burned it to the ground. Inspired by this example another guerrilla leader, Pak Chin, determined to recapture Kyŏngju, but was initially less successful. He burned some outbuildings, but the Japanese sallied out by the north gate and attacked them in the rear, causing many casualties. Nothing daunted, Pak Chin returned later with a secret weapon. According to Yu Sŏng-nyong's Chingbirok something was fired over the walls of Kyŏngju and rolled across the courtyard. Not knowing what it was, the 'robbers', as he calls the Japanese garrison, rushed over to examine it. At that moment the object suddenly exploded, sending fragments of iron far and wide and causing over thirty casualties. Such was the alarm it caused that Kyŏngju was evacuated, and the 'robbers' pulled back to the safety of the coastal fort at Sŏsaengp'o.[12]

It is possible to identify this mysterious weapon quite precisely as the Korean version of the delayed-action explosive iron shells called by the Chinese pi li hu pao (heaven-shaking thunder). It was not the first time that these devices had been used against the Japanese, as the earliest form of them had been fired from catapults during the first Mongol invasion in 1274, but the Korean model was much more sophisticated. According to Yu Sŏng-nyong, 'This was a new weapon. It was developed by the firearms maker Yi Chang-son to shoot in a large bowl mortar. The shell covered a distance of 500 paces and caught fire upon landing.'[13] The shells, called pig yŏk chinch'ŏllae in Korean, were also distinguished by a clever double fuse system, a fast-burning fuse for the mortar, and a slower one for the bomb itself, which the operator would light simultaneously. For mobility the mortars, which came in various sizes, were mounted on wooden carriages.[14]

The firing of pig yŏk chinch'ŏllae (explosive delayed-action bombs) into a Japanese camp, such as was done in the celebrated attack on Kyŏngju by Pak Chin. The explosive nature of the projectiles is clearly shown, but they would have been fired from a mortar, not a cannon. (ETK)

One of the most dramatic gestures made against the Japanese occupation of Kyŏngsang came not on land but on the sea in the person of Admiral Yi Sun-sin, who carried out a brave attempt to destroy the Japanese fleet lying at anchor in Pusan. Before this time Yi had not dared venture to the east of Kadŏk island, but on 8m 23d he joined forces with Yi Ŏk-ki and Wŏn Kyun to sail right into the hornets' nest. The scale of the challenge facing the Korean fleet at Pusan is quite amazing. In none of his previous victories had Yi had to contend with more than 100 enemy ships at any one time, but his arrival off Pusan the following day revealed an enemy armada of over four hundred vessels. They were under the command of Wakizaka Yasuharu, Katō Yoshiaki, Kuki Yoshitaka and Tōdō Takatora.

'Yi Ŏk-ki and I roared, "Do or die!" and waved our war flags,' writes Yi in his report to the Korean court.[15] Four Japanese ships lying outside the main anchorage became easy targets, but when the Korean fleet sailed in closer they came under heavy fire both from the ships themselves and from shore batteries, and Yi realised to his dismay that the Japanese fortifications in Pusan had been equipped with cannon seized from captured Korean castles, because 'cannon balls the size of Chinese quinces, or large stones as big as rice bowls' came flying over. Yi returned fire, and managed to silence the shore positions.[16]

Admiral Yi's Memorial to Court about Pusan is curiously brief compared to the long report he supplied about Hansando, but his account of this epic struggle contains some telling points. He was under the erroneous impression that the large number of Japanese ships in Pusan, none of which ventured out on to the open seas, meant that the Japanese were planning to evacuate Korea. He therefore stressed in the report that he was reluctant to destroy the Japanese fleet totally because he feared that the troops left behind on land would simply terrorise the local population. In fact, the situation was not one of evacuation but the exact opposite. The furious activity in the harbour was due to reinforcement and re-equipping, and the reason the fleet did not sail out was that they were transport vessels and did not wish to engage Admiral Yi.

In spite of these self-imposed limitations Yi counted 100 enemy vessels destroyed by his raid, and many of his men were 'mentioned in despatches', including a certain Cho Chŏng, who was a 'horse farm supervisor of Sunch'ŏn, who fitted out a boat with his own funds and participated in the battle with his slaves and cowherds as volunteers'.[17]

Yi also lamented the death of Chŏng Un, a captain from Nokto, who had fought beside him at every sea battle. In a separate memorial he recommends that Chŏng Un's memorial tablet should be installed next to that of Yi Tae-wŏn, a Korean patriot killed fighting against a Japanese pirate raid in 1587.[18] Chŏng Un was killed by being hit by 'a large fire ball of the enemy', which implies that among the artillery pieces acquired by the Japanese were some specimens of the mortars with delayed action fuses. Alternatively the expression could mean the simple fire bombs used in Japanese naval warfare that were flung by hand or with the help of a net on a pole to give greater range. Five captured Korean cannon are, however, mentioned in Yi's list of weapons taken from captured Japanese ships. Two were 'earth mark' cannon, and two of the others were of the 'black' variety.[19]

In the end Yi's concern for the local inhabitants, together with the size of the Japanese fleet, prevented Pusan from being a more complete victory than it actually was. Yi was wise enough to realise that an operation like Pusan could only be really effective if he was acting with the support of ground troops, and as of September 1592 such an action was not yet possible.

THEIR FINEST HOUR

Although the Pusan attack was not completely successful, it served to isolate still further the troops under Hashiba Hidekatsu who had been given the task of garrisoning Pusan. As the renewed momentum of the guerrilla armies gained pace, Korean volunteers were venturing to within a few miles of Pusan itself, and Japanese possessions on the south coast of Kyŏngsang, which had never been extensive, grew even fewer. Following pressure from guerrillas Kamei Korenori, who had lost his precious golden fan at the battle of Tangp'o, abandoned his castle at Sach'ŏn for the stronger fortress at Kŏsong, only to leave

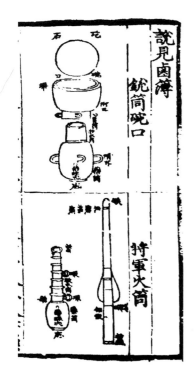

A Korean mortar (ch'ongt'ong wan'gu) shown in its constituent pieces according to the specifications in the Ch'ongt'ong tŭngnok (Complete records on firearms) published in 1448. The bowl which holds the mortar bomb is a separate section from the barrel with the explosive charge, and when in use the two pieces are fastened together with ropes. In the lower illustration is a wooden arrow.

Kosŏng in turn when nearby Ch'angwŏn fell to a Korean attack on 8m 24d. He then withdrew to Pusan, and Hashiba Hidekatsu placed him in charge of Kijang, a coastal fort to the east of the town. Finally, on 11m 13d Kijang came under attack. Being understandably unwilling to retreat again Kamei Korenori led a sally out of the castle and attacked the Koreans with relays of picked troops. The assault was beaten off, and the Japanese took 800 heads. The battle of Kijang was an example of that increasingly rare event – a Japanese success – but it was one that failed to extinguish the shame they had already experienced a month before at the first battle of Chinju, an epic struggle to which we will now turn.

It will be recalled that pressure from Korean attacks had forced Ukita Hideie to send reinforcements to Kyŏngsang from Seoul, and towards the end of October the three generals concerned, Hosokawa Tadaoki, Hasegawa Hidekazu and Kimura Shigekore decided that the best means of defence against the guerrillas was attack. They considered their position. The Japanese held Kimhae, together with coastal forts at Ungch'ŏn and Kosŏng, but since the loss of Ch'angwŏn both of these could only be reached by sea and were vulnerable to attack from Admiral Yi's fleet. It was therefore decided to make an attack by land westwards from Kimhae to liberate Ch'angwŏn and then head on to capture the Koreans' strongest point in western Kyŏngsang: the town of Chinju.[20]

Chinju lay on the Nam river upstream from Ŭiryŏng. It was a fortified town with a long high wall that touched the Nam river on its southern side. Between Chinju and the line of the Naktong was Kwak Chae-u's guerrilla territory, and up to that moment in the war the garrison of this strong fortress had never seen a Japanese soldier. Ukita's generals reasoned that if Chinju could be taken then the recaptured castles would fall back into Japanese hands,

The reconstructed wall of Chinju. The castle of Chinju withstood a ferocious attack in 1592. Much use was made of scaling ladders in the attempt to become ichiban nori (first to climb into the castle), a common samurai obsession.

A bas relief at Chinju of the heroic defence of the castle during the siege. On the left the Japanese are being knocked off their scaling ladders.

the guerrillas would lose rear support, and a new road to Chŏlla province would finally be opened. A Japanese army of 20,000 men therefore left Kimhae on 9m 25d for its first objective, which was the recently lost castle of Ch'angwŏn. On receiving news of the Japanese advance the Korean commander took his army out of the castle and drew up in battle formation on a nearby hill. Defeating him easily, the Japanese regained Ch'angwŏn the following day. The Koreans then fled to Haman, which the Japanese took on 10m 1d and made the survivors beat a final retreat towards mighty Chinju.

The castle of Chinju was under the command of Kim Shi-min, who led a garrison of 3,800 men. Kim was a fine general, and was not willing to provide the Japanese with their customary experience of a weak Korean castle defence. Instead he had acquired 170 newly forged Korean arquebuses made to quality standards equivalent to the Japanese ones, and had trained his men in their use. Chinju was the first occasion when these weapons were tried in battle. Kim also had many 'black' mark cannon and a supply of mortars and bombs of the same type that had caused such devastation at Kyŏngju. On 10m 4d the Japanese army left Haman, crossed the Nam river and approached Chinju from three sides. The stragglers from Haman had not had time to reach Chinju until then, and when they arrived at the gates they found them tightly closed against the expected attack, so they were overrun by the Japanese during the first assault on 10m 5d (8 November). Here was a chance for samurai glory once again, and the *Taikōki* tells us that a certain Jirōza'emon 'took the first head and raised it aloft. The other five men also attacked the enemy army and took some excellent heads.'[21]

When the Japanese reached the walls Kim's troops hit back at them with everything in their possession – arquebus balls, bullets, exploding bombs and heavy stones. It was not the reaction Hosokawa and his men had been expecting so, changing their plans, they made shields out of bamboo and under the cover of massed volleys of arquebus fire approached close to the walls, where long scaling ladders were set up. As the samurai scrambled up the ladders the defenders ignored the bullets and bombarded them with rocks, smashing many ladders to pieces. Meanwhile delayed action bombs and lumps of stone fell into the mass of soldiers awaiting their turn to fight for the special honour of being first into the castle. The *Taikōki* gives a vivid account of one such endeavour:

As we [Japanese] try to become ichiban nori (first to climb in) they climbed up as in a swarm. Because of this the ladders almost broke, and comrades fell down from their climb, so they could not use the ladders. Hosokawa Tadaoki's brother Sadaoki was one such, accompanied by foot soldiers on ladders on his right and left, and strictly ordered 'Until I have personally climbed into the castle this ladder is for one person to climb. If anyone else climbs I will take his head!' then he climbed. Because of this the ladder did not break and he got up, and the men who saw him were loud in his praise. Consequently, before very long he placed his hands on the wall, but when he tried to make his entry from within the castle, spears and naginata were thrust at him to try to make him fall, and lamentably he fell to the bottom of the moat.[22]

None of the Japanese army was to earn the accolade of ichiban nori that day, although many tried, and as the forward troops clawed at Chinju's battlements Japanese labourers behind them were bullied into hurriedly erecting a crude siege tower from which arquebuses could shoot down into the courtyard.

For three days this bitter battle, which was unlike anything seen up to that point in the Korean campaign, deposited heaps of Japanese dead in the ditch of Chinju castle. On the night of 10m 8d a guerrilla army under Kwak Chae-u arrived to witness the spectacle. It was a pitifully small band to be a relieving force, so Kwak ordered his men to light five pine torches each and hold them aloft as they blew on conch shells and raised a war cry at the tops of their voices. The arrival of a further 500 guerrillas from another direction added to the illusion of a mighty host, then they too were joined by 2,500 more. But the Japanese were not to be diverted from their main objective. Disregarding this newly arrived threat for a short while Hosokawa flung his men into a final attempt to take the castle by storm as he led attacks on the northern and eastern gates during the night of 10m 9d (12 November).

While fighting beside his men on the north gate Commander Kim Shi-min received a mortal wound from a bullet in his left forehead and fell unconscious to the ground. Seeing this the Japanese diverted all their troops to the northern side of the Chinju's ramparts, trying to gain a handhold on top of the walls, but from the ground below the Koreans swept the walls with arrows and bullets and drove them off. The Chinju garrison were perilously short of ammunition, but just then a Korean detachment arrived by boat up the Nam river bringing welcome supplies of weapons, powder and ball, an event that greatly heartened the garrison.

By now all of the Japanese troops had been committed to the assault. They had no rearguard, and were deep inside enemy territory, so to their great chagrin (and the fury of Hideyoshi when he heard about it), the Japanese generals decided to abandon the siege of Chinju and returned to Ch'angwŏn, licking their wounds after the greatest Korean success on land of the entire war. A sudden rainstorm covered their withdrawal, and there was no Korean pursuit. To the Japanese compiler of the *Taikōki*, the storm was proof that Hachiman Dai Bosatsu himself, the god of war who had taken part in Empress Jingō's Korean campaign while still in his mother's womb, had personally crossed the seas again to protect the Japanese army.[23]

REVOLTS IN THE NORTH

By the late autumn of the Year of the Dragon it was becoming increasingly obvious that the invasion of China was now a forgotten dream, and as for territorial gains in Korea, it was clear that the Japanese army held a chain of forts between Pusan and Py'ŏngyang and nothing else. Chŏlla was enemy territory into which the Japanese ventured at their peril, while Kyŏngsang and Ch'ungch'ŏng were hotbeds of guerrilla activity along the Naktong line.

The news from the north was just as bad, because the Japanese occupation of northern Korea had begun unravelling almost as soon as it had been established. In Hwanghae, Kuroda Nagamasa, who was supposed to be providing the rearguard for Konishi Yukinaga in P'yŏngyang, had problems of his own. He was based in the provincial capital Haeju, from where he had sent out a series of threats to the locals to pay their taxes or be beheaded. The reaction was a local uprising which began at the end of September. The insurgents fortified themselves inside the castle of Yŏnan, which was halfway between Haeju and Kaesŏng. It soon acted as a magnet for all the local stragglers from defeated Korean armies and guerrillas from the Righteous Armies. Cannon were mounted on its walls, and food and fodder crammed into every available storage area. Its garrison only consisted of 500 fighting men, while a further 2,000 civilians had also packed themselves inside, so a confident Kuroda Nagamasa advanced to the siege of Yŏnan on 8m 27d with 3,000 men.[24]

The reaction to the Japanese attack on Yŏnan may not have been quite on the scale of Chinju, nor did it involve such sophisticated weaponry, but it was no less enthusiastically delivered. A citizen's army manned the walls, and while soldiers made ready with bows and arrows their women and children stood next to them with stones and boiling water. Kuroda tried the stratagem that had won Kimhae for him at the start of the invasion by building a huge ramp against the walls using bundles of grass, sticks and lumber. At Yŏnan his ramp was countered with burning pine torches dropped from the battlements, which set fire to the dry materials. Kuroda then built siege towers from which to bombard the castle, and the defenders replied by excavating earthen ramparts from which they loosed fire arrows and burned the towers to the ground.

The Japanese assault on Yŏnan lasted four days and nights, and on 9m 1d (6 October) Kuroda gave up the attempt. The undefeated garrison at Yŏnan meant that his position in Haeju was now untenable. If he stayed there he would not be able to move to the assistance of Konishi should such a move be required, so Kuroda abandoned Haeju and moved the Third Division to Paech'ŏn, which was nearer to the main communications line.

The eastern province of Kangwŏn had also been very peaceful following its occupation by Mōri Yoshinari's Fourth Division, but after a few months guerrilla activity erupted here too, and in August Itō Yubei had to crush guerrillas threatening him at his base in Ch'ŏrwŏn. Shortly afterwards he crossed the Imjin river to attack Yŏnchŏn, while in September Akizuki Tanenaga put down a rising at P'yŏngch'ang and captured its leader alive. The boldness of the guerrillas in northern Kangwŏn even led them to threaten Seoul itself, so on 10m 18d Itō marched against their main base and attacked it at dawn the following day, catching the guerrilla leader asleep in his bed. Ishida Mitsunari, one of Hideyoshi's three Commissioners stationed in Seoul, was overjoyed at the news and asked Itō to send him the rebel leader's head.

Another group of guerrillas were operating in Kyŏnggi province from their base on Kanghwa island to the north-west of Seoul. This was the place to which the Korean Kings of Koryŏ had fled during the Mongol invasions, and from where they subsequently ruled as a government in exile. Now it became a haven for Korean irregulars, who scored their greatest triumph on 10m 24d when Nakagawa Hidemasa went out on a hawking expedition near Suwŏn. He was surrounded by Korean guerrillas and killed – an ignominious death for a bold samurai.[25]

Finally, and indicative of the increasing pressure that the Koreans were able to exert all along the Japanese line, Kwŏn Yul of Chŏlla, the former victor of the battle of Ich'i, marched north and established himself at the castle of Toksan, which had been taken from Japanese hands. This was to be his first base for the important events that were to occur around Seoul in 1593. Toksan was also the setting for one of the more entertaining legends of the Korean War, because Kwŏn Yul was besieged there by a Japanese army and ran perilously short of water. The Japanese knew this and prepared for an attack when the garrison grew desperate. Kwŏn Yul thereupon took his horse up to a prominent and very visible point of the castle complex, and had his men pour buckets of rice over it. From a distance it looked as though the horse was being washed with water. The Japanese concluded that the garrison must have water to spare, and lifted the siege![26]

The other major daimyō family to be based near Seoul were the Shimazu of Satsuma, who made up a large part of the Fourth Division. In November Shimazu Tadatsune's base at Ch'unch'ŏn came under attack. He requested

help from his father Yoshihiro, who was based at Yŏngpy'ŏn, and this relieving
force drove the guerrillas away, but no sooner had Yoshihiro withdrawn than
the Koreans attacked again. This time Tadatsune could not be bothered to
wait for a relieving force to be summoned. Instead he opened the gate and
led a sally out in typical Shimazu style, destroying the Korean army.

Although these actions were all Japanese successes, the overall pattern in
Kangwŏn and Kyŏnggi provinces was the same as in the rest of the country.
The Japanese held the castles and defended them well, but everywhere else
was slowly slipping back under Korean control. In early January 1593 Shimazu
Yoshihiro moved his base to Kŭmhwa and defended it against a raid, but by
that time the four fortresses to the east of Seoul at Wŏnju, Ch'unchŏn,
Kŭmhwa and Ch'ŏrwŏn were all that Mōri's Fourth Division had to show
for six months of occupation.

Immediately to the north, in southern Hamgyŏng province, Nabeshima
Naoshige, whose main concern until then had been civil administration and
tax collection, suddenly found himself thrown back into military activity. The
indignation of the local populace had been roused as much by the collaboration
of Korean officials with the Japanese as with the depredations wreaked by
the Japanese themselves, and in early December Nabeshima became the target
of a guerrilla raid on his base in the provincial capital of Hamhŭng. The
Koreans had taken up positions on nearby hills, so Nabeshima led a pre-
emptive strike against them on 11m 10d (13 December), an attack that seems
only to have whetted their appetite for Nabeshima's destruction. Two days
later they were back, but this time Nabeshima made sure of his complete
victory, and Hamhŭng was safe again.[27]

The quickest reversal of fortunes in northern Korea happened to the all-
conquering Katō Kiyomasa, the invader of China. Almost as soon as his back

was turned the castles he had placed into the hands of Korean traitors began to fall to Korean loyalists. Within eight days of Katō's arrival back in Hamhŭng on 9m 7d, where he no doubt recounted to Nabeshima all the glorious details of his conquest of the Jurchens and his aesthetic experience on the beach at Sŏsup'o, Korean rebels took Kyŏngsŏng castle. One by one the line of forts fell like dominoes, with their collaborator garrisons being liquidated. Soon Korean armies reached Kilchu, the most northerly of the coastal forts in which a Japanese garrison was stationed, and in December attacks began on Kilchu, Sŏngjin and Tanch'ŏn under the overall leadership of Chŏng Mun-pu. All three castles were heavily defended, but at Kilchu the Koreans had the good fortune to encounter and destroy a Japanese raiding party out foraging. A similar attack happened at Ssangp'o to a foraging party from Sŏngjin, and then in January 1593 Chŏng defeated a Japanese army whom he had enticed out of Tanch'ŏn, completing a campaign known as the 'Three Consecutive Victories'.[28]

The siege of Kilchu was to continue for a little while longer, but it was now the depths of the Korean winter, when the freezing winds blow straight down from Manchuria. 'The common soldiers suffered frostbite and lost hands and feet,' wrote the chronicler of Kiyomasa's adventures, 'while others developed snow blindness and could see nothing',[29] but as the last few days of the Year of the Dragon began to give way to the new Year of the Snake, a major new factor entered the haphazard equation of regulars, volunteers, guerrillas, monks and sailors. It is the Western calendar, rather than the Chinese one, that provides the most dramatic date for this development, because it was on New Year's Day 1593 that the vanguard of a massive Chinese army prepared to cross the Yalu river to liberate Korea from the Japanese yoke.

This painting from the Ch'ungyŏlsa at Tongnae shows Korean guerrillas launching a raid on a Japanese camp. In the right background a large wooden fire arrow heads towards the invaders' lines.

chapter seven

THE YEAR OF THE SNAKE

THE decision by the Korean government to seek help from Ming China had not been lightly taken. No request for help was lodged at the time of the landings at Pusan, and it was only when the fall of Seoul made the matter pressing that war minister Yi Hang-bok pointed out that assistance from China was the only way Korea could survive. Certain misgivings that went beyond the usual knee-jerk reaction of factionalism were then aroused when it was pointed out that the troops of Liaodong, who would be the most likely to be sent, were known to be both unreliable and ill-disciplined, and could prove to be a problem to Korea rather than her salvation. Nevertheless, Korea's position at that stage in the war looked so perilous that such niceties had to be dismissed.

The first Chinese troops to cross the Yalu arrived in Korea on 6m 15d, the same day that the Korean garrison at P'yŏngyang had deserted their posts and handed the city over to an exultant Konishi Yukinaga. The Japanese do not appear to have had a great respect for China's military capabilities, although this, as in so many other aspects of the Japanese attitude towards their continental adventure, was rooted as much in woeful ignorance as in up-to-date intelligence. The Ming army was certainly not the force it once had been. The traditional system of frontier defence of the early Ming had come to an end after the Tu-mu incident of 1449, and the regular army, the core of which was formed by mercenary troops, had deteriorated in both quality and quantity. However, military organisation was generally good and well provided with reinforcements which could be moved readily by land. In the Ningxia campaign which immediately preceded the Korean operation the Ming army successfully transported 400 artillery pieces over 300 miles of difficult terrain. The army had also been reorganised successfully by a certain Qi Jiguang, who had fought against the wakō in 1563 and had published a book on military matters in 1567 which later came to the attention of the Koreans. Qi's system, controlled by strict discipline, divided the infantry into five groups: firearms, swordsmen, archers with fire arrows, ordinary archers and spearmen, all of whom were backed up by cavalry and artillery crews. Many of the cavalry were mounted archers, and although army equipment resembled Korean items, there was no use made of the flail, and the Chinese foot soldiers used crossbows and were also much better supplied with firearms, including arquebuses.

As the first Chinese expeditionary force to move against P'yŏngyang was only 3,000 strong there was an understandable reluctance to advance against a Japanese army that had been so victorious so quickly. On crossing the Yalu the Chinese did not leave the frontier town of Ŭju until 7m 14d, having by then been reliably informed that the Japanese had already left P'yŏngyang. By the time they reached Anju the Ming commanders realised that their intelligence was seriously at fault. The Japanese garrison was still there and was large in number, and having been warned of the Chinese arrival they were frantically enhancing P'yŏngyang's defences, although not by extending the Korean-style walls of the city. Instead, with a contempt for Korean military architecture that the experience of the past months had done little to dispel, the squads of labourers press-ganged into the First Division took to the spade to create earthworks on the north and west of P'yŏngyang as a cheap and cheerful alternative to the classic Japanese model of excavated hillsides faced with stone. Like the yamashiro model they had left behind at home, the interlocking and overlapping system of inner and outer baileys reinforced with trenches and palisades would allow a clear field of fire for the Japanese arquebus squads, and the packed earth would also provide absorbency for the cannon balls that would be fired against them by the Chinese field artillery.[1]

As it happened, the Ming army decided upon a sudden assault rather than a steady bombardment. Boasting that he had once defeated 100,000 Tartars with 3,000 horsemen, the Chinese general took advantage of a heavy rainstorm to attack Py'ŏngyang at dawn on 7m 16d (23 August) while the earthworks were still far from being finished. He seems to have taken Konishi completely by surprise, and Yoshino Jingoza'emon writes of 'the enemy entering in secret'.[2] Most of the Japanese army did not have time to put on their armour and just seized whatever weapons lay to hand as the Chinese flung themselves against the walls. Matsuura Shigenobu was but one of the First Division's commanders who became personally engaged in combat, and received an arrow through his leg. But the Chinese success in entering P'yŏngyang by storm was to prove their undoing. When the Japanese realised that they outnumbered the attacking army by six to one, the defenders allowed the Liaodong troops to spread freely into the narrow streets of the walled town. Soon what had been a hammer blow action against one section of the wall rapidly diffused into hundreds of small groups of isolated Chinese soldiers who could be picked off at will by

Ming armour as depicted on the statue of a Ming officer in court uniform on the approach to the Ming tombs near Beijing. He holds a commander's baton in his right hand and his left hand rests on his sword. He wears heavy boots under his robe. (Photograph by Ann Paludan)

Japanese arquebuses. A retreat was called, and the survivors were allowed to flood out of the opened gates to be cut down in their dozens by mounted samurai.[3]

During the summer of 1592 the first Chinese attack on P'yŏngyang is beaten off. (ETK detail)

The defeat of the Chinese expeditionary force produced mixed reactions among the Japanese commanders. There was certainly a feeling of elation at having beaten off the first serious challenge to be mounted against them since the war had begun, and as reinforcements were daily expected this dramatic confirmation of Japan's superiority only added to their readiness to press on for the Yalu. But as the days grew into months the feeling also grew that the Chinese would be back, and in far greater numbers. This was a concern shared at the highest level of the Japanese command, and on 8m 7d Konishi Yukinaga journeyed to Seoul for a conference with Ukita Hideie and the three bugyō. Kuroda Nagamasa and Kobayakawa Takakage also attended. The conclusion was reached that if, or when, P'yŏngyang was attacked again, defence in depth would be needed along the line back to Seoul. Kaesŏng, the old Koryŏ capital just north of the Imjin, was weakly defended by Toda Katsutaka with only 3,000 men, so it was decided to bring Kobayakawa's Sixth Division north to Kaesŏng while Toda would move south to Sangju. Neither move happened immediately, because Kobayakawa was in the middle of the Kŭmsan campaign, but by the end of October the line between P'yŏngyang and Seoul was strengthened by Kobayakawa's large contingent at Kaesŏng. By this time Kuroda Nagamasa had also moved his base from Haeju to Paech'ŏn, the fort to which he had been driven by the guerrillas of Yŏnan.

The first Chinese attack on P'yŏngyang had taken place within a few days of Admiral Yi's victory at Hansando, so it cannot have been very long before news of that disaster was conveyed to Konishi Yukinaga. By this time too Katō Kiyomasa had only got as far as Sŏngjin on his long campaign into Hamgyŏng, but once the impact of the news from Hansando sank in, the dream of a march into China was over. The protection that Katō was giving to Konishi's right wing was already irrelevant. No troops, no supplies and no weapons were ever going to be ferried up the Taedong from the Yellow Sea, so Konishi had to content himself with the fact that the province of Py'ŏngan, which he had been granted as his fief and into which he had advanced only a few miles, was to remain immune for some time from the customary round of cadastral surveys, sword hunts and oppressive taxation that fellow generals like Mōri and Nabeshima were carrying out elsewhere. For Konishi, as for the entire Japanese army, P'yŏngyang was to be the end of the line.

THE TURNING OF THE TIDE

Cooped up for months in P'yŏngyang, illness began to take its toll, and Yoshino Jingoza'emon describes its effects:

> Some got sick in their bodies, some others (developed) rausai [pulmonary tuberculosis]. Every day our troops became thinner. Someone suffering the misery of these illnesses (received) rice, salt and sake as food for the throat, and after a while chestnuts and millet. Even the horses were unwell. No matter which daimyō they served the men grew weak and had a dark skin. If they couldn't drink sake there was nothing with which to comfort their spirits.[4]

Under these gloomy conditions Konishi Yukinaga held on to P'yŏngyang for the next six months as the last outpost of a premature Japanese empire until, as the first year of Bunroku gave way to the second, the Chinese returned. The slaughter of their token force from Liaodong had been a salutary lesson, and they had spent the next eight months putting matters right The rebellion in Ningxia prevented the Ming from giving Korea their undivided attentions until late in 1592, and at one stage a fifty-day truce was agreed with Konishi to gain time in which to organise their forces. In October China received an offer of help from an unexpected quarter when the King of Siam sent a mission offering to send the Siamese navy against Japan. It was February 1593 before the gesture was finally rejected, by which time Siam was engaged in war with Burma, but the episode shows how destabilising such an event as the Japanese invasion of Korea was to East Asia in general.[5]

Meanwhile on 9m 14d Xie Fan, an imperial emissary who had witnessed the Japanese in action at P'yŏngyang, recommended to the Ming Emperor that China should send another force immediately. Failure to do so, he warned, would lead to Japan advancing into China itself, so agreement to proceed was given on 9m 16d. In place of the meagre 3,000 men of August the Ming would now send 43,000, and it was at the head of this number of troops that General Li Rusong crossed the frozen Yalu to arrive in Anju on the first day of the first month of the new Year of the Snake.

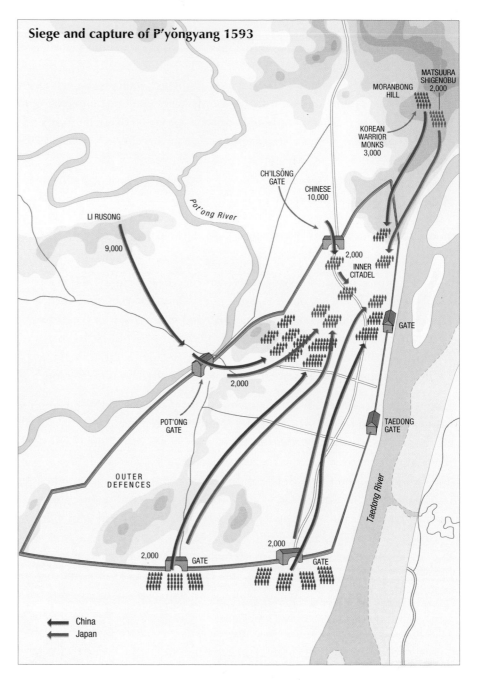

Siege and capture of P'yŏngyang 1593

MATSUURA
SHIGENOBU
2,000

MORANBONG
HILL

KOREAN
WARRIOR
MONKS
3,000

CH'ILSŎNG
GATE

CHINESE
10,000

Pot'ong River

LI RUSONG

9,000

2,000

INNER
CITADEL

GATE

POT'ONG
GATE

TAEDONG
GATE

Taedong River

OUTER
DEFENCES

2,000

2,000

2,000   GATE

2,000   GATE

← China

← Japan

*Map of the siege of
P'yŏngyang, 1593.*

On 1m 5d (5 February) 1593 Li drew up his ranks outside P'yŏngyang.
The Japanese earthworks and palisades were now complete and frozen rock
hard, but they drew only scorn from the Ming officers, who compared the
mounds of earth unfavourably to their own elegant Great Wall of China. These
crude defences were more like the earthen walls thrown up by the barbarous
Jurchens, but that was before these Chinese officers had experienced the volleys

of Japanese bullets that were to be discharged from behind these bleak and primitive-looking defences.

In addition to the earthworks and its own stone walls, P'yŏngyang also possessed certain natural features which added greatly to its defence. Reference was made earlier in the description of the Japanese capture of P'yŏngyang to the importance of the Taedong river, but in January 1593 the Taedong was of less importance than the narrower Pot'ong river, which flowed on the other side of the city and acted as a moat against an attack from the north-west. Another crucial area was to the north of P'yŏngyang, where a hill called Moranbong overlooked the walls and the river. A Buddhist temple, the Yŏngmyŏngsa, lay on its southern edge, and the whole complex was defended by walls and two gates, the Hyŏnmu Gate and the Chŏnkŭm Gate. In peacetime Moranbong (Botandai in the Japanese chronicles) was a popular place from which to enjoy the attractive view of the river over the tree peonies on its slopes. Now the pavilion called the 'Tree Peony Bower' which graced its summit provided a command post for Matsuura Shigenobu and his 2,000 men, and was to see some of the fiercest fighting of the forthcoming battle.

From the foot of Moranbong the walls of P'yŏngyang formed a crude and elongated right-angled triangle lying against the Taedong river, two sides of which would receive the Chinese attacks. The northerly point of this triangle

View of Mount Moranbong, the hill to the north of P'yŏngyang, showing the river and the temples at its foot. This beautiful scenic location was the site of some of the fiercest fighting of the siege of P'yŏngyang, led by Korean warrior monks.

The lively defence of the river-viewing 'Tree Peony Bower' on the summit of Mount Moranbong by the troops of Matsuura Shigenobu. (ETK)

was just below Mount Moranbong, while the hypotenuse, the north-west side of the walls, was pierced by two important gates: the Ch'ilsŏng (Seven Stars) Gate, just south of Mount Moranbong, and the Pot'ong Gate, where the wall touched the Pot'ong river. On the shorter, southern side of the triangle were two more gates, and each of the four gates was defended by 2,000 Japanese troops. The remainder of the 15,000 soldiers under Konishi's overall direction were within the walls and ready to be moved wherever they were needed, although a small number may have been stationed on the island in the middle of the Taedong as a rearguard to cover the crossing points in case of a retreat.

By now Li Rusong's 43,000-strong army had been swollen by an additional 10,000 Korean troops, some regulars, some volunteers, and 5,000 warrior monks, in a rare example of inter-unit cooperation. Li occupied some high ground to the west of the Pot'ong river with 9,000 men of his headquarters staff, and deployed 10,000 Chinese troops against the Ch'ilsŏng Gate and 11,000 against the Pot'ong Gate. A further 10,000 Chinese tackled the south-eastern gate, while 8,000 Koreans were to attack the south-western gate. The 3,000 warrior monks, whose fighting qualities were greatly respected by Li Rusong, were allocated to attacking Moranbong hill. The Korean monk army was under the command of Hyujŏng, the leader who had first called the religious contingent to arms, and on 1m 5d (6 February 1593) he led his men up the steep slopes in the face of fierce arquebus fire from the Japanese positions to begin the battle for Py'ŏngyang. There were hundreds of casualties, but the monks persevered, and received support rather late in the day from a Chinese unit under Wu Weichong who began scaling the western slope. The fight at

Mount Moranbong lasted two days and nights, with both sides suffering heavy losses, but at the end of that time the Japanese were driven down the reverse slope into P'yŏngyang's walls.[6]

While the fight for Moranbong was still in its second day Li ordered a general assault from all sides. On 1m 6d the allied armies advanced and were met by a withering arquebus fire from the earthworks. But the superior numbers of the Chinese told, and by the following morning the Chinese and Koreans were attacking the old stone ramparts themselves with Li Rusong at their head. Eyewitnesses of the scene described how the Chinese corpses piled up so densely outside the walls that they made a ramp up which their comrades clambered. With such determination, and at such a heavy cost in casualties, each of the four landward gates was taken, and the surviving Japanese were driven back into the citadel that filled the northern tip of the triangle to provide P'yŏngyang's last defence. Yet even with their backs so much to the wall the Japanese launched a fierce counterattack under Sō Yoshitomo, determined to die only as the noble samurai of old, overwhelmed by impossible odds.

By this time the winter's night was drawing on, and as Li Rusong had his enemy cornered he was loth to provoke any more desperate sallies, so he called off his men to rest until morning. That night Konishi Yukinaga made the decision to retreat. Under cover of darkness, and taking advantage of the frozen surface of the Taedong river, the entire Japanese garrison slipped out of the eastern gates and evacuated the city without either the Chinese or Korean armies knowing anything about it. As the chronicler Yoshino Jingoza'emon tells us:

The capture by the Chinese of the Ch'ilsŏng (Seven Stars) Gate. Note how a representation of the constellation of the plough has been painted on to the lintel. (ETK)

> There was hardly a gap between the dead bodies that filled the surroundings of Matsuyama castle [Mount Moranbong]. Finally, when we had repulsed the enemy, they burned the food storehouses in several places, so there was now no food. On the night of the seventh day we evacuated the castle, and made our escape. Wounded men were abandoned, while those who were not wounded but simply exhausted crawled almost prostrate along the road.[7]

The destination for this ragged, tired, frozen and wounded army was the first of the communications forts that lay back along the line towards Seoul. The castles had been built a day's march apart from each other, and the nearest was P'ungsan, held by Ōtomo Yoshimune of the Third Division. But an unpleasant surprise lay in store for Konishi's men, because to their

The evacuation of P'yŏngyang by the Japanese army across the frozen Taedong river by night. This fateful decision by Konishi Yukinaga was the beginning of a long retreat that was eventually to see the Japanese leave Korea completely. (ETK)

astonishment P'ungsan had been abandoned. Patrols sent out by Ōtomo had reported to him that Konishi was under attack from over 100,000 Chinese troops, and that both fields and mountains were filled with enemy soldiers. Ōtomo Yoshimune's conclusion was that Konishi had probably been defeated already by the time his scouts had ridden back. No relief march was conceivable with his tiny garrison, nor could they withstand the huge force that must be bearing down upon them, so Ōtomo decided to burn P'ungsan and retreat to Seoul. Yoshino puts into words the hardship this extraordinary decision caused to the wounded and frostbitten survivors of Konishi's army:

Because it is a cold country, there is ice and deep snow, and hands and feet are burned by the snow, and this gives rise to frostbite which make them swell up. The only clothes they had were the garments worn under their armour, and even men who were normally gallant resembled scarecrows on the mountains and fields because of their fatigue, and were indistinguishable from the dead . . . [8]

The diary kept by a member of the Yoshimi family adds snow blindness to the list of afflictions from which the wounded men were suffering.[9] These unfortunates were now faced with a further day's march through the wind and snow to the first of Kuroda Nagamasa's forts, which had not been abandoned, but his colleague's cowardice in the face of an enemy could not easily be forgiven. Ōtomo's family, one of the oldest and noblest in Kyushu, and one of the first and greatest of the Christian daimyō, was now disgraced irreparably and forever. When the news was reported back to Japan their fief of Ōita was stripped from them by Hideyoshi and given to another, and the mighty Ōtomo effectively passed out of history.

Konishi's retreat to Seoul took nine painful days. P'yŏngsan was reached on 1m 10d, Paech'ŏn on the 11th, Kaesŏng on the 13th, while the frozen and exhausted vanguard finally entered Seoul on 1m 18d (19 February). Rearguard cover was provided along the march by Kuroda Nagamasa who, in contrast to Ōtomo's appalling actions, had sent troops forward to engage the Chinese when he received the news of the Ming advance. In one such action a contingent under a certain Awayama Toriyasu had marched a few miles north from

Kuroda's base at Paech'ŏn to reinforce the little fort of Kangui, which controlled a river crossing. Other Third Division troops had fallen back on Kangui, and the decision was made to send a letter to Kuroda explaining the situation and requesting further help:

> ... the enemy army have crossed the river in the middle of the night and are establishing lines on this side, which suggests that soon we will be crossing swords in a battle. Please send out troops quickly.[10]

But Awayama would have none of it. He knew there was no time for troops to be sent from Paech'ŏn, so taking a brush he crossed out the final sentence of the letter and wrote 'Rest easy', then led his men out to hold back the Chinese advance. The Japanese casualties were frightful, but like every rearguard action fought over those fateful few days it served to buy time along the road towards Seoul, so that the retreat from P'yŏngyang did not become a panic-stricken rout.

When Kangui fell Kuroda Nagamasa evacuated Paech'ŏn and followed Konishi's army south. Everywhere the Japanese army was in full retreat, and with Kuroda's departure Hwanghae became the second Korean province to be given back to the enemy. The next strong point along the line was Kaesŏng, held since October by Kobayakawa Takakage. News of the fall of P'yŏngyang had reached Seoul on about 12 February, and a delegation from Ukita's Chiefs of Staff was sent up to Kaesŏng to discuss the situation with Kobayakawa. The old warrior was for making a stand, but Ōtani Yoshitsugu suggested to him that a wiser course of action might be to abandon Kaesŏng and put the Imjin river between the Japanese and the advancing Chinese army. Kobayakawa agreed and the armies pulled back, allowing the Chinese and Koreans to enter Kaesŏng in triumph on 1m 18d (19 February). There was now no major fortress between their armies and the city of Seoul.

THE BATTLE OF PYŎKJE

By late February all the units of the Japanese army that had been stationed north of the capital had arrived in Seoul, and about 50,000 men were now inside the city or encamped around it. Even the Second Division under Katō and Nabeshima, who were now perilously isolated, received an order to pull back to the capital, and evacuated Anbyŏn under cover of rain on 1m 21d for an eight-day march over the mountains. The news of the Chinese advance had also permeated down to the citizens of Seoul, who hoped to assist their coming liberation by attacking Japanese bases in the capital. As a result, towards dawn on 1m 23d, fires were started in various places, but the Japanese troops reacted savagely with extensive killings and burning of Korean places in

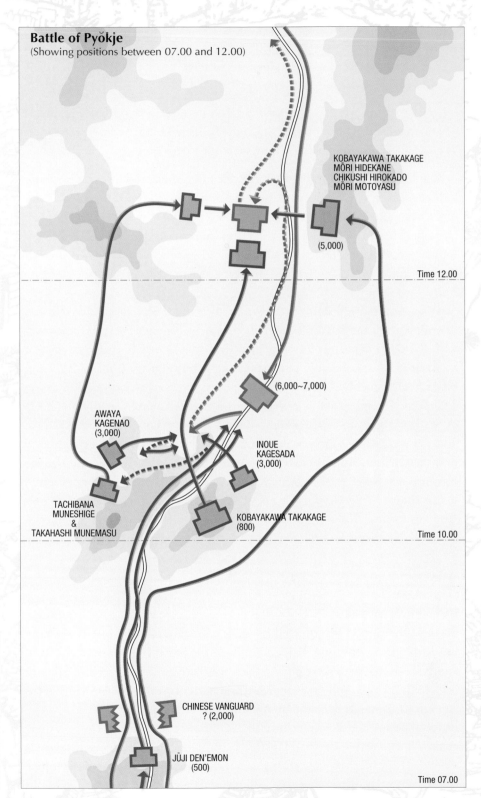

Battle of Pyŏkje
(Showing positions between 07.00 and 12.00)

KOBAYAKAWA TAKAKAGE
MŌRI HIDEKANE
CHIKUSHI HIROKADO
MŌRI MOTOYASU

(5,000)

Time 12.00

(6,000~7,000)

AWAYA
KAGENAO
(3,000)

INOUE
KAGESADA
(3,000)

TACHIBANA
MUNESHIGE
&
TAKAHASHI MUNEMASU

KOBAYAKAWA TAKAKAGE
(800)

Time 10.00

CHINESE VANGUARD
? (2,000)

JŪJI DEN'EMON
(500)

Time 07.00

Map of the battle of Pyŏkje, the largest battlefield engagement of the Korean War.

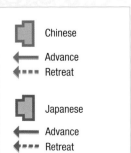

Chinese
Advance
Retreat

Japanese
Advance
Retreat

reprisal to ensure that there was no Korean fifth column in the city. There could well have been a complete massacre of all Seoul's inhabitants, were it not for the fact that the Japanese effort had to be directed towards monitoring the movements of the Chinese and Koreans in Kaesŏng, where that same day Li Rusong held a council of war to plan the attack upon Seoul.

The Chinese vanguard set off early on 1m 25d, full of confidence about engaging an enemy who had been in steady retreat since P'yŏngyang. For Ukita Hideie the decision now had to be taken over where the defensive line should be drawn. The Imjin river would provide but a small obstacle to the Korean army who were familiar with its layout. Should it be Seoul itself, with the prospect of a long siege? Guerrilla bands were active all round the capital, and to leave Seoul and retreat further would be a tremendous admission of failure. It was Kobayakawa Takakage, the veteran commander in the Japanese army, who forced the decision. In his opinion they had retreated far enough anyway, and it was time to take the fight to the advancing enemy. His Sixth Division would lead an attack on the Chinese somewhere along the road back to Kaesŏng.

The Chinese and Korean movements were being carefully monitored by Japanese troops, whose scouts kept their distance. On the morning of 1m 26d this scouting role was replaced by a flying column under young Tachibana Muneshige, who led Kobayakawa's force out to intercept the Chinese with a main body following some distance behind. The total strength of the Japanese army was about 40,000 men. Konishi Yukinaga remained in Seoul, along with the disgraced Ōtomo Yoshimune. At dawn the same day Li Rusong left P'aju and headed for Seoul with his allied army of 20,000, led by his vanguard of 1,000 men who crossed the pass that followed a well-established road and dropped down steeply towards the village of Koyang.

The road passed along its way, in a place called Pyŏkje, one of several lodging houses that had been set up along this main road to China for the use of envoys between the two countries. Much of the subsequent fighting took place near this lodging, so that the battle is commonly called the 'battle of the Pyŏkje lodging' (Pyŏkje-yek or Byokchekwan). The site of the battle is still a main communications artery. Just before Pyŏkje the road heading north from Seoul forks at a major traffic intersection. The left fork heads towards Munsan and the DMZ, while the right fork is a busy dual carriageway that begins to climb through Pyŏkje along the old road to China until it reaches the top of the pass, only the gradient and the hills on each side retaining any element of the location that existed in 1593.

That morning the freezing February fog was so dense that it is doubtful if anyone could even see the road properly, let alone the famous lodging house. The lack of visibility therefore made Pyŏkje one of those battles where units

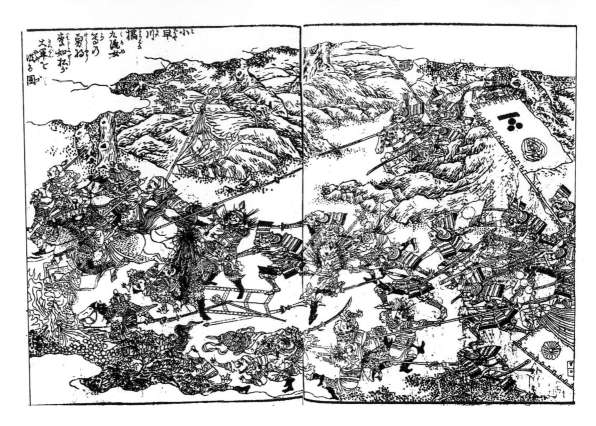

Kobayakawa Takakage at the battle of Pyŏkje. Kobayakawa is at the right of the picture under his standard bearing the Mōri badge. Tachibana Muneshige is depicted to his right. (ETK)

collide and disengage with little knowledge of overall developments. The first of a series of such encounters began at about 7.00 a.m. when Tachibana's forward troops, a unit of about 500 men under Jūji Den'emon, blundered into a mass of Chinese soldiers. Fierce fighting took place and the Chinese broke, at which Jūji led a vigorous pursuit to the north through the fog where, somewhere between Koyang and Pyŏkje, they ran into a further body of Chinese numbering 6–7,000. Over a hundred Japanese were cut down, including Jūji himself who sustained multiple wounds. Tachibana Muneshige and Takahashi Munemasu then hurried up with the rest of their troops and a bitter engagement developed with the Chinese, who rotated their front line from seemingly inexhaustible supplies of men. By 10.00 a.m. the remainder of Kobayakawa's Division arrived, and Tachibana and Takahashi withdrew exhausted to a nearby hill to the west to rest their men.[11]

Leading Kobayakawa's troops were Awaya Kagenao and Inoue Kagesada, each of whom had 3,000 men. They were for making a joint frontal attack, but Kobayakawa's subordinate commander Sayo Masakatsu persuaded them to deploy as two forward wings with Awaya on the left and Inoue on the right. The lack of visibility helped to confuse the Chinese as to the actual size of the Japanese army, and they turned their attentions against Awaya, who soon began to give ground. Inoue prepared to move over in support, but Sayo restrained him, suggesting that he should wait until Awaya had begun to pull back, at which point Inoue could take his pursuers in the flank as they advanced up the hill. This is precisely what happened, and when both forward wings of his army were engaged Kobayakawa saw the opportunity to develop a further phase in the struggle. Far from merely holding their own, Awaya and Inoue were driving the Chinese vanguard back up the pass. When they had gone about half a mile Kobayakawa ordered into action his brother Mōri Hidekane, his nephew Mōri Motoyasu and Chikushi Hirokado, who approached cautiously at some distance from the right. Meanwhile the troops of Tachibana and Takahashi, who had been resting from their earlier efforts on the hill to the left, made a wide sweep round on to the Chinese right flank to join in the fighting once again. While these flank manoeuvres went on Kobayakawa Takakage advanced up the pass behind his vanguard with Kikkawa Hiroie in the lead, and somewhere within the fog, in the environs of the Pyŏkje lodging house, they encountered the rest of the Chinese army.

Li Rusong had been following closely behind his vanguard. On crossing the ridge he had fallen off his horse and injured his face, but quickly mounted another so as not to demoralise anyone who had seen the incident. On making his first contact with the Japanese under Kobayakawa, Li ordered an immediate advance down the road, his troops spreading out across the narrow strip of land on either side. For a short while Kobayakawa let them advance. The ground, made sodden from mountain streams and melting snow, became chewed up under the impact of thousands of feet. Horsemen could not move their mounts, whose hooves became mired. At that point the three units of the Japanese converged upon them from three sides. A Chinese account takes the story on:

> There seemed to be several tens of thousands of them. Swords flashed, and flags and banners seemed to cover the sky. The Ming soldiers saw this and everyone's heart missed a beat. Suddenly the Japanese soldiers brandished their swords and began a charge, completely surrounding them. The soldiers who were under the Commander were all northern Chinese horsemen who had no firearms and carried short swords. The Japanese came up close and plunged into them, killing and cutting in all directions. Both men and horses trembled with fear at having to go and face the point of those swords.[12]

In the fierce hand-to-hand fighting it was the relative efficacy of the rival swords and spears that decided the issue. The razor-sharp edges of the Japanese blades cut deep into the heavy coats of the Chinese, while Japanese foot soldiers tugged mounted men from the backs of their horses using the short cross blades on their spears. The chronicle goes on to say that the fight lasted from the Hour of the Snake (10.00 a.m.) until the Hour of the Horse (12.00 noon), and even the Chinese commander Li was in the thick of the fighting, because,

The Chinese General Li Rusong is wounded at Pyŏkje in an encounter with the samurai Inoue Gorō Kagesada, who led the right wing of Kobayakawa's vanguard. Li lies on the floor, protected by his bodyguard. (ETK)

'The Japanese General, who wore a golden helmet, was about to capture the Commander, when his second-in-command covered him with his own body and received a great number of Japanese blades, but then his horse was struck by a bullet and he fell off and died.'[13]   The parallel Japanese account suggests that it was Inoue Kagesada who almost won the accolade of taking the enemy general's head, but the brave subordinate general's sacrifice had not been made in vain, because it enabled Li Rusong to escape from the field.[14]

At about this time it started to rain, and the broken ground grew more and more to resemble a swamp, as men and horses trampled together and helmets, spears and halberds were scattered on the ground. Changing tactics, Kobayakawa drew back his samurai to allow a field of fire for his arquebus squads, who shot bullets into the mass of Chinese and Koreans. The Japanese then pursued the defeated enemy back up the pass to its highest point, and after a few more hours of fighting Kobayakawa ordered the advance to cease as darkness fell. The army made its way back to Seoul, carrying 6,000 Chinese heads with them as trophies.

Pyŏkje was a stunning victory by an army that had looked beaten, a reversal of fortunes that Kobayakawa readily attributed to the divine protection that Japan had enjoyed since the time of Empress Jingū's invasion of Korea. On the defeated side a heartbroken Li Rusong fled back to P'aju and eventually reached Kaesŏng on 1m 29d. So catastrophic was the battle of Pyŏkje that he endeavoured to keep the disaster secret for as long as he could, but we read of him being back in P'yŏngyang on 2m 16d (18 March), by which time it must have been common knowledge.

THE SIEGE OF HAENGJU

During the days which followed the victory at Pyŏkje the Japanese garrison in Seoul were further heartened by the safe arrival from Hamgyŏng province of the exhausted survivors of Katō and Nabeshima's Second Division. It was now time for a decisive effort to take out the fortress of Haengju, the one remaining enemy threat to the capital, the background to which is as follows.

After the recapture of P'yŏngyang the Korean monk soldiers had moved south to join up with guerrilla armies and prepare for a joint attack on Seoul with the Ming. Four contingents of monks had then fought bitterly contested skirmishes with Japanese troops to secure their positions around the capital, and in one at Chasŏng the monks lost half their number.[15]   The monk leader

Yujŏng fought a particularly celebrated action at Suraksan, and other contingents fought at Ich'on and Uhwan-dong, but the most important acquisition was the fortress of Haengju, a sansŏng on a hill eight miles north-west of Seoul which overlooked the Han river and covered all approaches down from the Pyŏkje area, a few miles to the north. On hearing of the Chinese advance against Seoul, Chŏlla's skilled general Kwŏn Yul had left his base at Toksan, near Suwŏn, and marched round the west of Seoul to take over this dilapidated castle which possessed steep cliffs on the river side and abrupt slopes in all other directions. Kwŏn Yul's 2,300 men, who included a monk contingent under Ch'ŏyŏng, strengthened Haengju's fortifications with ditches and palisades and waited for the signal to join the Chinese attack on Seoul, but the ensuing battle of Pyŏkje ensured that none was to come.

Having won one battle so decisively at Pyŏkje, Ukita Hideie decided to make Haengju his next target, and at dawn on 2m 12d (14 March) he led a massive 30,000 strong Japanese army out of Seoul to crush this minor annoyance. Konishi Yukinaga and Kobayakawa Takakage are two of the famous names who took part. The attack began about 6.00 a.m. with little overall plan – just a steady advance up the steep slopes of Haengju from all directions. But the Koreans were waiting for them. Dug in behind earthworks and palisades they replied with bows, arquebuses, delayed-action mortar bombs, rocks and tree trunks. Pride of place in the Haengju armoury, however, were a substantial number of the curious armoured artillery vehicles called hwach'a (fire wagons). The hwach'a was the brainchild of a certain Pyŏn I-chung, and consisted of a wooden cart pushed by two men on level ground, or four on steep ground. On top of the cart was mounted one of two varieties of a honeycomb-like framework from which either 100 steel-tipped rockets or 200 thin arrows shot from gun tubes could be discharged at once. Timing was of course crucial, because a hwach'a could not be

A reconstructed hwach'a, Kwŏn Yul's 'secret weapon' at Haengju, which is displayed in the grounds of the Tŏksugung Palace in Seoul.

The successful defence of Haengju castle by Kwŏn Yul. A hwach'a is fired downhill at the advancing Japanese, and the women carry rocks in their aprons to the men. (Courtesy of the Haengju Memorial Shrine)

easily reloaded, but the Japanese attack at Haengju was delivered in the form of dense formations of men marching slowly up a steep slope, so conditions could hardly have been better.

Haengju is regarded with Hansando and the first battle of Chinju as one of the three great Korean victories of the war. In an action that has passed into legend, even the women of the garrison played their part, carrying stones to the front line in their aprons or their skirts.[16] In spite of the hail of missiles the overwhelming superiority in numbers of the Japanese forced Kwŏn Yul's troops on to their second line of defence, but they went no further back. Nine attacks in all were made against Haengju, and each was beaten off for a total Japanese casualty list that Korean sources claim may have reached 10,000 dead or wounded. Among the commanders wounded before the attack on Haengju was suspended were Ukita Hideie, Ishida Mitsunari, Maeno Nagayasu and Kikkawa Hiroie.

The result of the Haengju débâcle was that within a space of less than twenty days the Japanese had gained one tremendous victory and suffered one humiliating defeat, with the inevitable result that the military effects of each cancelled the other out. The Chinese army had withdrawn, but they were expected to return, and the Korean position was stronger than ever after the engagement at Haengju. Namsan, the rocky hill in the centre of Seoul, had already been fortified in anticipation of a possible Korean attack on the capital, and the subsequent Japanese defeat at Haengju meant that a large and confident Korean army were now poised on Seoul's doorstep, so a bridge of boats was laid across the Han river just in case a retreat should be needed. As Ukita had correctly anticipated, the despondent Chinese general Li Rusong resolved to return to the fray when he heard of the triumph at Haengju, and Chinese troops began to move south towards Seoul once again.

THE EVACUATION OF SEOUL

Li Rusong was not alone in feeling that, in spite of Pyŏkje, the tide of war had turned decisively against the Japanese. The experience of the actual fighting at Pyŏkje and Haengju may have encouraged Ukita Hideie to think that he could hold on to Seoul in a battle, but the additional factor of the rapid deterioration in the physical condition of the Japanese army was beginning to give him real concern. On 3m 23d the Japanese Chiefs of Staff carried out an assessment of what men they still had under their command, and their conclusions were alarming. A mere eleven months had passed since over 150,000 Japanese troops had landed in Korea. Now the best estimate of the army's strength was 53,000 men. 'All the soldiers based in Seoul in particular have run out of provisions and are facing starvation,' wrote the author of *Matsui Monogatari*, 'and on top of this okori (fever) and ekibyō (plague) are prevalent, and many men have died.'[17]   The expressions 'fever' and 'plague' probably indicate typhus, and Konishi Yukinaga's long-serving First Division had suffered the most. From an original strength of 18,700 men his army now consisted of 6,626 effectives, a decline in numbers of almost 65%.[18]   Death and wounds from numerous battles, sieges, frostbite, guerrilla raids and typhoid fever had taken a huge toll, and the Second Division had fared little better. As the troops of Katō and Nabeshima straggled into Seoul after their long trudge across the peninsula the chronicler noted how the common soldiers who had defended Kilchu castle to the end had suffered frostbite and snow blindness, and one or two had even been eaten by tigers while on sentry duty. The review noted above revealed that Katō's army had been reduced in strength by 45% and Nabeshima's by 36%.[19]

It is therefore not surprising to read that after much heart-searching the decision was made to evacuate Seoul and regroup within the castles and harbours of Kyŏngsang province. To cover the preparations for withdrawal a message was sent to the Korean Prime Minister proposing a peace conference, which was eventually held in mid-stream on the Han river at Yongsan to the south of Seoul. The Japanese side were in no position to make extravagant bargains. The Koreans insisted on the evacuation of Seoul and a withdrawal to Kyŏngsang province by all Japanese units, which was fully acceptable as that was what the invaders had been planning to do, and their other demand,

The Japanese burn Seoul and withdraw south towards Pusan. (ETK)

which was for the Japanese to hand back their two royal hostages, was opposed only by Katō Kiyomasa, who had captured them in the first place. With the prospect of a safe retreat untroubled by guerrillas the Japanese negotiators agreed with alacrity. To the background of an eerie truce, which was frequently broken by both sides, the Japanese army headed south, its vanguard crossing the Naktong at the end of May, and finally pulled their rearguard into the safely of the 'Pusan Perimeter' in early June.

Seoul was officially liberated by the Chinese army on 4m 19d (19 May), and their arrival revealed the horrors that the Japanese had left behind, because the starvation and typhus that had afflicted the Japanese troops had been visited tenfold upon the Korean population. The pile of dead bodies that the Chinese heaped up for cremation beside the city wall topped the ramparts, and emaciated people crawled along the streets where smoke rose from the embers of burned-out homes, workshops and palaces, because the Japanese had fired the city before they left to cover their withdrawal. Only one royal residence was still inhabitable. This was the Tŏksugung Palace, where King Sŏnjo re-established his authority amid the blackened wastes. Yu Sŏng-nyong described the ghastly scene in *Chingbirok*:

The Tŏksugung Palace in Seoul, the only royal palace to survive the Japanese capture of the city in 1592, became the temporary home of King Sŏnjo when he returned to the capital in 1593.

The moment I entered the castle, I counted the number of survivors among the citizens, who totalled only one out of every hundred. Yet they looked like ghosts, betraying their great sufferings from hunger and fatigue. The corpses of both men and horses were exposed under the extreme heat of the season, producing an unbearable stench which filled the streets of the city. I passed the residential districts, both public and private, only to find remnants of complete destruction. Also gone were the ancestral shrines of the royal family, the court palaces, government offices, office buildings and various schools. No trace of the old grandeur could be seen.[20]

A Japanese monk in the retinue of Nabeshima Naoshige confirms the stench from the dead bodies, and blames this for the outbreaks of illness among the troops before the evacuation. Ill-health also appears to have affected the Chinese army. At the time of the Pyŏkje action an epidemic of horse fever had spread through the Chinese army, and most of their horses died. A similar thing then happened to the Chinese army that returned to Seoul and consequently hindered any pursuit of the retreating Japanese.[21]

THE UNGCH'ŎN RAIDS

While the capital was being reclaimed Admiral Yi Sun-sin had been making his own contribution to the overall trend of victory a few hundred miles to the south. Yi had kept himself well informed about the fall of P'yŏngyang and the Chinese advance. Lacking the force with which to assault Pusan, he patrolled the sea around Kadŏk and Kŏje islands as before, and observed large Japanese troops concentrations around Ungch'ŏn, where ships were gathering and fortifications were being built. No Japanese warship was tempted to come out and engage the Korean fleet, so Yi went on to the offensive and launched his first assault on Ungch'ŏn on 2m 10d (12 March).

The enemy had built long walls on the eastern and western mountainsides where he took up positions planted with multi-coloured war banners, and rained gunfire towards us in a haughty manner. Our warships darted forward with one accord from right and left while shooting cannonballs and arrows like thunder and lightning. This was done twice a day, killing the enemy robbers in countless numbers.[22]

Over four successive raids on Ungch'ŏn Yi inflicted much damage from a distance, but his reports also record his frustration at being unable to do more. For example, during his third raid on 2m 18d he notes with satisfaction the performance of a turtle boat, whose crew killed 100 Japanese:

Among them was a Japanese commander in golden helmet and scarlet armour who shouted 'Row back fast!', but before finishing his words he fell dead on his boat by a direct hit of our leather-winged arrow.[23]

Set against this is his clear exasperation at the absence of Korean or Chinese ground troops with whom he could have carried out a combined operation. In spite of several requests the only response was the arrival of Kwak Chae-u's guerrillas, whose small force Yi regarded as insufficient. Yi therefore mounted a limited amphibious operation of his own. 'I ordered out a dozen warships manned by monk captains and sharpshooters to make landings at strategic points,' he writes. 'Our valiant monk soldiers jumped up brandishing swords and thrusting spears and charged into the enemy positions, shooting guns and arrows from morning to night.'[24]

The accounts written by both sides of the raids on Ungch'ŏn provide several illustrations of the often chaotic nature of contemporary warfare. After successfully attacking some enemy vessels two of Yi's ships turned back to join the fleet and collided side on, so that one of the Korean ships capsized with great loss of life.[25] Yi was highly critical of such carelessness brought on by exuberance, and devoted an additional memorandum to the matter but, taking full responsibility for the tragedy, he added, 'I do hereby prostrate myself in shame to await Your Majesty's punishment.'[26]

The Japanese samurai spirit also produced its own problems during the fourth raid, where Japanese accounts reveal that Wakizaka Yasuharu and Katō Yoshiaki were once again in action. Wakizaka 'captured the guard ship (a Korean vessel) by throwing a grappling rope on to it', but,

> Kuki was on a fast ship too, and once more the guard ship was secured by a grappling rope. He disputed over the precedence. While the debate continued Yasuharu, who was carrying his spear in his hand, ordered that Kuki's grappling rope to the ship should be cut. Yasuharu's retainers Mibusuke and Sokuji, who were seventeen years old, went forward and cut Kuki's rope.[27]

The account goes on to say that in the ensuing squabble over precedence the Korean ship escaped.

Admiral Yi's chief complaints to the Korean court concerned the non-appearance of soldiers of the Chinese army who, he had been assured, were pursuing the retreating Japanese following the recapture of Seoul. 'No news has arrived from the Ming Chinese army,' he writes on one occasion,[28] the most exasperating aspect of the situation being the evidence before his own eyes that the Japanese army was in a very sorry state and could have been easily swept into the sea. In one of his reports on the Ungch'ŏn actions, he noted that 'the enemy's fighting strength has recently been greatly weakened with many war dead and wounded',[29] and his diary for 5m 17d (16 June) contains the angry comment that, 'Ming General Li (Rusong) stayed in Ch'ungju while the Japanese enemy attacked everywhere, plundering, raping and burning. My hair stood on end with indignation.'[30]

Later in the same report Yi Sun-sin quotes from interviews he conducted with liberated Korean prisoners of war, who stated that infectious diseases were rife in the Japanese army and had already claimed many lives.[31] This was indeed true, and as the former invaders marched back to Pusan along the road they had once trod in triumph, the health of their army continued to deteriorate. A letter dated 7m 21d sent home by Date Masamune, who had arrived in Korea with reinforcements, reports an outbreak of beri-beri, which killed eight out of ten sufferers, and in another letter three days later he refers to deaths occurring 'because the water in this country is different', which may imply an outbreak of cholera.[32]

If any of the Japanese troops who staggered back through Kyŏngsang were expecting a spell of 'R and R' in Pusan their hopes were shortly to be cruelly dashed. Date Masamune's newly arrived contingent had not been sent to Korea to cover a withdrawal, but were but a small part of the reinforcements that the war-weary generals were to lead into one final and epic battle at Chinju. This new offensive strategy called for a further shrinking of the line, so the units stationed in Sangju were redeployed in strength around the Kimhae/Ch'angwŏn area to the west of Pusan. Meanwhile the Ming army had slipped into the castles abandoned by the retreating Japanese, and Chinese garrisons were now located in an offensive ring from Kyŏngju through Sŏngju, Sŏnsan, Koch'ang and Namwŏn, the total number of Chinese in Kyŏngsang and Chŏlla provinces now being about 30,000. There were also about 50,000 Korean troops in the two provinces.

THE SECOND BATTLE OF CHINJU

The failure by the Japanese army to capture Chinju castle in November 1592 appears to have infuriated Hideyoshi more than any other defeat suffered at Korean hands. The débâcle at Haengju could be seen to have been offset by the great victory at Pyŏkje, while Hansando had happened as victories on land were being gained elsewhere. Chinju stood alone as a Japanese humiliation. It was a fortress apparently no different from any that had fallen so easily to Japanese attack during those triumphant first months of the march on Seoul, and in view of the great strength of the Japanese forces that had been brought against it, the failure to take it was a disgrace that had to be expunged. The new Japanese strategy against Chinju seems to have been quite straightforward – to destroy this powerful and hitherto untouched Korean base before the Chinese could intervene, and with Hideyoshi's anger in mind Ukita Hideie committed a total of over 90,000 troops to the Chinju campaign, the largest Japanese force mobilised for a single operation in the entire war. At least half of these were reinforcements brought over from Japan, and they were placed under the generals who had already fought from one end of Korea to the other.[33]

In mid-July 1593 the local Korean commanders held a council of war in Ŭiryŏng. Kwŏn Yul's victory at Haengju had given them new confidence, so their first move against the new Japanese line was an advance on Haman, in spite of words of caution from the reliable Kwak Chae-u. The sudden approach of the Japanese vanguard heading for Chinju confirmed Kwak's misgivings, so the Koreans pulled back to use the Naktong as a defensive line in the Kigang area, the site of Kwak's earliest guerrilla operations. But with a massive Japanese force approaching from Ch'angwŏn the defence of fortresses was a more promising strategy, so the Korean forces spread themselves between the castles of western Kyŏngsang and Chŏlla provinces.

Not knowing what might be the Japanese objective, Kwŏn Yul headed for Chŏnju while Kim Ch'ŏn-il entered Chinju, and took charge of its defences against a possible attack. Chinju had a permanent garrison of 4,000, which soon grew to a possible 60,000 through the arrival of guerrillas, volunteers and many civilians, including women and children, who packed themselves into its walls. Its layout was exactly the same as it had been in 1592. It was protected to the

Map of the second siege of Chinju.

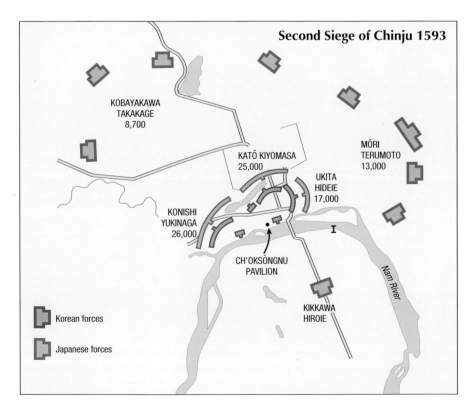

Second Siege of Chinju 1593

KOBAYAKAWA
TAKAKAGE
8,700

KATŌ KIYOMASA
25,000

MŌRI
TERUMOTO
13,000

UKITA
HIDEIE
17,000

KONISHI
YUKINAGA
26,000

CH'OKSŎNGNU
PAVILION

KIKKAWA
HIROIE

Nam River

Korean forces

Japanese forces

south by cliffs overlooking the Nam river, and the long perimeter walls with towers and gateways that stretched round the city on the other three sides made it look like a miniature version of P'yŏngyang. Like Py'ŏngyang Chinju had a bower for viewing the river, the Ch'oksŏngnu pavilion, which looked over the Nam on the castle's southern side. On 6m 19d some Chinese troops, who claimed to be the vanguard of a great force that was approaching from the north, entered the castle amid great rejoicing.

On hearing that the Korean army had pulled back from Ŭiryŏng the Japanese advanced on Haman, and on 6m 18d crossed the undefended Naktong at Kigang to occupy Ŭiryŏng without a struggle. The march westwards continued, and by 6m 22d (20 July) the Japanese vanguard were constructing bamboo bundles and setting up wooden shields in sight of the walls of Chinju. The names of the commanders disposed around Chinju confirms the importance attached to the Chinju operation. Every general of note was present for this last great and vengeful battle of the first invasion. Three units were deployed for the actual assault. To the west was Konishi Yukinaga with 26,000 men. To the north was Katō Kiyomasa with 25,000 troops, while to the east was Ukita Hideie in command of a further 17,000. Beyond them was another ring of Japanese soldiers whose eyes were turned as much in the direction of a possible Chinese advance as to the castle itself. On the hills to the north-west, watching for movements from Namwŏn and Chŏnju, stood Kobayakawa Takakage with 8,700 men, while Mōri Terumoto and 13,000 troops covered the north and east in case of hostile moves from Sŏngju and Sŏnsan. Finally, across the Nam to the south was Kikkawa Hiroie from the Mōri division, ready to cut off any Korean guerrillas coming from that direction.

The gate of Chinju from the inside. Note the typical Korean style of an arched tunnel entrance of stone. The capture of Chinju was the last battle of the first invasion, and one of the most bloody encounters in the entire war.

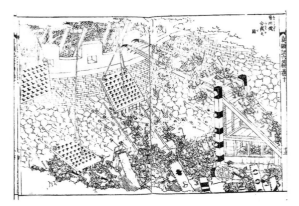

The Japanese use a Chinese-style 'cloud ladder' (depicted hopelessly out of scale!) against Chinju, whose defenders hit back using fire and 'wolf's tooth striking boards'. (ETK)

The Chinju garrison had tried to augment their defences by diverting the Nam river round the walls to the north to flood the ditch, and on the first day of the Japanese attack on 6m 23d (21 July) advance troops broke the edges of the dyke and drained off the water. As they proceeded to fill the ditch with rocks, earth and brushwood, assault parties drew steadily nearer to the walls under cover of shields made from bamboo bundles, some of which may have been mounted on a wheeled framework. The Koreans replied with arquebuses, cannonballs and fire arrows, shattering or burning the bamboo defences. On the 25th day the Japanese tried the same technique that had been used during the first siege of Chinju by erecting a static siege tower, to which the Korean responded by increasing the defences within the castle and firing back. 'His Lordship (Kim Ch'ŏn-il) knew that all the robber generals had gathered on the mountain top to the east of the castle, and secretly fired the cannons,' says a Korean account. 'The cannon balls hit the lines, and the enemy generals fell to the ground.'[34] At about this time a local Righteous Army arrived in support, but were driven off by the Japanese rearguard.

On 6m 27d Ukita Hideie sent a message into the castle calling upon Kim Chŏn-il to surrender and arguing that if one general submitted then 10,000 peasants' lives would be saved, but the request drew no response. Instead the inspiring figure of Kim Chŏn-il urged his men to fight to the last:

His Lordship had an inherent weakness in his legs and could not walk, so in the castle he travelled in a shoulder palanquin, but took little rest by day or night. He prepared rice gruel with his own hands, and made sure that the members of the garrison ate it. All the soldiers were inspired, and pledged themselves to the death.[35]

It was now time for a major Japanese assault to be led by kikkōsha (tortoise shell wagons), which were stout wooden contraptions on wheels that were pushed up to the edge of the walls. Under the protection of the kikkōsha's boarded roofs, foundation stones would be dug out of the ramparts, leading to the collapse of a section.

at Kuroda Nagamasa's duty station they built up almost the whole width (of the ditch) by working day and night. This was done by throwing grass into the ditch to make a flat surface. They tried to attack, but from inside the castle pine torches were thrown that set the grass alight. The soldiers inside the tortoise wagons were also burned and retreated.[36]

The burning of the wagons, which was done by the simple expedient of dropping bundles of combustible material soaked in oil or fat from the battlements, drove off this assault. Nothing daunted, Katō ordered other kikkōsha to be prepared and had their roofs covered with ox hides for fire prevention. On 6m 29d a new attack began that concentrated on the wall's corner stones in the north-east, and a fortuitous rain storm helped dislodge the foundations. The customary rush to claim the distinction of being ichiban nori commenced as soon as the stones in the wall began to slide, with samurai pushing each other out of the way. The competition at Chinju was between Katō Kiyomasa and Kuroda Nagamasa. Seeing that Gotō Mototsugu, one of Kuroda's retainers, was likely to be the first to climb in, Katō's standard bearer, Iida Kakubei, threw the great Nichiren flag over the wall to claim his place. According to the *Taikōki*, the ruse succeeded:

Katō Kiyomasa's use of kikkōsha (tortoise wagons) to undermine the walls of Chinju proved to be the decisive act of the siege. (ETK)

> Katō's unit broke into the castle. The first to climb in were the standard bearers Shobayashi Shunjin, Iida Kakubei and Morimoto, followed by Kuroda's horō-wearing man Gotō Matabei [Mototsugu]. The three men removed themselves from the group and quickly entered the castle. All the men attacking saw this and were deeply impressed by such a splendid act.[37]

The Korean account of Chinju quoted earlier states that by this time the garrison were so short of weapons and ammunition that they were fighting with wooden sticks, but at least one senior defender still had a sword. This was General Sŏ Ye-wŏn. When the Japanese broke in he opened one of the gates and sallied out twice to fight an individual combat with a certain Okamoto Gonojō, a retainer of Kikkawa Hiroie. On the second occasion, however, Okamoto pursued him back to the gate and forced his way into the courtyard, where the injured and exhausted Sŏ was sitting on the stump of a large tree. 'Pausing for breath he unsheathed his sword, leapt upon him and struck off his head. To one side of this place was the edge of a steep cliff, and Sŏ's head tumbled down into the grass beneath.'[38] As it was unthinkable for a noble samurai to lose such a prized head a search was made of the river bank:

> Okamoto's two soldiers searched for and located Sŏ's head among the grass, and sent it for identification. Some men who had been captured alive said that this was indeed General Sŏ's head, and Hiroie rejoiced greatly. It was pickled in salt, and with Okamoto Gonojō in attendance it was sent to Japan and presented to the Taikō.[39]

The Ch'oksŏngnu Pavilion overlooking the Nam river at Chinju. This was the site of the celebrated self-sacrifice by the heroine Nongae, who dragged a Japanese general to his death.

This dramatic depiction of Nongae's sacrifice has exaggerated the drop from the pavilion to the river. (ETK detail)

The overall Korean commander Kim Ch'ŏn-il met death at his own hand. He was watching from the top of one of Chinju's towers, and descended to the courtyard when he saw that the battle was lost. Accounts differ as to how he died. One chronicler tells us that he 'bowed to the north, threw his weapons into the river, and killed himself beside the well at the foot of the tower'.[40] Another states that he simply jumped into the river.[41]

The latter alternative to being taken alive by the Japanese was favoured by many of the garrison, as noted by the chronicler of Katō Kiyomasa's exploits, which states that 'All the Chinamen were terrified of our Japanese blades, and jumped into the river, but we pulled them out and cut off their heads'.[42] Kikkawa's men on the far bank of the Nam took a particularly active part in pulling escapees out of the river and beheading them. Some Japanese accounts note the taking of 20,000 heads at Chinju. Korean records claim 60,000 deaths, and both figures imply a massacre of soldiers and non-combatants alike.[43] The *Taikōki* claims that 15,300 heads were taken, and that the total number of deaths was 25,000, of whom the balance 'fell from the cliffs and were drowned',[44] but all the Japanese accounts are very reticent about identifying who these other victims were.

That night, while the Nam river downstream from the castle walls flowed red, and headless corpses still choked its banks, the victorious Japanese generals celebrated in the Ch'oksŏngnu pavilion, from which the best view of this hellish scene could be appreciated. The kisaeng (courtesan) girls of Chinju were pressed into the service of the conquerors, and entertained them in the pavilion above the now ghastly river. That night one kisaeng struck a blow for Korea. A courtesan called Nongae became a target for the amorous affections of Keyamura Rokunosuke, a senior officer in the service of Katō Kiyomasa. Luring him close to the cliff edge, Nongae locked her arms into his passionate embrace of her, and flung herself suddenly backwards into the river, clinging on to her victim until both she and he were drowned. Nongae now has a memorial shrine next to the pavilion on Chinju's cliff, a female heroine of the massacre of Chinju, Korea's worst military disaster of the entire Japanese campaign.[45]

Chinju also proved to be the last battle of the first invasion. Throughout the time of the Chinju campaign Admiral Yi Sun-sin had continued to monitor Japanese movements along the south coast. The evacuation that he was daily expecting to see was indeed carried out after this final victory, but there were certain disturbing features to it. Far from simply loading their men on to the ships and

The eaves of the Buddhist temple built inside the Chinju castle complex as a memorial to the Korean warrior monks who helped defend it during the siege of 1593. The outside of the temple is ornately decorated in typical Korean fashion.

carrying them home to Japan, the Japanese appeared to be strengthening their coastal positions, rather than progressively demolishing them. An escaped prisoner of war even told him that, 'The enemy is increasing in number and he is building bunkers and spreading tents twice as much as before; at present there are no signs of his intended crossing of the sea.'[46]

On 8m 14d a reconnaissance party strengthened Yi's suspicions that although many troops were leaving, the Japanese were building a series of forts along the coast east and west from Pusan. These were the places that became known as the wajō (the castles of the people of Wa, as in 'wakō'), which for the next few years were to remind the Korean people that the war against them was still continuing. The work proceeded at a furious pace, and another escaped Korean prisoner described the scene near to his home on Kŏje island:

> They felled trees on (Mount) Pukpong and levelled the ground to build a wide circular mud wall, inside which houses were being built. About one third of the Japanese, with some Koreans, were engaged in carpenter work. The Japanese boats continually carry war provisions and winter clothing from their home country by voyages of two or three days.[47]

This account is very revealing. First, it shows that the wajō were being built in the labour-intensive Japanese style of converting excavated hills into overlapping baileys, complex work that was intended to last. Second, the reference to winter clothing confirmed Admiral Yi's worst fears about the Japanese intentions. 'He is going to pass another winter in our country, to our great mortification,' he writes in a report.[48] But Yi was wrong on one point. It was not just one more winter that the Japanese were going to spend in occupied Korea, but five.

车

chapter eight

THE STRANGE OCCUPATION

ROM 1593 to 1597 Korea was to find itself in a strange and unenviable position. The departure of Japanese troops, which began with the evacuation of Seoul on 4m 18d (18 May) 1593 was carried out with such destruction in its wake that it caused more unease than relief to the war-weary Koreans. There was therefore no element of ignominious withdrawal about this operation carried out by an apparently retreating enemy. It was instead more an act of defiance and an expression of confidence by a force that needed to re-group and re-arm, but which felt able to return at any moment. Also, as Yi Sun-sin had observed so accurately, the Japanese evacuation was only partial, because a large stretch of the south coast of Kyŏngsang was to remain under Japanese occupation for the whole of the four-year period until the armies returned. The other important factor to note concerning this time is that long peace negotiations began even before Seoul was evacuated, and were then continued for several years at a level of farce that even exceeded the fiasco of the talks that had preceded the first invasion. When these discussions broke down the second invasion became almost inevitable, and by then the Japanese had reorganised their army and were set to return in force with a fresh invasion plan.

THE PHENOMENON OF THE WAJŌ

The limited Japanese occupation of Korea between 1593 and 1597 was centred around the string of coastal fortresses that were known as the wajō or waesŏng, and the ruins of these unique historical fossils may still be seen in Korea today. From a distance they have the appearance of irregularly shaped hills from which sections have been scooped out and removed. In some cases rice fields planted on land reclaimed from the sea now touch the remains of huge sloping stone walls where waves once lapped. In other places farm entrances make good use of the gaps between massive gateways, while elsewhere the flat tops of the hills, once levelled at an enormous cost in labour and suffering, now

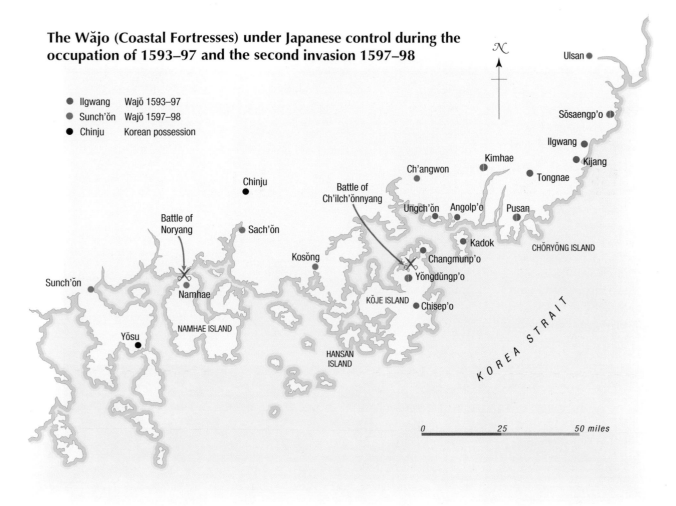

The Wăjo (Coastal Fortresses) under Japanese control during the occupation of 1593–97 and the second invasion 1597–98

- ● Ilgwang Wajŏ 1593–97
- ● Sunch'ŏn Wajŏ 1597–98
- ● Chinju Korean possession

entertain local people for cherry blossom festivals where towers once dominated the lives of their ancestors.

The ruins of the wajō are the most prominent physical reminders of the Japanese invasions to exist in Korea today. They covered the initial Japanese withdrawal from Korea in 1593, and were then garrisoned as the sole remaining Japanese presence on the peninsula for the next four years. Some were extensions of existing Korean fortresses, while others were newly created, but all were characterised by the imposition of Japanese styles of fortification on to the Korean landscape. The Korean sansŏng style had been shown to be too vulnerable, and the occupation forces were taking no chances. The Japanese historical records have preserved the names of the wajō commanders, and as most of them had once ruled vast tracts of occupied Korean territory the reduction of their fiefs to these tiny coastal enclaves shows how complete was the Japanese withdrawal. From east to west the wajō and their garrisons were as listed in Table 4.[1]

Map showing the location of the coastal wajō fortresses during the occupation of Korea between 1593 and 1597, and the new line of wajō established after the second invasion in 1597.

Table 4: Garrison commanders of the wajō in 1593

Sŏsaengp'o	Katō Kiyomasa
Ilgwang	Mōri Yoshinari, Shimazu Tadatoyo, Itō Yubei, Takahashi Mototane, Akizuki Tanenaga
Kijang	Kuroda Nagamasa
Tongnae	Kikkawa Hiroie
Pusan	Mōri Terumoto
Kimhae (Chukdo)	Nabeshima Naoshige
Kadŏk	Kobayakawa Takakage, Tachibana Muneshige etc.
Angolp'o	Wakizaka Yasuharu, Kuki Yoshitaka, Katō Yoshiaki etc.
Ungch'ŏn (three wajō)	Konishi Yukinaga, Sō Yoshitomo, Matsuura Shigenobu
Kŏje - Yŏngdŭngp'o	Shimazu Yoshihiro
Kŏje - Changmunp'o	Fukushima Masanori, Toda Katsukata, Chōsokabe Motochika
Kŏje - Chisep'o	Hachisuka Iemasa, Ikoma Chikamasa

The important wajō of Sŏsaengp'o, which formed the eastern end of the Japanese line during the occupation. The traditional sloping Japanese stone walls backed onto an excavated hillside is shown to good effect. As the wajō would have had little in the way of superstructure above them their appearance has remained virtually intact for four centuries.

Table 5: Garrison strengths of the wajō in 1593

	Large (e.g. Kadŏk)	Small (e.g. Yŏngdŭngp'o)
Garrison size	5,000	2,000
Firearms, (including)	200	100
Large calibre	1	1
50 monme	10	10
30 monme	10	10
20 monme	10	10
13 monme	4	3
6 monme	10	10
2.5 monme	150	72
Saltpetre	450 kin	400 kin
Gunpowder	800 kin	400 kin
Bullets	4,500	4,000
Lead	450 kin	400 kin
Sulphur	45 kin	40 kin
Bows	300	100
Arrows	6,000	2,000
Swords	450	400
Suits of Armour	17	15
Helmets	10	7
Spears	200	100

These commands remained roughly the same for the occupation period, except that certain generals, including Kobayakawa Takakage and Mōri Terumoto, eventually retired to Japan on health grounds. In August 1593 a review was carried out of the size of garrisons to be stationed at each fort, and it was decided to place 5,000 men in the larger castles and between 2–3,000 men in the smaller ones, making a grand total for the occupying forces of about 43,000 men.[2] Records also exist of the breakdown of weaponry in the two grades of wajō, as shown in Table 5.[3] The separate mentions of saltpetre and sulphur probably indicate that these chemicals were kept for revitalising old gunpowder stocks.

An escaped Korean POW said of the wajō: 'Half of their numbers defend their fortified walls and half returned home. Those who defend the walls will also go home in the third moon of next year on arrival of their reliefs',[4] and in a later Memorial to Court dated 11m 17d (8 January) 1594, Admiral Yi reported:

The retreating Japanese robbers still occupy the southern coastal area without the least sign of evacuation. Judging from their movements no one can tell their unfathomable strategic plans. The increasing Japanese robbers on Kǒje island dig more dens, with their vessels moored deep in the ports as their boats busily ply up and down the sea entrances, threatening to come out with surprise attacks at any moment.[5]

A month later Yi received a report which recorded active building work taking place on Kǒje island, by 'hundreds of Japanese taking positions in barracks outside Chisep'o and Okp'o, pitching tents in fours and fives in never ending lines at strategic points in the fields'. The Japanese were also seen 'moving about in scattered companies in the daytime and signalling to each other with torches at night'.[6] A separate report from Wǒn Kyun supported the observations that the barrack construction was in full swing, and that 'the enemy's torches illuminate the long sea coast from Pusan and Tongnae to Ch'angwǒn and Chinhae amid the booming of guns'.[7]

Later in the January report cited above Yi was able to compare Korean observations with an account given to him by a captured Japanese soldier called Magoshichi. Yi naturally suspected the man of being a spy, or even a double agent who would give them false information, but his description of the location of the wajō and the names of the commanders tallied with what was already known. The prisoner also gave a very colourful account of how he had ended up in Korea in the first place. At the end of 1592, he claimed, 3,000 men had deserted from the ranks of Chōsokabe Motochika, and he was one of 600 replacements hurriedly recruited. Magoshichi claimed to have been taken on as a gunner, but then continued:

> I can shoot arrows, and at the time of my recruitment in Japan they promised to give me liberty from the life of slavery with rewards of gold, silver and many other treasures if I showed military prowess at battles in Korea, but when I came to Korea they gave me very little food and forced me to do many drudgeries, the burden of which was too heavy to bear. One day I talked with Yasaburō, one of my friends: 'We had better surrender to Korea than work in starvation.'[8]

The two men therefore decided to desert, but Magoshichi's account goes on to say how his friend was caught by a Japanese soldier as they made their escape. Magoshichi got away, but before he was able to defect he was captured by a group of Korean women picking oysters. They handed him over to the Korean army who brought him to Yi as a prisoner. Magoshichi added some interesting information about life in the wajō when he reported that on 11m 4d (26 December) 1593 about a hundred ships had sailed for

Japan loaded with sick and injured men.[9]

The discrepancies in Magoshichi's account concerning his role in the Japanese army excited Yi's suspicions, so Magoshichi was kept in chains, but we do know that some Japanese did go over to the Korean side, and Yi's diary for 10m 13d (14 November) of 1595 is surprisingly matter-of-fact over the activities of a group of surrendered Japanese whom he employed to plaster the ceiling of his headquarters![10]   Three months later we read:

> Early in the morning five surrendered Japanese entered camp. On being questioned about the reasons for their escape, they explained that their commanding officer was a cruel fellow, driving them hard, so they ran away and surrendered. The large and small swords in their possession were collected and put away in the attic of the pavilion. They further confessed that they were not Japanese from Pusan but Japanese under the command of Shimazu on Kadŏk island.[11]

These entries may appear surprising given the popular view of the death-defying Japanese samurai, but such defectors were probably simple peasants from samurai estates, press-ganged into the role of labourers in a daimyō's army, and treated as brutally as the defeated Koreans. They sometimes made their grievances felt, and on 1m 18d (16 February) 1596 Yi reports hearing of a 'conspiracy to mutiny in the Japanese camp'.[12] Concerning the lives of those who defected or were captured, there is an extraordinary entry in Yi's diary for 7m 13d of the same year which reads:

> After dark the surrendered Japanese played a drama with the make-up of actors and actresses. As Commanding Admiral I could not attend, but since the submissive captives wished to entertain themselves with their native farce for enjoyment of the day, I did not forbid it.[13]

The Japanese chronicles give their own versions of life in the wajō, where the troops performed the tea ceremony, played go, and generally tried to behave as if they were back in Japan. As the *Wakizaka ki* notes, 'It was very peaceful inside our camps, so on occasions some people amused themselves by putting on sarugaku performances.

Katō Kiyomasa fights a tiger in Korea. This print is one of many to deal with this popular topic, but Kiyomasa's name has been changed in the cartouche to circumvent a contemporary ruling that woodblock prints were not to depict actual historical characters.

In more serious vein, Katō Kiyomasa shoots the tiger that has killed a man inside his camp. (ETK)

Others danced, or passed the time with tea ceremonies and the pleasures of drinking bouts.'[14]

Of all the activities in which the occupying forces indulged themselves, none was more dramatic than tiger hunting. Tigers first became a threat to the Japanese forces in 1592 when Katō Kiyomasa led his division into Hamgyŏng, and a scene of Katō Kiyomasa hunting a tiger with his famous cross-bladed spear became a popular topic for print makers, but in the account in *Jōzan Kidan* Kiyomasa's quarry was a man-eater that had already taken a horse from inside the camp and then returned and killed a man. Spears may have sufficed for sport, but guns were the choice for this very serious expedition:

A single big tiger forced its way through a thick growth of miscanthus reeds and spotted Kiyomasa. Kiyomasa was standing on top of a large rock and took aim with the gun he had ready. When he did this the tiger came to a stop at a place with about 30 ken between it and Kiyomasa, and glared at him.[15]

Kiyomasa's followers lowered their arquebuses and took aim, but Kiyomasa ordered them to hold their fire so that he could kill the tiger himself. 'The tiger opened its mouth and leaped upon him fiercely. At that moment Kiyomasa's gun roared. The tiger was hit in the throat and fell to the ground.'[16]

Hunting the tiger. Apart from the relaxation tiger hunting gave to the occupying troops, Hideyoshi believed that tiger meat would restore his flagging vitality. (ETK)

That tiger hunting was also carried out for reasons other than sport or self-preservation is confirmed by documentary evidence of Hideyoshi's belief that tiger meat had the capacity to restore his failing health. In a letter to Kikkawa Hiroie of 12m 25d (4 February) 1595, the recipient is ordered to send Hideyoshi the 'head, meat and entrails of a tiger, well salted, leaving out nothing but the skin'.[17] Tiger skins had other uses, as shown by the numerous paintings of daimyō seated grandly on tiger pelts draped over their camp stools. On one memorable occasion Hideyoshi's generals excelled themselves by taking back to Japan not merely tiger meat, but a complete tiger, which had to be held on the end of a chain by eight strong men:

Looting by Japanese troops, an activity which led to much resentment throughout the war and during the occupation. (ETK detail)

> At that particular time all the generals from the Korean vanguard had returned to Nagoya, and when they were gathered together it pulled with the strength of many men, and all of a sudden ran off, heading into the midst of the assembled generals. Everyone was frightened and excited, but among them Katō Kiyomasa shifted his kneeling posture, clenched his fists, bent his elbows, and fixed his glare sternly on it, and for a little while the tiger also glared at Kiyomasa, who held his ground as it came over.[18]

Aside from these diversions, some Japanese raided Korean settlements, and one of Yi's reports from 1594 reads, ' . . . they kill, rape and steal in a more cruel manner than before', but illness still took its toll, and the same report continues, 'The Japanese in Ungch'ŏn took new positions, stationing 1,000 men or 800–900 men in each place. Many of them have died of illness or fled home while undergoing hardships in building houses and city walls.' [19]

THE ROLE OF THE KOREAN NAVY

Throughout the time of occupation the Korean navy, assisted by guerrilla bands, largely succeeded in achieving the Korean government's overall aim of keeping the Japanese confined to barracks, and Yi's diaries and reports contain much detail about these operations. It would appear that Hideyoshi was quite content to accept the status quo, with no advance being made by Japanese troops while peace negotiations continued. As a result, the areas immediately adjacent to the wajō remained the only pieces of Korean territory that could be regarded as 'occupied'. It would, however, be a mistake to regard all wajō as isolated fortresses hemmed in by hostile troops. In some cases many

Korean people who had initially fled before the Japanese advance returned to the wajō and settled there, giving the areas directly adjacent the appearance of a castle town. At its height the wajō of Kimhae (Chukdo) was surrounded by over six hundred houses, and at Ungch'ŏn trade flourished.

Throughout this time of uneasy and spurious peace Admiral Yi took every opportunity to monitor, harass and even attack the Japanese fleet. There were sporadic clashes, particularly when the Japanese attempted to run supplies to the wajō or to raid local villages, but not all these incidents were everything that they seemed to be. Yi's diary entry concerning one such raid in 1593 says that 'the supposed Japanese were found to be a large group of Korean refugees fleeing from Kyŏngsang province, who, having disguised themselves like the Japanese war dogs, plundered private homes as they ran amok in all parts of the town'.[20] Towards the end of the occupation the heightened tension caused by the threat of a new invasion gave further opportunities for bands of Korean renegades to take advantage of their fellow countrymen. In October 1597, by which time the second invasion had already taken place, Yi's diary noted:

> During breakfast some Tangp'o abalone divers stole the cattle in the field with the false alarm, 'The Japanese thieves have come! The Japanese thieves have come!' Since I knew it was a ruse I had two fellows among the shouting false alarmists arrested and ordered their heads to be cut off and hung up high for a public warning. The sailors and people calmed down.[21]

Most incidents, however, were unquestionably Japanese raids. In March 1594 we read of 'torch-bearing robbers' haunting Haeundae, the beach area near Pusan, and five enemy sailors being apprehended and one killed at Nokto,[22] and Wŏn Kyun also reported to Yi that his men had killed more than three hundred Japanese.[23]

The largest armed clash between the Korean fleet and the occupying forces happened in the spring of 1594 with a naval battle at Tanghangp'o, the site of Yi's great victory of 1592. The garrisons of Kŏje and Ungch'ŏn had been out raiding inland, and on 3m 3d (23 April) Yi was informed of six enemy vessels from Yŏngdŭngp'o on Kŏje lying at anchor near Tanghangp'o. He immediately sent a large flotilla to investigate, while despatching an additional request for ground troops to be made ready on the coast. Early the following morning the six Japanese ships were captured and destroyed. Meanwhile Yi led his main body to make a demonstration against the wajō of Yŏngdŭngp'o and Changmunp'o, where they surprised some Japanese ships heading home. The crews abandoned the ships for the safety of

The bell tower of the Chondungsa temple on Kanghwa island. The bell that hangs inside it dates from 1097 and, having survived the Japanese invasion of 1592, was taken to be melted down as scrap by another occupying Japanese army in 1945. Fortunately the war ended before this could be done, and the bell was restored.

land, so Yi's men destroyed their fleet. Some Korean captives were freed, but 'the Japanese cut off the heads of two other Korean prisoners of war and threw them down before they fled'.[24]   Two days later other attacks were made on Japanese ships, but Yi concludes his Memorial to Court with the words:

> Had we attacked the defeated enemy from sea and land in a united action we could have annihilated him, but the positions of the navy and the army were so far apart no swift liaison was possible, so we failed to catch the whole bag of the birds in a cage.[25]

But there was greater frustration for Yi than that caused by simple problems of coordination. The two nations were theoretically at peace, and talks were continuing, a situation that was particularly delicate for Korea's Ming allies. 'I opened the envelope,' writes Yi concerning one such incident on April 1594, 'and found a message from Dan Zongren, Commanding General of the Chinese Armed Forces, instructing me to refrain from attacking the enemy because he had just had a truce talk with the Japanese at Ungch'ŏn. Being annoyed at his news I did not know how to control myself.'[26]   In another diary entry of October 1594, Admiral Yi longs for the opportunity to attack the enemy:

> Though I swore with other captains of war to avenge our slaughtered countrymen upon the enemy by risking our own lives, and we pass many days on land and at sea in this resolution, the enemy has taken his positions in deep trenches and high fortresses on steep hills inaccessible to us.[27]

A month later, however, Yi disregarded any possible Chinese qualms and made another demonstration off Changmunp'o, but there was no reaction from on land so the Koreans simply burned two Japanese ships.[28] A few days later he attacked Changmunp'o again, having made a useful alliance with some very effective Korean ground troops:

> After making appointments with Kwak Chae-u and Kim Tŏk-nyŏng, I ordered out several hundred sharpshooters to land at Changmunp'o to challenge the enemy. Late in the day I led our central force to the scene of battle for a joint action on sea and land. Much frightened, the disheartened enemy hordes scattered and ran . . .[29]

But two days later he sadly records that the Japanese had planted a sign outside Changmunp'o which read 'Japan is now talking peace with Ming China so we need not fight'. As a result there are no further accounts of conflict as the winter of 1594/5 draws on, but the welfare of the brave Korean navy is clearly in the thoughts of their government, because 'The Field Marshall forwarded some winter-proof ear-muffs made of rat skin to each Naval Station', a gesture that was clearly appreciated.[30] Still Yi continued to monitor troop movements and analyse intelligence reports. In April 1595 he notes receiving information that 'Hideyoshi has resolved to send more reinforcements across the sea in order to build permanent forts and barracks at Pusan',[31] but this is followed by reports concerning the evacuation of the forts on Kŏje in August. This indicated to Yi that the occupation forces were being concentrated into fewer areas, but there were still occasional armed clashes, and during the first month of 1596 a Japanese ship trying to land was driven away by Yi's blockading force.

KOREA'S CHRISTIAN VISITOR

For a final comment on life in the wajō of occupied Korea we turn to the testimony of a remarkable eyewitness, Father Gregorio de Cespedes SJ, who went to Korea in the winter of 1594/95 in the capacity of visiting chaplain to the Christians among the Japanese troops. This Spanish Jesuit was born in Madrid in 1551 and was admitted to the priesthood in Goa in 1575. He arrived in Japan in 1577, and we first hear of him in Ōmura in Hizen province, the territory of the Ōmura daimyō who went to Korea with the First Division, where he appears to have played an active part in missionary work in Japan, and is credited with the baptism of the famous Gracia, wife of Hosokawa Tadaoki, in 1587.

At the end of 1594 Father Gregorio went to Korea via Tsushima, where he was received with great joy by Maria, the Christian wife of Sō Yoshitomo, who was also the daughter of Konishi Yukinaga. It was to Konishi's wajō in Korea that Father Gregorio then headed, where, according to a Spanish account, 'The Father and his companion had much to do, as all these Christians had neither heard mass nor sermon nor confessed themselves since they had left Japan for Korea'.[32] Konishi's wajō is referred to as Camp Komangai, an attribution which is probably due to a Japanese reading of the Chinese characters for Ungch'ŏn as 'Kumagawa' being subsequently misheard by European ears. Father Gregorio describes it as follows in the first of two letters sent from Korea:

> The fortress of Komangai is impregnable, and great defensive works have been erected there which are admirable, considering the short time in which they were completed. They have built high walls, watch towers and strong bastions, at the foot of which all the nobles and soldiers of Augustin, his subjects and allies are encamped. For all there are well built and spacious. Houses with stone walls are built for the chiefs.[33]

In his second letter he adds that Ungch'ŏn is built 'on a very high and craggy slope. When I have to go down for some confessions at night, it gives me much work, and when I go back I ride a horse and rest many times on the way.'[34] The solidity of the wajō was echoed by their interior décor, and when Father Gregorio visited Sō Yoshitomo, 'I was astonished to see the beautiful things he has; they surely did not seem to be of temporary use but looked as if they were intended to stay there all one's life.'[35] The Korean winter was, however, an enormous trial to him:

> The cold in Korea is very severe and without comparison with that of Japan. All day long my limbs are half benumbed, and in the morning I can hardly move my hands to say mass, but I keep myself in good health; thanks to God and the fruit that our lord is giving.[36]

By the time Father Gregorio arrived in Korea the original Japanese defensive line had been shortened, and he reports that near to Ungch'ŏn was the fortress of Kuroda Nagamasa, whose piety comes in for special praise. His men listened to two sermons a day, and in the case of Nagamasa himself:

> in order to meditate on them at his leisure, he withdrew each day at certain hours, which were set aside for this purpose, to read his books of devotion . . . Being such a great lord and such a leading soldier and commander, and busy in affairs of war, never did he abstain from fasting all the days ordered by the Church, without counting others which he added on account of his devoutness, all of which he accompanied with the secret disciplines which he practised.[37]

The unbeliever Katō Kiyomasa was also not far away:

> Toranosuke, the arch enemy of Augustin, is staying north of here, about fifteen leagues away. He has made some attacks upon the Koreans, one of them in a certain place where, according to reports, there were more than one thousand monasteries of bonzes (Buddhist priests), and where, he had heard, there was great wealth and an abundance of food. However, when he arrived he destroyed everything, burning and demolishing all . . .[38]

As Father Gregorio was the first European visitor to Korea it is a pity that the only Koreans he ever came into contact with were those unfortunates captured by the Japanese and destined to be sent to Japan into slavery, but the account of Father Gregorio's mission notes an act of charity on the part of at least one member of the occupying forces:

> There was a knight, a native of Bungo, who, being in the war in Korea, and taking pity on the many creatures who were dying destitute of their parents, took it upon himself to baptise them because, since he could no longer make their bodies whole, they should not lose their souls. Thus all those whom he saw in probable danger of death he immediately baptised.

The full-dress costume of a high-ranking military official of the Chosŏn dynasty as depicted at the Korean Folk Village near Suwŏn.

For this purpose he had a servant of his always carry a bottle of water hanging from his belt and by these means he sent to heaven more than 200 souls.[39]

Father Gregorio concludes his brief correspondence with some personal yet perceptive observations of the Korean scene:

> All these Christians are very poor, and suffer from hunger, cold, illness and other inconveniences very different from conditions in other places. Although Hideyoshi sends food, so little reaches here that it is impossible to sustain all with them, and moreover the help that comes from Japan is insufficient and comes late. It is now two months since ships have come, and many crafts were lost.[40]

KOREAN MILITARY REORGANISATION

While Admiral Yi Sun-sin fought on against the occupying forces as best he could, the notional period of truce gave the Korean government an opportunity to examine the reasons why they had been defeated by Japan. Yu Sŏng-nyong, the Prime Minister, took an active role in the process, and came to an early recognition that the superior tactical organisation of Japanese military units had played a large part in their initial success. He noted how the Japanese vanguard which engaged an enemy was always backed up by two wings and a main body, and how, as at Pyŏkje, the advancing army spread into two enveloping arms while the centre company weakened their opponents by arquebus fire ready to deliver the killing blows with sword and spear. By contrast, the Korean army had tended to move forward as one body. Yu also cited the weakness of the Korean leadership, so that 'when all of a sudden they do meet with a powerful enemy, the officers do not know their troops, nor the troops their officers, and they are broken up like clods of earth and smashed like tiles'.[41]

The deficiencies of the Korean army had also been noted early on by their Ming allies, and the Chinese general Luo Shangzhi had recommended to Yu that a new unit should be set up to train the Korean soldiers in the 'three skills' of musketry, swordsmanship and archery. The result was the half-hearted and inadequately financed establishment of the Military Training Agency in September 1593, which initially had only 72 men allocated to it, a number which later grew to 10,000. Their military manual was the *Jixiao Xinshu* of Qi Jiguang, the Chinese general whose work Yu Sŏng-nyong greatly admired.

Qi's recommended scheme (called the sog'o system in Korean) divided larger units into smaller ones according to a strict military hierarchy and chain of command. In the resulting Korean model the theoretical size of the various units began from the basic grouping of the tae (squad), which consisted of eleven men under a Taech'ong (squad leader). Three of these squads formed a ki (platoon or banner) of 33 men under a Kich'ong, while three banners made a ch'o (company) of 99 under a Ch'ogwan (company commander). Five companies together made up the standard large unit, which was the sa (battalion) of 495 soldiers under the battalion commander or P'ach'ong. These planned numbers were not always realised, and in his writings Yu notes the creation of some battalions that had a complement of only 360 men.

In some cases a battalion would represent the contribution to the army that was provided by a single administrative district within a province. Otherwise it might be that two or three districts combined to make up a battalion, which then joined with other battalions to make a total provincial command of 25 battalions with a theoretical manpower of 12,375 soldiers. Thus the army of Kyŏnggi province consisted of five yŏng (regiments), one for Seoul and four from other subdivisions, each yŏng being made up from five battalions.

As to the breakdown of weaponry within the army, the three 11-man tae that made up an individual ki were supposed to consist respectively of one squad of 11 salsu ('killers', i.e close combat edged weapons), one squad of 11 sasu (archers) and one squad of 11 p'osu (gunners). We have already noted Yu Sŏng-nyong's firm commitment to the adoption by Korea of the European-style arquebus, which had outranged Korean bows on many occasions. 'When soldiers are lined up against the enemy ranks,' wrote Yu, 'our arrows do not reach the enemy while their musket balls rain down on us.'[42] Yet once again the numbers set out by the planners were not always achieved, and the organisation of the army for P'yŏngan province in 1596 reveals that within a battalion that was already under strength, (having only 36 squads rather than the prescribed 45), instead of the theoretical dozen squads for each weapon, only eight were squads of gunners, five were edged weapons, and 23 contained archers. According to Yu, it was the innate conservatism of the Koreans, so

This Korean foot soldier is a life-sized fibreglass figure on guard duty outside a restaurant (!), but neverthe-less gives a good indication of the simple costume and lack of defensive armour given to the common soldiers who fought the Japanese.

mistrustful of change, that was the problem, so that 'the silk clad gentry' considered the idea of arquebus squads as 'something laughable'.[43]

The social composition of these regiments under the sog'o system represented a marked change from previous practice. No longer would slaves and the sons of yangban be exempt from military service. Instead both social groups would be subject to conscription. At the same time Yu argued for a return to the locally based chin'gwan system of military responsibility, which, he believed, would provide a series of lines of defence across the country should the invasion be repeated. Hence the troops mobilised in southern Kyŏngsang would be automatically backed up by further levies based around Taegu, and behind them Sangju, Ch'ŏngju and the garrisons around the capital. 'The strength of the country would be like a double door or a double wall,' wrote Yu, 'and even though the enemy might be able to penetrate one of the layers, there would always be another.'[44] That was the ideal, but one wonders how useful a system based on provincial forces of only about 12,000 effectives would have been in 1592 against an army that had been able to land 150,000 men at Pusan within the space of one month.

The final matter to which Yu Sŏng-nyong directed his imaginative mind was the vexed question of wall construction and maintenance. Reference was made earlier to the inadequacies of Korean fortifications, both in design, construction and repair. Musing on the subject by the banks of the Ch'ŏngch'ŏn river near Anju, Yu came up with a proposal for walls that contained gun portals and towers separated by six or seven hundred paces, with a pile of cannon balls stacked ready beside the big guns 'like chicken's eggs':

> Then when the enemy approaches the walls, he will be hit by a cross fire from the guns. Not to speak of men and horses, even metal and stone could not escape being pulverised by this . . . All you would have to do is to have several dozen men man the gun turrets, and the enemy would not dare draw near.[45]

It is clear that with this reference to artillery cross fire Yu Sŏng-nyong has worked out a Korean version of the 'trace italienne', the system of angled bastions with no blind spots that was becoming the norm in contemporary Europe. Had his ideas been adopted, and both time and the devastated Korean economy were clearly against him, then the returning Japanese in 1597 might have had to face strongly fortified towns that echoed the defences of the contemporary Netherlands. Namwŏn certainly had towers that allowed some flanking fire when the Japanese attacked it in 1597, but this was probably due to the rapid rebuilding carried out by the Chinese army rather than as a result of Yu's recommendations. Instead a lack of will, and an even more acute lack of resources, meant that Korea would face its next invasion largely under the

The main gate of the Ch'angdŏkkung Palace, which is believed to have survived the capture of the city by the Japanese, thus making it the oldest original palace gate in the city. It was built in 1405.

traditional policy of 'strengthen the walls and clear the countryside', which required the peasantry to take refuge not in modern fortified towns with strong artillery walls but in distant sansŏng.

To a very large extent, therefore, the reforms of Yu Sŏng-nyong remained a paper exercise, held back by a lack of finance and manpower, and political torpor. As a result Korea received the second Japanese invasion in little better shape overall than that which existed when they had suffered the first. Writing a century later, Yu Hyŏng-wŏn, the great reformer of the seventeenth century, was able to look back in despair on two Japanese invasions and the wars against the Manchus, and note sadly that in Korea, really, nothing ever changed:

> ... once they hear that the enemy is coming, without waiting for the enemy to spread around, the whole country becomes an empty wasteland and the government has no one to whom it can issue orders. The fighting troops have nothing to fear or avoid: they just make it their business to take flight and scatter. Enemy bandit cavalry in groups of three or four men roam over all the eight provinces and plunder the country at will ... [46]

HIDEYOSHI'S P'ANMUNJŎM

While Yi fought and Yu reformed, the two nations who had entered their country and fought on its soil talked to each other in a world of their own from which Korea was excluded. The Sino-Japanese peace negotiations, which frustrated Admiral Yi and formed a backdrop to the uneasy atmosphere of the years of truce, had actually begun very early in the campaign. As far back as August 1592, following the disastrous defeat of the small Chinese expeditionary force sent against P'yŏngyang, the Ming rulers approached Konishi Yukinaga and negotiated a fifty-day truce. The Chinese motives were quite simple. A Mongol rebellion in Ningxia was preventing them from devoting the necessary men and resources to the Korean theatre. As a rest from hostilities was by no means unwelcome to the Japanese also, an agreement was reached.

The Ming negotiator, one Shen Weijing (written as Chin Ikei in the Japanese accounts) returned to P'yŏngyang when the truce period was up, and made strong demands of the Japanese, secure in the knowledge that a huge Chinese army was now ready to cross the Yalu. These negotiations came to nothing, and it was not until Konishi had been driven from P'yŏngyang and the Chinese had been defeated at Pyŏkje, that Shen again put in an appearance. The result of this fresh diplomatic effort was the withdrawal of the Japanese from Seoul to the coast as discussed in the previous chapter. Other matters on the respective agendas, such as the investiture of Hideyoshi as King of Japan and the opening up of the port of Ningbo to Japanese trade, were discussed but vaguely recorded, leading to a series of assumptions and counter assumptions that were eventually to reduce the whole procedure to an empty pantomime. The result was that neither side appreciated nor cared what the other's demands actually were, a failure that was to prove disastrous.

The Ming envoy Shen Weijing arrives at Ukita Hideie's headquarters in Seoul to negotiate the Japanese withdrawal. Virtually all the important diplomatic exchanges of the war were conducted between Japan and China without Korean involvement. (ETK detail)

Conspicuously absent from any of the above meetings were representatives of Korea, whose government was neither informed of the process nor invited to participate in it. In fact, the decision reached in the final round of the talks, which included the withdrawal of Chinese forces from Korea, was directly counter to Korean wishes. The Koreans felt that the Japanese were on the run, and were determined to finish off the wounded enemy. However, Ming wishes prevailed, and Korea was to find itself shut out from the conference table for the whole of the truce period. Instead Shen Weijing, together with two government agents masquerading as official Chinese diplomats, travelled back to Nagoya with the Japanese army, arriving on 5m 15d (14 June) 1593. Here they were received in grand style and met Hideyoshi, who entertained them in his golden tea room.

The result of the previous obfuscation during the negotiations so far had meant that the Chinese believed that Japan was willing to make itself a vassal of China, while Hideyoshi was under the firm illusion that the Chinese envoys had come to Nagoya to surrender. Somehow the talks continued, and when Shen and his colleagues were about to depart at the end of the month they were presented with a document setting out Hideyoshi's seven conditions for lasting peace between the two countries:

1. A daughter of the Ming Emperor would be married to the Emperor of Japan.
2. The system of licensed trade would be revived.
3. Chinese and Japanese ministers would exchange pledges of amity.
4. Japan would give back the four northern Korean provinces to Korea, and keep the four southern provinces for itself.
5. Following this, one Korean prince and two Korean ministers would go to Japan as hostages for good behaviour.
6. The two captured Korean princes would be released.
7. The ministers of the Korean King would give a solemn and binding pledge of acceptance to the above conditions.[47]

From Hideyoshi's point of view, which was that he was receiving a surrendered enemy, his conditions were most generous, and it was even suggested during the talks that he was willing to drop the claim to Korean territory if the marriage with the Ming princess was guaranteed. Apart from this, the only other item of any consequence was the opening up of the port of Ningbo, which was little more than restoring the ancient status quo.

To the Ming envoys, however, all seven demands were highly presumptive, and not the sort of behaviour that the Celestial Kingdom expected from one of its vassal states. Yet they should not have lingered for long under any delusions over Hideyoshi's underlying motivation, because he included with the seven points a memorandum, addressed to Konishi Yukinaga but meant for the Ming envoys.[48] It began with the now familiar assertion that Japan was 'The Land of the Gods', and continued with a further reminder of Hideyoshi's belief in his mystical conception when the wheel of the sun had entered his mother's womb. And how had Hideyoshi exercised this divine mission? Why, by ridding Japan of the menace of the pirates, for which he had received no thanks from the Ming, who persisted in treating Japan as a third-rate vassal state. He had therefore despatched an army to show Japan's greatness, but as the Koreans had ungraciously refused to cooperate in this inspired programme their country had been destroyed. In other words, there had been a totally unnecessary war, and it was all the Koreans' fault.

Hideyoshi's negotiating team had therefore painted themselves into a very tight corner. The combined effects of stringent demands and erroneous beliefs from the two sides, each of whom was ignorant of the true wishes and understanding of the other, ensured that agreement was virtually impossible. Meanwhile the Japanese were building their wajō at a furious pace, which did little to encourage a Chinese belief in Japanese good faith. Matters were then suddenly brought home to Konishi Yukinaga when his envoy Naitō Tadatoshi, (a fellow Christian daimyō baptised as João), was unable to get any nearer to the Ming court than the Liaodong peninsula because his diplomatic credentials did not include a message of submission from Japan.

Instead of reporting back to Hideyoshi, Konishi Yukinaga resolved to settle the business himself from his fortress at Ungch'ŏn. Konishi realised that the opening up of trade through Ningbo was an interest vital to Hideyoshi, but that for this to succeed the Ming would expect Japan to follow the same procedure that had once been accepted quite happily by the great Ashikaga Yoshimitsu, who had submitted to a largely notional status as vassal of China. As Hideyoshi would never agree if such a move was presented to him openly, Konishi and Shen Weijing hoped that if they forged a letter of submission and presented it to the Ming, and if Hideyoshi could be invested by the Ming in some way that would not cause him to explode with rage, then the resulting trade concessions would be such a welcome prize that Hideyoshi might not even notice that he had been manipulated, or might even dismiss the matter if the truth did come to light.[49]

The plot was so risky that the decision to proceed can only have been made because the negotiators on both sides realised the serious predicament into which they had placed themselves. The false document they concocted repeated the assertions about quelling pirates and unruly Koreans, and ended with Hideyoshi 'prostrating himself' before the Great Ming, begging him to bestow upon humble Hideyoshi 'the title of an imperially invested vassal king'.[50] After another delay en route to Beijing, Naitō Tadatoshi finally presented the letter early in 1595, and it is interesting to note that the Ming court first suspected that the document might have been forged when they noticed that it contained no reference to Hideyoshi's solar conception, a piece of bravado that had clearly become his trademark. Naitō however assured them that all was well, and even went much further than his diplomatic mission had intended when he stressed that it was investiture as King of Japan, and not trade, that was Hideyoshi's prime aim. The Ming therefore decided to grant to Hideyoshi that which he so earnestly desired, and wheels were set in motion to produce a golden seal and suitably ornate robes for the grand ceremony of investiture that would follow.

The Japanese envoys had therefore achieved the strange result of having negotiated a peace settlement with China on the basis of a condition that

Hideyoshi had never asked for, and in fact opposed, yet without a single one of the conditions that he had actually insisted upon. That the ignorant Hideyoshi also doubted the supposed Chinese intentions is clear from a letter he wrote to Kikkawa Hiroie in Korea, urging him to strengthen his defences and stock up with food, because 'I do not believe that the words of apology of the Chinese are sincere'.[51]

Late in 1595 Naitō accompanied the Chinese ambassadors on their journey from the Ming court to Japan via Korea. On arriving in Seoul they abruptly ceased their progress, and stated that they would not proceed to Japan until all Japanese troops had been removed from Korea. Konishi Yukinaga accordingly made a great show of evacuating three of the wajō and conspicuously shipping home a large number of sick and wounded. This appears to have satisfied Li Zongcheng, the chief envoy, who moved on to Pusan, where he appears to have been informed about the true nature of the situation which awaited the investment party in Japan. Li was so alarmed at the revelation that he promptly disappeared, leaving the golden seal and the robes of state behind him. Soon afterwards nature itself gave its own verdict on the looming diplomatic disaster when a huge earthquake flattened the newly built audience hall at Fushimi castle in the late summer of 1596.

It was therefore 9m 2d (23 October) 1596 when the Ming ambassadors finally appeared before Toyotomi Hideyoshi in Ōsaka castle. The Japanese ruler was delighted with the robes and the seal, but the Chinese took offence when he did not bow before them. A quick-thinking Japanese explained that Hideyoshi had a boil on his knee, and the catastrophe was postponed. The following day Hideyoshi held a banquet for the Ming envoys. He wore his Chinese crown and robes, and sat surrounded by the generals who had served him in Korea, all of whom were now gaily decked in the trappings of Chinese princes. All was well until Hideyoshi ordered his diplomatic expert, Saishō Shōtai, to read aloud in translation the document of investiture from the Ming Emperor. As the Zen monk concluded his peroration Hideyoshi realised for the first time that not one of his seven demands was included, and that the whole ceremony he had just undergone was no more than an insulting attempt to try to make him, the conqueror of Korea, a vassal of China! There was no trade agreement, no provinces and certainly no princess. In a tremendous rage as furious as it was understandable Hideyoshi tore the robes off his back and flung the crown on to the palace floor. The peace negotiations were at an end. From that moment on it would not be to the false yet conciliatory tones of Konishi Yukinaga that Hideyoshi would listen, but to the bellicose assertions of his rival Katō Kiyomasa, who had urged all along that the Chinese and Koreans were not to be trusted. To Katō there was only one way out of the insulting situation into which Japan had been plunged by this incompetent Christian meddler. The war with Korea would have to start all over again.

chapter nine

THE KOREAN WAR

THE second Japanese invasion of Korea in 1597 marked the beginning of a new phase in a conflict that had now changed from being a convoluted and much delayed invasion of China to an operation with much simpler objectives. Korea, and only Korea, was now the target, the partition of the country and the seizure of its southern provinces being Hideyoshi's only war aim. The second invasion was therefore destined to become what the first invasion had never been – a Korean War. Poor Korea had insulted Hideyoshi by refusing to cooperate in the invasion of China, and was therefore labelled as a provocateur that had brought the response upon itself. As a result this unfortunate country, stripped of most of its resources by the first invasion, was the chosen victim for the second, and half its territory was to be the conqueror's prize.

Hideyoshi's treatment of the unfortunate Ming Embassy in 1596 had sent to Seoul all the signals that were necessary to clarify his renewed intentions for war, and the Korean government could only prepare for the worst. Reference was made in the previous chapter to the steps taken by Prime Minister Yu Sŏng-nyong towards reorganising the army and their defence systems during the time of truce. The results of these heroic endeavours were meagre, and the only other significant item of preparation by Korea was the carrying out of an act of supreme folly, because early in 1597 the factionalism that was rife within Korean society led to the greatest and most astonishing blunder of the entire campaign when it claimed as its victim the victorious and unimpeachable Admiral Yi Sun-sin.

The background to this extraordinary development is as follows. A Japanese double agent conveyed to Kim Ŭng-sŏ, one the commanders of Kyŏngsang province, a sensational message that had apparently come from Konishi Yukinaga. The gist of the communication was that Katō Kiyomasa was planning to invade Korea again, but because Konishi hated Katō so much he was warning the Koreans of the exact timing and location of the operation so that Admiral Yi could intercept the fleet and destroy Katō, thereby removing

Konishi's rival. Not suspecting that the message was a patent forgery designed to lure the Korean navy into a trap, Kim forwarded the intelligence to General Kwŏn Yul, who in turn sent it on to Seoul, so the middle of March 1597 was to find Kwŏn Yul in Yi's base at Hansando urging the incredulous admiral to take advantage of this golden opportunity.[1]

Yi declined to act on the very sensible grounds that it would be unwise to deploy his fleet on the open sea without any confirmation of Japanese movements other than a spy's letter. The area of operation claimed for Katō in the letter was also one that aroused Yi's suspicions, because it was a potential death trap for a Korean fleet lured out of its home port. In fact by the time the interview with Kwŏn Yul took place the object of their discussions had already landed on Kŏje island, but instead of providing confirmation that Yi had been right, his opponents, again prompted by the Japanese agent, took Katō's arrival as proof that Yi had neglected his duties by failing to intercept him! What had been common sense therefore became an act of cowardice. Yi had disobeyed his sovereign's orders, and, by command of King Sŏnjo, he was to be brought to Seoul to stand trial.

The battle of Ch'ilch'ŏnnyang was Japan's only naval victory of the entire war. It resulted in the death of the incompetent Wŏn Kyun, the destruction of the Korean navy, and an unopposed Japanese landing. (ETK)

Early in April 1597 therefore, in a bloodless victory for the Japanese forces, the greatest obstacle that lay between them and a successful renewal of the war was removed from office. Yi was replaced at his base of Hansando by the ineffective and pathetic figure of Wŏn Kyun, who proceeded to use his new position as an opportunity for drunkenness and debauchery. When Yi's trial took place only his distinguished record saved him from the death penalty, and his sentence was reduced to that of being degraded in rank and sent to serve in Kwŏn Yul's army as a common soldier. Here he spent a short but frustrating time until the subsequent battle of Ch'ilch'ŏnnyang forced the King to grant Yi a pardon and to reinstate him to his former office. Such a complete reversal of a royal decision suggests a disaster. In fact, the sequence of events during Yi's absence could hardly have been worse for Korea.

The battle of Ch'ilch'ŏnnyang, which was fought before dawn on 7m 16d (28 August) 1597, was Japan's only naval victory of the entire war. Because of Wŏn Kyun's incompetence, the engagement was conducted like one of Admiral Yi's campaigns in reverse. Present were the usual elements of intelligence gathering, careful scouting, the luring of the enemy into a position chosen by the victor, a sudden attack and the use of overwhelming firepower, but at Ch'ilch'ŏnnyang all these factors were brought to bear from the Japanese side against Korea.

Ch'ilch'ŏnnyang is a narrow strait that divides tiny Ch'ilch'ŏn island from the north-west coast of Kŏje, and in the Japanese accounts the battle is known as the battle of Kŏjedo. Wŏn Kyun was in overall command, and under him fought many of Yi Sun-sin's loyal commanders, including Yi Ŏk-ki, the Right Naval Commander of Chŏlla, who had distinguished himself in many battles, and Pae Sŏl, who had been appointed as Right Naval Commander of Kyŏngsang following Wŏn Kyun's unexpected promotion. Being informed of the approach of a large Japanese fleet, but not of its precise location, its size, its composition or its likely intentions, Wŏn Kyun resolved to lead into battle against it the entire Korean navy.[2]

The Korean fleet left its base at Hansando on 7m 7d, and contact was made with the enemy on the open sea off Chŏryŏng island near Pusan. At this point Wŏn Kyun suddenly appreciated the size of the new armada, which is variously described as being between 500 and 1,000 strong, but in spite of having crews that were already tired after their long journey, and with a storm brewing, Wŏn Kyun ordered the Korean navy into the attack. Thirty ships were lost from the quickly dispersed fleet before Wŏn Kyun called a withdrawal and pulled his men back to the apparent safety of nearby Kadŏk island. Unfortunately, Kadŏk was one of the islands which the occupying Japanese had chosen to fortify, a colossal blunder of intelligence that was to cost Wŏn Kyun dearly, and the garrison under Chikushi Hirokado and Takahashi Munemasu wasted no time in attacking the Koreans as they came ashore in search of water and provisions. Four hundred men were lost in this brief action, after which the Korean fleet hastily set sail again, and rounded the north coast of Kŏje to seek a temporary sanctuary in the narrow straits of Ch'ilch'ŏnnyang.

By now General Kwŏn Yul had been informed of Wŏn Kyun's earlier reversal, and made ready to support him from land as he withdrew to Hansando, but Wŏn Kyun would not budge from Ch'ilch'ŏnnyang. Meanwhile the Japanese, who had received such a stunning demonstration of the lack of military skill that was now at the helm of the Korean navy, moved several hundred of their ships from Pusan to the safety of Ungch'ŏn and Angolp'o, and decided to launch a night attack. The assault on the fleet at Ch'ilch'ŏnnyang was planned for 7m 15d (27 August), when the moon would be full. As well as the usual names we have encountered before in naval fighting such as Tōdō Takatora and Katō Yoshiaki, the battle honours at this unique event were to be shared with Konishi Yukinaga and the Shimazu family, all eager to gain their sea legs in this unprecedented opportunity. While the Japanese fleet approached, the wajō garrison on Kŏje island, whose position lay very close to Ch'ilch'ŏnnyang, made ready to receive any survivors. Soon after midnight three guns were fired, the agreed signal for an attack. 'Everyone pricked up his ears on hearing it,' wrote the chronicler of the Tōdō family.[3] 'In the middle of the night the robber soldiers sneaked in among our ships,' said a Korean chronicler, who added, 'But neither officers nor men were greatly concerned about it.'[4]

It was the sort of naval battle at which the disgraced Admiral Yi Sun-sin had always excelled. Hardly deserving their easy victory, the Japanese fleet bore down upon the hapless Koreans, whose state of shock prevented them from using their traditional tactics of destroying the Japanese fleet from a distance with superior artillery fire. 'Wŏn Kyun was startled as they beat drums, sounded gongs and shot fire arrows,' says the Korean account,[5] the element of surprise allowing the Japanese troops to triumph using their own traditional tactics of close combat by boarding parties, a form of naval warfare that Admiral Yi had never allowed to gain the upper hand. When the battle was over more than two hundred Korean ships floated in the straits as pieces of burnt wreckage, and any survivors who had struggled ashore had fallen prey to the sword blades of the Kŏje garrison. Among them was Wŏn Kyun himself and the redoubtable Yi Ŏk-ki. Pae Sŏl of Kyŏngsang was one of the few to escape. To the fury of Wŏn Kyun, who regarded him as a coward deserving of court martial, Pae Sŏl slipped away when the battle was just beginning and hurried back to Hansando with twelve ships, a tiny remnant that for many months would represent the sum total of the southern coastal fleet of the Korean navy. Not wishing to see the resources of the Hansando base fall into Japanese hands, Pae Sŏl burned its buildings and withdrew far to the west. The humiliation was now complete.

THE SECOND INVASION

It soon became obvious that the removal of Admiral Yi and the débâcle of Ch'ilch'ŏnnyang had created a defenceless void at the precise location into which, during the first invasion, no Japanese had dared advance. The presence of Yi on the sea, and guerrillas on land, had ensured that Chŏlla province had been virtually spared from attack in 1592 and 1593. Its towns, its granaries and its fields, which had been worked so hard to feed the rest of Korea's

The Second Invasion 1597

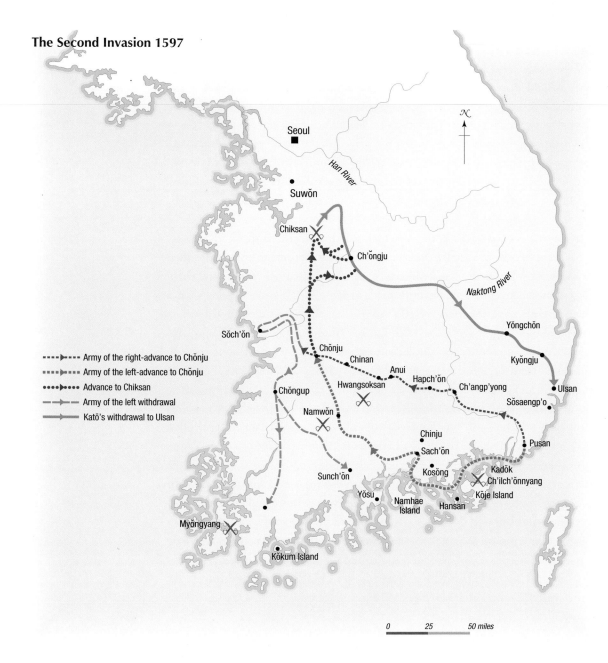

Map of the second invasion in 1597.

devastated provinces, remained untouched by either destruction or plunder. Its roads and castles were intact both for pillage and occupation, and its population had yet to be enslaved. It is therefore not surprising to learn that the Japanese advance on Seoul in 1597, an assault planned to be as rapid and as devastating as the blitzkrieg of 1592, should be conducted through this virgin territory.

The primary objective inside Chǒlla was its provincial capital Chǒnju, upon which two armies would converge. The so-called Army of the Right would march directly north-west from Pusan via Ch'angnyǒng, cross the Naktong to Hapch'ǒn, and proceed through Anui and Chinan, while the Army of the Left would be ferried round the now peaceful south coast from Pusan to Sach'ǒn, where it would march through Konyang and Hadong towards the untouched fortress town of Namwǒn.[6]

These two Japanese armies were the 1597 version of the nine divisions of 1592, and are listed in detail in Appendix II. The roll call contains many familiar names, but with certain very noticeable omissions such as Kobayakawa Takakage, who had gone to be a 'Guest in the White Jade Pavilion' in 1596. In overall command of the invasion was his heir Kobayakawa Hideaki. Ukita Hideie led the Army of the Left, while the former First Division of Konishi, Sō, Matsuura, Arima, Ōmura and Gotō were also present. Several other stalwarts of the first invasion such as Mōri Yoshinari and the Shimazu family made the total up to 49,600 men.

In the Army of the Right, of which 30,000 men supplied by Mōri Hidemoto (who replaced his cousin Terumoto) made up nearly half the strength, the old Second and Third Divisions loomed large in the persons of Katō Kiyomasa, Nabeshima Naoshige (now accompanied by his son Katsushige) and Kuroda Nagamasa, all of whom brought extensive combat experience to a total of 64,300 troops. These two divisions were also shortly to receive unexpected reinforcements, because the defeat of Wǒn Kyun at Ch'ilch'ǒnnyang rendered the 7,200 men earmarked for naval duties quickly redundant, so the troops under Wakizaka and Kurushima were soon to find themselves fighting on land. By this time the wajō garrison strength already in Korea was about 20,000, making the full Japanese army approximately 141,100 men, a number nearly up to the 158,700 of 1592.

The numbers and the leaders of the second invasion may have been roughly the same, but it was soon to become obvious that the nature of the 1597 campaign was very different from its predecessor. Korea was no longer just the road to China. It was itself the final objective, and the mixed emotions of revenge, plunder and conquest conspired to lift the savagery that had attended the first invasion to new heights of energy, and to plumb new depths of horror. The fury that at Pusan had led the invaders to decapitate dogs and cats was now channelled and made clinical, as Korea began to suffer from what can only be described as planned mayhem. Somehow the accounts of the second invasion also have a different feel to them. Gone is any wider vision of a distant and noble objective, of China subdued under the swords of the 'Land of the Gods'. The individual glory of the moment becomes all, and while the pages of the numerous chronicles and diaries produced for the second campaign still ring with the clash of samurai arms and the glories of individual combat, there is a background echo not apparent in the accounts of the first invasion which speaks of hidden horrors. On occasions these terrible scenes bubble to the surface amid what are admittedly some of the finest descriptions of battles to be found in the whole of Japanese military history, producing the strange combination of idealised samurai warfare and its brutal reality.

In the pages which follow I shall make use of these dramatic texts produced by men who were often eyewitnesses to the deeds of their noble masters, but in addition to such hagiographic accounts there exists one remarkable historical source which presents a mirror to Japanese warfare in a way that is almost unique. The work in question is *Chōsen Nichinichiki* ('Korea Day by Day'), which was complied by a Buddhist monk called Keinen.[7] Keinen was a Jōdo Shinshū priest of the An'yōji temple in Usuki in Bungo province in Kyushu. This had once been the fief of Ōtomo Yoshimune, who had been stripped of it following his disgrace at P'ungsan in 1593. The territory had been handed on to the minor daimyō Ōta Kazuyoshi, who took Keinen with him to Korea in 1597 in the capacity of personal physician and chaplain.

While he was in Korea Keinen kept a diary, sometimes written from memory, and on other occasions, one suspects, written very shortly after the vivid and disturbing events that he had just witnessed. As a devout Buddhist Keinen had absolute faith in the redeeming power of Amida, even in the terrible scenes he saw around him where the world of men seemed to have been transformed into the realm of beasts. The diary entries range from the personal, when he complains about the bitter cold of the Korean winter, through the lyrical, where he rhapsodises over the necklace of jewels formed by icicles on the mooring rope of a boat, to the uncomprehending horror of an innocent observer who has come upon a scene of unbelievable cruelty. It is these passages that jolt the modern reader, because Keinen pulls no punches in his descriptions of what he has seen. In fact his observations of Japanese cruelty were such a sensitive matter for successive Japanese governments that Keinen's diary was to remain in manuscript form and unpublished for nearly 400 years.

The terror begins from the moment of Keinen's arrival at Sach'ŏn with the Army of the Left on 8m 4d (15 September) 1597. 'I had hardly disembarked from the ship when the men were stealing things and butchering people,' he writes. 'It was a situation of plunder, and my feelings could easily be discerned from my expression.'[8] The following day, by which time the vanguard had reached Hadong, he records seeing houses being burned, and expresses his emotions through one of the many short poems that are included in the diary to encapsulate the events of the previous days. In this one he alludes to the fact that Chŏlla province was called 'The Red Country' by the Japanese:

'They call this the Red Country
But black is the smoke that rises
From the burning buildings'[9]

Over the next few days Keinen accompanied Ōta Kazuyoshi and his men as the Army of the Left made their slow and savage progress. 'On both field and mountain, castles notwithstanding, they are burning everything, putting an end to the people or fastening chains or bamboo collars around their necks. Parents are slaughtered while the children weep.'[10] His poem for that day refers to the mountains resounding to the voices of soldiers that he likens to fighting demons. On 8m 7d he uses the words 'violent' and 'disgraceful', and writes of 'very serious crimes', and in his entry for the following day he compares the sight of parents being slaughtered in front of their children, who are then taken into slavery, as comparable to 'the tortures of hell's tormenting demons'.[11] 'Forty days have elapsed since I left my hut of rushes and boarded the ship,' he laments on 8m 10d as crops burn in the fields of Chŏlla.[12] Then finally, on 8m 12d, the army came near to its first military objective, the town of Namwŏn:

> As for the high mountain we crossed on the way to Namwŏn, I have not seen the like in Japan to this day. The huge crags stick up like sword blades. Here also there is a ferocious waterfall. Seeing this waterfall makes one's hair stand on end, as would the ferry across the Saigawa to the mountain of death.[13]

It is this image that provides the motif for that day's poem, symbolising the awful spiritual journey that he felt he was making through this horrific landscape:

'I cross the cloud-covered peak
Of the terrible mountain of death'

'We pitched camp about five ri from the castle of Namwŏn,' he writes the following day. He has obviously been talking to an army officer because he adds, 'In an attempt to bring about the fall of this castle an attack will be carried out this evening', and finishes with the verse:

'Before the castle of the Red Country
Everyone in the camp
Joyfully rested his weary limbs'[14]

Keinen was about to see one of the largest and most savage battles of the entire Korean War.

THE SIEGE OF NAMWŎN

Of all the defended places in Korea, Namwŏn most resembled the classic Chinese model of a fortified town, being located on a flat plain within encircling mountains, and therefore possessing none of the mountain features of the typical Korean sansŏng. To the south flowed a river, but this acted only as a distant moat and played little part in the defensive plans, which are known quite precisely because of a detailed map prepared by a certain Kawakami Hisakuni, who probably intended it as an aid to identifying the locations of his brave deeds for which reward was to be claimed. The map, which is now displayed in the museum of the commemorative shrine in Namwŏn, shows the town's layout to be that of a rectangle of stone walls, pierced at the centre of each side by a gateway. Between each gate and corner the wall was built outwards in the form of a simple square-sided rectangular bastion to provide flanking fire on to the gates, giving it a more formidable appearance than the conventional sansŏng. Little remains of the wall today, but a short restored section is about fourteen feet high and is almost vertical on the outside with a more pronounced slope inside. The whole must have presented a very striking appearance in 1597, as it was apparently plastered with shell-lime, and tiny fragments of shells made its surface glitter.[15]

A few miles to the north, however, lay an alternative defensive position in the shape of the sansŏng of Kyŏryŏng. Erected about half-way up the 1600-foot-high mountain, the fortress wall extended for over three thousand yards round the contours of the hillside in the typical serpentine model. The decision about where to make a stand was settled with the arrival in Namwŏn on 6m

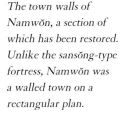

The town walls of Namwŏn, a section of which has been restored. Unlike the sansŏng-type fortress, Namwŏn was a walled town on a rectangular plan.

12d of the Ming general Yang Yuan at the head of 3,000 troops. The Korean garrison were for moving to Kyŏryŏng, but Yang Yuan overruled them and began an extensive programme to strengthen Namwŏn's walls, adding another ten feet to their height, and excavating a wide ditch twenty feet deep enclosed by a wooden palisade. An abattis of tree trunks was laid at the base of the ditch to slow down the attackers. When the Japanese drew near on 8m 9d the new defences had just been completed, and fearing lest Kyŏryŏng should be occupied by the invaders, Yang Yuan ordered the destruction of its fortifications.[16]

The following day, as Japanese scouts began to appear, the defenders of Namwŏn were joined by the military commander of Chŏlla province Yi Pok-nam, the Kwangju magistrate Yi Ch'un-wŏn, and generals Sin Ro and Kim Kyŏng-no. There were now within the walls 6,000 defenders in total, split equally between Koreans and Chinese, together with almost as many civilians. As noted above in Keinen's diary, the Japanese established their lines at Namwŏn on 8m 13d. Ukita took the southern sector, together with Wakizaka Yasuharu, Tōdō Takatora and Keinen's master Ōta Kazuyoshi, while the western side was covered by Konishi's old First Division. Kurushima Michifusa and Katō Yoshiaki provided the contingent to the north, where they joined the Shimazu force, while eleven other generals prepared lines to the east. A full list of names appears in Appendix III. While the Japanese were still preparing their positions the defenders sallied out against them, but they were met by detachments of arquebusiers, and speedily withdrew. The following evening, as on so many occasions at the beginning of the first invasion, a delegation was sent to the defenders calling upon them to surrender and allow the Japanese a free passage through, and as on all those occasions this was again rejected.

The monk Keinen's first comment about the actual siege concerns the weather. On 8m 14d it rained 'like a waterfall', turning the whole Japanese camp into a swamp, and Keinen only had 'paper', presumably the oiled variety spread on the floors of Korean houses, to keep him dry. In his concluding poem he compared the appearance of the drenched samurai to the demons

The Ming general Yang Yuan defies the Japanese, from a painting in the Manin Uich'ŏng shrine at Namwŏn. As on several previous occasions, the Japanese army at Namwŏn in 1597 presented their demand for a safe passage through Korea and, as had always happened before, it was refused.

in *Ise Monogatari*, but on the following day he had his first sight of combat, which filled him with sadness. 'From along the whole line firearms and half-bows are being fired. One cannot but feel sympathy for those men who suffer death.'[17]

A very different view of the attack on Namwŏn comes from the brushes of those who took part in the fighting during the successful night attack on 8m 15d (26 September), and one of the most detailed and vivid accounts is by

another follower of the same Ōta Kazuyoshi, whose descriptions have a very different emphasis from those of Keinen. Ōkōchi Hidemoto was a serving samurai, and his *Chōsen ki* (Korean Chronicle) was designed to glorify the exploits of his master and also, quite plainly, Ōkōchi himself, because his personal role in the fighting is related with great prominence. In addition to Ōkōchi's account of operations on the southern side of Namwŏn, we have another on the

The gateway of the mountain fortress of Kyŏryŏng, abandoned by order of the Chinese in favour of the town walls of Namwŏn.

south (Wakizaka), one from the west (Matsuura) and one, by the chronicler of the Shimazu family, of the operations against the northern wall. What the descriptions have in common is the prominence given to 'their' unit, with an almost complete disregard for the rest of the action. In the case of Ōta and Matsuura some very forceful claims are made that one of their number was the warrior who attained the supreme accolade of ichiban nori, the first to enter the castle, an achievement for which there was the usual intense and often violent competition.

All the accounts agree on one thing. The earlier rain had cleared, and had been replaced by a fresh, bright moonlit night that was ideal for an assault. The attacks began at 10.00 p.m., when 'everything could be seen in minute detail' according to the Shimazu chronicler, whose army, together with Katō Yoshiaki, had in fact been ordered not to attack but to move north from Namwŏn to guard against a possible relieving army coming from Chŏnju. The Shimazu appear to have been engaged in the fight at some stage, however, because the account tells of them engaging the enemy in 'an honourable spectacle, and particularly eminent in it were the men of Satsuma',[18] but it is more than likely that this operation was conducted against members of the garrison fleeing north after the town had fallen.

The *Wakizaka ki* describes Wakizaka Yasuharu fighting on the southern wall alongside Tōdō Takatora:

From within the castle great stones were thrown and fell like rain, and there were many wounded and dead. To add to this the stone walls were high and coated over with plaster, so they could not easily make their entry. His Lordship and Takatora had scaling ladders set up, and although one or two men fought over them, they succeeded in making their entry.[19]

Meanwhile, on the western wall, Matsuura Shigenobu had secured an area of the ramparts and, following a suggestion from his hata bugyō (flag commissioner) Nishi Kiyo'emon, sent his standard bearers in to raise the Matsuura flags on high from the walls. This would encourage the other attackers, and also inform them that the

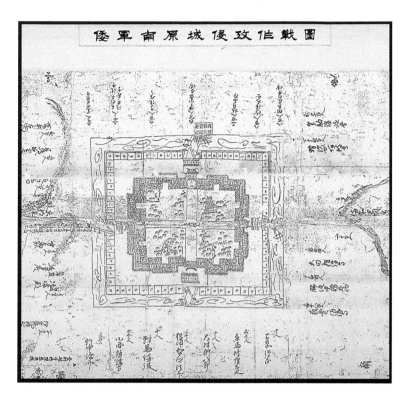

Matsuura troops had got there first. Shigenobu's chronicler in the *Matsuura Hōin Seikan nikki* therefore claimed the prize of ichiban nori for the brave Nishi Kiyo'emon, followed shortly by his master Matsuura Shigenobu.[20]

It is only in Ōkōchi Hidemoto's long and highly personal account in *Chōsen ki* of the attack on the southern wall that we read of the stratagem for which the siege of Namwŏn is best remembered. In preparation for the assault the Japanese foot soldiers scoured the nearby fields, cutting the rice crop which would otherwise soon have been harvested, and tying the stalks into large bundles which were thrown into the moat at a chosen position. So many were collected that a huge and unsteady mound extended to the level of the ramparts. While arquebuses raked the walls with fire, bamboo scaling ladders were added to the pile ready for a determined assault. As the ramp neared completion fire arrows were loosed at the nearest tower, and when this was set alight the samurai rushed on to the huge heap of rice bales. Kishi Rokudayu, later to be credited with taking the first head at Namwŏn, was among the leaders, to be passed on his progress along the ramp by Ōkōchi Hidemoto, who became the first to actually touch the wall. Together with Danzuka Genshirō, Ōkōchi heaved his body on to the parapet while behind them swarmed the Japanese foot soldiers, whom Ōkōchi refers to as 'our inferiors'. Like Matsuura on the western wall, Ōkōchi shouted for the flags to be brought up as quickly as

A map of the siege of Namwŏn prepared by a Japanese called Kawakami Hisakuni. North is to the left, and the names of the commanders on the four sectors may be found in Appendix III. (Courtesy of the Memorial Shrine, Namwŏn)

possible and, led by his lord Ōta Kazuyoshi, Ōkōchi and the rest of the vanguard dropped down into Namwŏn, each warrior proclaiming his name like the samurai of old.[21]

Different flags now flew triumphantly from various parts of the wall. The dark blue banners of Ōta, with the Chinese ideograph that formed the first syllable of his name, were prominent on the southern wall, and when they descended into the town numerous single combats began as the civilians huddled in their homes. Kishi Rokudayu obtained the first head, then Ōkōchi killed two other men, and:

The siege of Namwŏn, from a painting in the shrine at Namwŏn. Yi Pok-nam, the military commander of Chŏlla province, is shown in red armour, while in the background the Japanese have taken the walls.

> Graciously calling to mind that this day was the fifteenth day of the eighth lunar month, the day dedicated to his tutelary kami (Hachiman) Dai Bosatsu, he put down his bloodstained blade and, pressing together his crimson-stained palms, bowed in veneration towards far-off Japan. He cut off the noses and placed them inside a paper handkerchief which he put into his armour.[22]

Very soon the Japanese assault party were faced with a counterattack from mounted men, yet even in all this confusion and danger the personal credit for taking a head was all-important:

> Using his two shaku one sun blade Ōkōchi cut at the right groin of the enemy on horseback and he tumbled down. As his groin was excruciatingly painful from this one assault the enemy fell off on the left-hand side. There were some samurai standing nearby and three of them struck at the mounted enemy to take his head. Four men had now cut him down, but as his plan of attack had been that the abdominal cut would make him fall off on the left, Ōkōchi came running round so that he would not be deprived of the head.[23]

Nearby a bizarre encounter took place between a group of Japanese and a giant Korean swordsman seven shaku in height. He was dressed in a black suit of armour, and as he swung his long sword a samurai thrust his spear towards the man's armpit, only to catch his sleeve instead. At the same time another Japanese caught the man's other sleeve with his spear, ensuring that the warrior was now pinioned like a huge rod-operated puppet. He continued to swing his sword arm ineffectively from the elbow 'as if with the small arms of a woman', but the reduction of this once formidable foe drew only scorn from Ōkōchi. Impaled on two spears, and waving his arms pathetically, he reminded Ōkōchi of the statues of Deva Kings in Buddhist temples with their muscular bodies and glaring eyes. With contempt and ridicule from his attackers the helpless giant was cut to pieces.[24]

Soon Ōkōchi himself became a casualty. Attacked by a group of Koreans he was knocked to the ground, and as he was getting up several sword cuts were made to his chest, leaving him crouching and gasping for breath. His comrade Koike Shinhachirō came to his aid while Ōkōchi parried five sword strokes with the edge of his blade. A sixth slash struck home, cutting clean in two the middle finger of Ōkōchi's bow hand, but Ōkōchi still managed to rise to his feet and quickly decapitated his assailant.[25]

Advancing more deeply into Namwǒn's alleys, Ōkōchi soon encountered another strong man dressed magnificently in a fine suit of armour on dark blue brocade. Ōkōchi 'was cut in four places on his sleeve armour, and received two arrow shafts that were fired deeply into his bow arm in two places', but in spite of these wounds he managed to overcome the man and take his head. Assuming that it belonged to a high-ranking warrior he took the trophy back to Ōta Kazuyoshi. No one on the Japanese side was able to identify it, but after a short while it was shown to some Koreans who had been captured alive. 'They were taken aback, and as they looked at it in anger tears began to flow' when they identified it as none other than the overall Korean leader, the Kwangju magistrate Yi Ch'un-wǒn.[26] In the register of heads for the day (included here as Appendix III) this auspicious prize, noted erroneously as the magistrate of Kyǒngju, appears proudly next to the name of Ōkōchi Hidemoto.[27]

Of the 3,726 heads counted that day, only Yi Ch'un-wǒn's was kept intact. The others were discarded after the noses had been removed, the beginning of the process of nose collection in lieu of heads that was to become such a feature of the second invasion. Insisting upon proof of his soldiers' loyalty and achievements like the reward-giving generals of the ancient civil wars, Hideyoshi began to receive a steady stream of shipments of these ghastly trophies, pickled in salt and packed into wooden barrels, each one meticulously enumerated and recorded by the yokome-shū (inspectors' unit) before leaving Korea. In Japan they were suitably interred in a mound near Hideyoshi's Great Buddha, and there they remain to this day inside Kyoto's least mentioned and most-often-avoided tourist attraction, the grassy burial mound that bears the erroneous name of the Mimizuka, the 'Mound of Ears'.

More nose-taking followed the capture of the walls when the troops of Katō Yoshiaki and Shimazu Yoshihiro, who were guarding the northern road,

The Mimizuka in Kyoto, the erroneously named mound where are interred the noses cut from the heads of Chinese and Korean victims and sent back to Japan as proof of duty done.

turned about to cut down any survivors fleeing in that direction. After a few hours of night fighting, when the moon and the white walls of Namwŏn both turned red from flames and blood, 'the torment was broken', to use the words of the monk Keinen.[28] Apart from noting that his unit under Ōta Kazuyoshi was the first to enter, a matter later relayed back to Hideyoshi in a vermilion seal letter, Keinen has no other comment to make on the actual assault. No doubt he was kept well clear of the fighting, but with the dawn he was free to go and see for himself the effects of the quick and savage assault. The civilian survivors were wailing bitterly as he walked in shock round the streets of the town, perhaps trying to reassure them of the unfailing mercy of Amida. Yet he himself was quickly plunged into despair. 'Things that yesterday were known to be permanent, today, as is the way of this world of uncertainty, become the smoke of impermanence,' he writes as his diary entry for 8m 17d.[29] Even the sights during the march across Chŏlla had not prepared him for the horrors of the aftermath of Namwŏn:

> 'Whoever sees this
> Out of all his days
> Today has become the rest of his life'[30]

Worse scenes were to meet him over the next two days when he left the town 'and saw dead bodies lying near the road like grains of sand. My emotions were such that I could not even glance at them.' As he walked further on he found more noseless corpses in nearby houses, 'and this went on into the fields and mountains'.[31] In his last entry before leaving Namwŏn for the advance on Chŏnju, Keinen concluded with the poem:

'Today in another place I did not know
I was thoughtful among the people in the empty houses
As dawn broke'[32]

To the *Wakizaka ki* chronicler, however, the slaughter of civilians was just another phase in the military operation:

From early dawn of the following morning we gave chase and hunted them in the mountains and scoured the villages for the distance of one day's travel. When they were cornered we made a wholesale slaughter of them. During a period of ten days we seized 10,000 of the enemy, but we did not cut off their heads. We cut off their noses, which told us how many heads there were. By this time Yasuharu's total of heads was over 2,000.[33]

The bad news from Namwŏn travelled quickly northwards to the other Korean garrisons, and after just two days the Japanese Army of the Left marched out of Namwŏn to the provincial capital of Chŏnju and found it abandoned. The great prize of Chŏlla province, the one piece of south Korean territory that had eluded them for the whole of the first invasion, was now securely in Japanese hands.

Following the victories at Namwŏn and Hwangsoksan, Chŏnju, the provincial capital of Chŏlla, was abandoned to the advancing Japanese. (ETK)

THE ADVANCE ON SEOUL

The cataclysmic battle at Namwŏn, which is so well known and well recorded by both sides in the conflict, has completely overshadowed another successful battle fought by the Army of the Right the following day. This army was the larger of the two Japanese contingents. It had marched without incident through Ch'angnyŏng (where Kwak Chae-u looked down on them from his castle of Hwawang), had crossed the Naktong river to Hapch'ŏn and Anui, and faced resistance only from the sansŏng of Hwangsoksan, an isolated mountain fortress which lay just east of the Chŏlla provincial border on top of a wooded hill about five miles north-west of Anui. Its defenders had hastily recruited an army from the neighbouring districts, and many thousands of Korean troops were packed inside it. While their comrades to the south-west prepared to take on the much more serious proposition of a siege of Namwŏn, the Army of the Right took up their post around Hwangsoksan. Katō Kiyomasa drew up his men to the south. Nabeshima Naoshige took the western station, while Kuroda Nagamasa covered the east. During the night of 8m 16d (27 September) the Japanese took advantage of the moonlight that had aided the capture of Namwŏn the day before, and began a full-scale assault. The victory was as quick and as complete as that of Namwŏn, and 350 heads were taken.[34]

There was no further opposition as the Army of the Right marched on to join their comrades in Chŏnju, where there was some reorganisation of the

Guerrilla leader Kwak Chae-u defies Katō Kiyomasa's army from his castle of Hwawang on top of a high mountain near Ch'angnyŏng. In the event, Katō Kiyomasa ignored this position and pressed on into Chŏlla province unmolested.

Japanese forces. The new arrangements resulted in the Army of the Left being reinforced by the units under Nabeshima and Chōsokabe from the Army of the Right, whose depleted numbers left Chŏnju and occupied Kongju, the abandoned capital of Ch'ungchŏng province. Their total strength was now about forty thousand men, which was made up largely from the contingents of Mōri Hidemoto, Katō Kiyomasa and Kuroda Nagamasa. Ōta Kazuyoshi joined them in his new capacity as yokome (inspector of forces) along with Takenaka Tanezane. At Kongju the army divided into two. Katō Kiyomasa, along with Ōta, swung to the east to approach Seoul via the former 'Japanese corridor' that passed through Ch'ŏngju, where they arrived on 9m 6d. The main body continued to head due north, and arrived at Ch'ŏnan the same day.[35]

As Ch'ŏnan lay just south of the provincial border between Ch'ungch'ŏng and Kyŏnggi provinces, the threat to Seoul was becoming obvious to the Koreans, so a largely Ming force was

The commander of Hwangsoksan kills his wife as the fortress blazes around him. (ETK detail)

hurriedly despatched towards Suwŏn to halt their progress. The Chinese general advanced cautiously towards Chiksan, where scouts informed him that the two armies were now but a short distance apart. Here he waited, and before long the Japanese force, which was under the overall command of Kuroda Nagamasa, also sent forward a vanguard unit. As dawn broke on 9m 7d (17 October) Nagamasa's vanguard reached a vantage point three miles north of Chiksan, from where they had a good view of what appeared to be an immense Chinese horde below them. It was also obvious that the Chinese had seen them too, which placed the Japanese leadership in something of a quandary, because if they retreated the Chinese would pursue them and occupy the favourable ground which would allow them to fall upon Kuroda's troops. If the Japanese vanguard attacked they were likely to be annihilated, but in so doing they would slow the enemy advance and perhaps hold them down on the plain while Kuroda's main body followed. The crucial strategic objective appeared to be a rough earthen bridge across the river, to which the Chinese were heading. So, comparing themselves favourably to the 'forlorn hope' troops who had goaded Takeda Katsuyori into attacking at the famous battle of Nagashino in 1575, the Japanese advanced. On coming within range of the Chinese the foot soldiers opened up with their arquebuses, and the samurai attacked through the clouds of smoke.[36]

The sound of firing reached Kuroda Nagamasa long before any of his messengers. A mounted unit under Gotō Mototsugu was sent directly forward, while Kuroda rode out in support with the rest of his army as other messengers hastily galloped back to Mōri Hidemoto. When Gotō arrived on the higher ground he immediately comprehended the situation. The Japanese vanguard had advanced across the earthen bridge to engage the Chinese. They were now fighting with their backs to the river and were being slowly pushed back. The chronicler of the Kuroda family puts the following heroic words into Gotō's mouth, '...if the bridge is crossed by that great army then surely they will attack Nagamasa's main body ... so, accepting that only one man may be left alive for every ten that are killed, we must defend the bridge and prevent the enemy from crossing.'[37]

Gotō therefore set off in a charge down the hill and led an advance across the river. The shock of the attack drove the immediate enemy back, and rallied the distressed Japanese. As soon as he was assured that the position had been reversed, Gotō withdrew his mounted force and returned to the high ground, where, according to the chronicler 'he came and went at various places, and gave the impression that the Japanese were a large force'.[38] Very soon this impression became a reality when Kuroda Nagamasa appeared with the rest of his army. They quickly engaged the Chinese, whom they began to drive back until the Chinese were reinforced in their turn by 2,000 troops from Suwŏn. Once again the fierce fighting continued with no advantage to one side or the other, but then the final set of reinforcements arrived. These were Japanese, and consisted of Mōri Hidemoto's army. The arrival of their overwhelming numbers made the Ming army withdraw towards Suwŏn, but as it was now growing dark the Japanese command felt it imprudent to pursue them, so both armies disengaged.

This little-known battle of Chiksan left the Japanese poised for a quick advance on Seoul and the achievement of Hideyoshi's war aims. But if Chiksan may have been an indecisive battle, it had decisive results. The post-Namwŏn panic that had seen Korean and Chinese armies abandoning positions at Chŏnju and Kongju had now been arrested, and it was clear that a large Chinese army was preparing to defend Seoul. Chiksan was therefore occupied by the Japanese to use as a base for the attack on the capital. But once again, just as at P'yŏngyang in 1592, the supporting troops never arrived, and Chiksan was to become another last outpost of a Japanese advance. Even more remarkably, the reason why the attack never happened was again the result of a naval victory gained by Admiral Yi Sun-sin.

The battle of Chiksan. Advance troops under Kuroda Nagamasa are seen crossing the river against the Chinese force. Chiksan was to become the limit of the Japanese advance in 1597. (ETK)

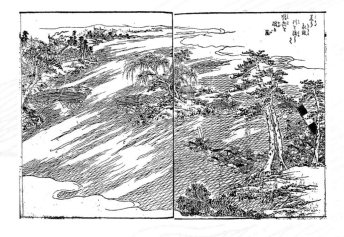

THE MIRACLE AT MYŎNGYANG

Shortly after the victory at Namwŏn the Japanese admirals were despatched to Hadong to plan how they would secure the sea route up the Yellow Sea to transport the troops that would be needed for the attack on Seoul. The plan was that the Army of the Left would be ferried up into the Han river to turn the Korean flank in a two-pronged assault, and the first phase of the operation went smoothly enough. With a strength of over 64,000 the Army of the Left departed Chŏnju on 8m 27d and headed away from the main road to the north for the proposed embarkation point at the estuary of the Kŭm river, which acted as the border between Chŏlla and Ch'ungch'ŏng provinces.

Meanwhile the Japanese admirals proceeded cautiously westwards into the unfamiliar seas off the coast of Chŏlla, and it was on 8m 28d that they renewed their acquaintance with the reinstated Admiral Yi, who had now taken command of the twelve ships saved by Pae Sŏl. The approach of a scouting party of Japanese ships alarmed the Korean sailors, but Yi put new heart into them and scattered the intruders. This incursion did however prompt Yi to withdraw further to the west to identify a more secure base. He selected Pyŏkp'ajin on Chindo island, which was separated from the mainland at the extreme south-western tip of Korea by a very narrow strait called Myŏngyang, otherwise known as Ultolmok, 'The Roaring Channel', because of the fierceness of the changes of its tides.[39]

The Japanese ships continued to press further along the coast, and by 9m 6d their advance party had reached the harbour of Oranp'o, where Admiral Yi sailed to meet them eight days later and forced them to retreat back to the east. That same night the Japanese returned for another attack, and were again beaten off. It was at this point that Yi began planning how he could employ the unusual tidal conditions in Myŏngyang to defeat the Japanese. The tidal race passing through the strait is one of the fastest in all Korean waters, running between 9.5 and 11.5 knots at its highest rate. It was also known to change direction from north to west and then back again every three hours. This phenomenon was the only advantage Yi had, because the Japanese possessed 133 ships, while he still had only the twelve vessels saved from Ch'ilch'ŏnnyang.[40]

The historic battle, which the Koreans call the 'Miracle at Myŏngyang', was fought early in the morning of 9m 16d (26 October) 1597. As Yi had anticipated, the Japanese fleet of 133 ships approached the strait from the direction of Oranp'o on a favourable tide, while Yi took up his position in the open sea just to the north of the strait. When the Japanese had advanced midway up Myŏngyang, Yi sailed into the attack, and his tiny flotilla was of course immediately surrounded, but Yi stuck firmly to his time-honoured

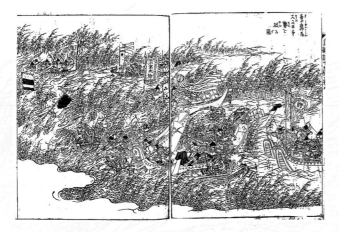

The sea battle that the Koreans call 'the Miracle at Myŏngyang'. The way in which the Japanese ships were ambushed in the narrow strait, and the fierce hand-to-hand fighting which followed, are clearly shown. (ETK)

tactics of keeping the Japanese ships beyond boarding distance and bombarding them with cannon and fire arrows. As a result only one of the Korean ships was boarded, and Yi's diary notes seeing 'the enemy hordes like black ants climbing up An Wi's ship'. But, using 'sharp-edged clubs, long spears or sea-washed stones' the boarders were repulsed.[41]

At one stage in the battle a captured Japanese soldier on Admiral Yi's flagship looked down at the struggling bodies in the sea and noticed a dead samurai floating in an ornate brocade robe. Recognising the man as his commander, the prisoner let out an exclamation of surprise which alerted the Koreans to the trophy that had come their way, so they hauled the corpse on board. 'I commanded my men to cut the body into pieces, and from that time the morale of the enemy was greatly affected,' wrote Yi.[42] The high-ranking victim was identified as Kurushima Michifusa, brother of the late Kurushima Michiyuki, killed in 1592 at Tangp'o.

As the fight progressed the tide turned, and began to carry the Japanese ships back along the strait. The Korean ships continued to harass them, destroying vessels out of all proportion to their relative numbers. In his diary Yi claims that 31 Japanese ships were lost before they retreated, but the total was probably much higher, and as it happened just nine days after the stalemate battle at Chiksan the extra psychological pressure the naval victory applied to the Japanese decision-making process was considerable.

A few days earlier, on 9m 8d, the Army of the Left had burned and occupied Sŏch'ŏn castle to secure their position on the Kŭm river, but the news reaching them from the Japanese naval forces was becoming increasingly discouraging, so a council of war was held at Chŏngŭp on 9m 16d, the same day that Admiral Yi was to seal their fate with the battle of Myŏngyang. Similar deliberations were being held much further to the north, Katō Kiyomasa having now advanced from Chŏnju to join the main Korean army at Chiksan, and when the news broke about the disaster at Myŏngyang all the commanders realised that the attack on Seoul could no longer take place. The army at Chiksan was perilously isolated, and there was no alternative but to return to the safety of the wajō.

The Army of the Right accordingly turned about and began a long march back through the centre of Korea, following the old line of the Japanese advance of 1592. At Sangju, the site of one of their greatest victories, the army divided. The main body under Mōri Hidemoto continued along the banks of the Naktong down to Pusan. Katō Kiyomasa and others headed further east towards his coastal wajō of Sŏsaengp'o, looting what was left to take, and burning what could not be stolen. The road took them through Kyŏngju, the capital of the old Silla kingdom and the treasure house of Japanese Buddhism. Kyŏngju had seen two battles since the Japanese had first landed, but had emerged relatively unscathed. With Katō Kiyomasa's last withdrawal vengeance was wreaked, and the entire city was put to the torch, including the wonderful Pulguksa temple. Loaded with plunder, Katō reached the sea coast at Ulsan, a harbour that had once been one of the 'Three Ports' when it was used as a Japanese trading post a century before. Katō immediately appreciated its strategic potential, so labourers were set to work to raise a wajō on this site that was to become the new eastern end of the Japanese defence line.

While this was going on the Army of the Left had made a similar decision to proceed to the coast of Chŏlla and occupy fortified positions, thus extending the existing line of wajō to twice its original length towards to the west. Shimazu Yoshihiro and Chōsokabe Motochika took over Sach'ŏn, while Konishi Yukinaga and Ukita Hideie went to Sunch'ŏn, where extensive building work began. Shimazu Tadatsune and Nabeshima Katsushige completed the line at Kangjin and Haenam, although both these sites were abandoned early in December. The coastal defence line had now returned to being the only Korean territory occupied by Japan and, within this line, particularly within its newly extended ends at Sunch'ŏn, Sachŏn and Ulsan, spades and axes were wielded as the invaders prepared to settle down for another long Korean winter.

The Pulguksa temple at Kyŏngju. On the retreat to the coast Katō Kiyomasa's men burned down this treasure of Korean Buddhism located in the ancient capital of the Silla Kingdom. The Pulguksa has since been completely restored.

chapter ten

THE WAJŌ WARS

THE Japanese armies of the second invasion had carved a swathe of destruction almost to Seoul and back again, and had now returned to the coastal fortresses that had served them so well during the occupation. But if anyone thought that this meant a return to the idyllic round of poetry parties, tiger hunts and drinking bouts which had formerly characterised Japanese life in the wajō, then he was in for a rude shock. The Japanese forces had marched out of their castles to relaunch the war and commit acts of aggression against Korea, and when they withdrew within those walls their pursuers were determined to give them no rest. One more year of bitter conflict was left of Japan's Korean War, a year that was to see huge armies of Chinese and Koreans battering against the walls of one wajō after another in an attempt to drive the invaders into the sea.

THE SIEGE OF ULSAN

The first Japanese stronghold to experience such a response was Ulsan, Katō Kiyomasa's newly acquired base that formed the eastern extremity of the Japanese line. Ulsan lay on a broad river estuary which gave easy access to the sea. It was 15 miles by boat from Sŏsaengp'o, the next wajō along the line, but unlike Sŏsaengp'o's carefully sculpted stone walls laid down during the more leisurely days of the occupation, Ulsan was largely unfortified when the Japanese arrived after their march through Kyŏngsang, so a rapid and extensive building programme began immediately.

Katō Kiyomasa delegated the defence of Ulsan to a garrison of about seven thousand men under Katō Yasumasa, Kuki Hirotaka, Asano Nagayoshi and others, and continued on his way to Sŏsaengp'o. The re-fortification of Ulsan was placed in the capable hands of Ōta Kazuyoshi, which is one reason why the whole Ulsan action is so well-recorded, as Ōta was still accompanied by his two chroniclers: the samurai Ōkōchi Hidemoto and the monk Keinen. Work began at a furious pace in late November 1597 to make a strong castle out of the prominent hill about one hundred and fifty feet in height that overlooked the river, so squads of Japanese began raising earthworks and ditches, cladding the sides of the hill in stone, and building fences and barracks from timber cleared from nearby forests.

Keinen, who was still in a state of shock after what he had witnessed in Namwŏn, wrote in his diary of the 'Buddha-less world' in which he now found himself.[1] With the arrival of the cold Korean winter Ulsan seemed to be a land 'like the seventh of the eight cold hells, all gloomy and shrivelled up',[2] but it was the constant noise of building work that first gave him concern:

> From all around comes the sound of the hammers of the blacksmiths and the workmen, and the swish and scraping of the adze. With the dawn it grows more and more terrible, but if it means we will not be defeated I can put up with the banging I am being subjected to even in the middle of the night.[3]

The constant labour was hard and unremitting, and was imposed particularly cruelly on the shoulders of the press-ganged peasants drafted from samurai estates in Japan, who were forced to work alongside Korean captives and treated equally badly. Their fate stirred Keinen to pity, and, while recognising that everyone in the Japanese army was involved in the desperate construction programme 'from whose who are in the arquebus squads or who wear horō (i.e. the samurai), down to the boatmen and the labourers', Keinen noticed a very different attitude being shown to those who were soldiers and those who were not. 'To prevent carelessness heads are cut off,' he writes, 'but blame is not shared equally, and to the sorrow of the peasants it is their heads that they

The site of Ulsan castle today. The hill of Ulsan, which withstood one of the fiercest sieges of the entire Korean campaign, is little changed in appearance from 1598. It lies on the edge of the city next to the river, and is the only piece of high ground for miles around.

cut off and stick up at the crossroads.'[4] In the intense pressure to have the walls of Ulsan finished before the Chinese army arrived these labourers were clearly regarded as expendable, and were worked until they dropped.

Few incidents illustrate the obsessive savagery of the Korean campaign better than Keinen's observations of the cruel treatment meted out by the Japanese army against their fellow countrymen. After all, the peasants they were flogging were men who would be expected to till the lands of these same samurai overlords when they returned to Japan, but in the unreal atmosphere of the Korean campaign there was no thought for the future other than the immediate short-term goal of completing the wajō's defences. 'With no distinction being made between day and night,' writes Keinen, 'men are made to exceed their personal limits. There are beatings for the slightest mistake in performing a task such as tying knots. In many cases I have witnessed, this is the last ever occasion on which the person gets into trouble',[5] and in his diary entry for 11m 15d (23 December) 1597, he makes one of his most despairing statements of all. 'I am fearful of these things,' he writes. 'Hell cannot be in any other place except here.'[6]

To add to the misery caused by overwork, the labourers also had to suffer attacks from the Chinese patrols that were beginning to appear in the vicinity. On 11m 16d Keinen writes of a group of peasants left in the forest to trim the branches off the newly felled trees. A Chinese unit came upon them and beheaded them all. 'Brought here from thousands of miles away,' he writes (thus confirming that he is talking of Japanese and not Koreans), 'they are tortured for even one single moment of carelessness. I do not see these as actions which human beings could devise.'[7] This theme, that by the actions he is witnessing the humans at Ulsan are losing their humanity and descending into bestiality, is one that he returns to a few days later. It is a process that Keinen sees operating at two levels, because the samurai are losing every trace of human compassion when they treat the peasants like the dumb animals that they increasingly resemble. In a vivid metaphor, prompted by seeing the labourers staggering under the weight of the supplies unloaded from the ships, Keinen writes:

> Yet even amidst all this, the carrying of heavy loads piled up like a hōrai [the 'treasure mountain' of Chinese mythology] between the harbour and the rear lines is an exceptionally terrible thing. They drag them along to (shouts of) 'Come on!', but when they reach the wooden palisade these dumb oxen are of no use anymore, and are slaughtered, their hides are flayed, and they are eaten. 'Is this not the realm of beasts?' thought I.[8]

Keinen, of course, does not mean us to take literally his words about the 'dumb oxen', which the peasants have become, being 'flayed and eaten', but the reality of the situation is almost as terrible. In spite of an order from Hideyoshi, noted by Keinen on 11m 17d, which stated that no labourer was to be left behind in Korea when the army returned, the Taikō's lieutenants in Ulsan were doing just the opposite because, when food supplies became a problem, the peasants 'were not given their rations, but were driven away up into the mountains and abandoned. I saw how this was done with my own eyes'.[9]

'I have endured the billows for a thousand miles since I set off to war and came here,' laments Keinen on 11m 18d.[10] At Namwŏn he felt that he had crossed 'the terrible mountain of death'. To reach Ulsan he had 'traversed the floating world ... moving from the heights to the depths', and to his comments about the treatment of their fellow Japanese he adds a poignant observation about the fate of captured Koreans:

> Among the various sorts of traders who have come over from Japan are those whose trade is in people. They follow along behind the ranks and buy up men and women, old and young. They tie ropes round their necks and drive them along. If they can no longer walk, they drive them on from behind and make them stand up by beating them with canes. I think this is how sinners must be tortured in hell by demons.[11]

Again the vision of a descent into the realm of beasts comes into Keinen's mind. The captives are tied together 'like monkeys'. They are led 'like horses and cattle, as just so much baggage'. The sight of these wretches, together with the 'dumb oxen', moves him to put into words a final cry of despair because, although he has used expressions comparing humans to animals, he appreciates that real animals do not behave in this cruel manner to one another. 'Nothing', he concludes, 'is as awful as the deeds carried out in this world by those who are normally referred to as humans.'[12]

By early January 1598 the increasingly severe winter weather was beginning to hinder the construction work. Keinen, who hailed from warm Kyushu, had little experience of cold, and several of his diary entries describe such wonders as ice on the river 'across which a horse could be ridden', which prevented the delivery of firewood, and the sound of the wind whistling through the walls of the temporary shelters built outside Ulsan's walls while the work went on. One day he looks across the fields white with snow and thinks he sees packhorses, but instead it is the labourers trudging through the snow with their painfully heavy burdens, and in another strangely lyrical passage he describes how the ropes by which the boats are tethered to the shore were hung with icicles like jewelled necklaces.[13]

The Korean winter therefore played its own part in reducing the time available to complete Ulsan's walls in preparation for an attack, and the arrival of the Ming just before dawn on 12m 22d (29 January) 1598 was to find a large proportion of the Japanese army still encamped in the flimsy barracks

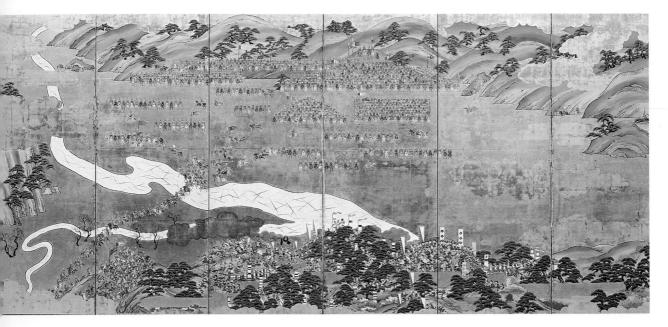

A huge Ming army marches against Ulsan as the Japanese garrison prepare to enhance their defences. From a painted screen in the collection of the Nabeshima family.

outside Ulsan's enceinte. Their advance seems to have taken the Japanese by surprise, and *Matsui Monogatari* provides one of the very few notes of humour discernible in this savage campaign when it tells how the sound of gunfire was heard coming from the Nabeshima camp:

> Near the camp was a huge marsh to which many swans came every night. At dawn they flew over the camp. The foot soldiers had been told about this by Nabeshima, and would fire their arquebuses at the flying birds, bringing down one or two. This happened every night, and when the sound of gunfire was heard that particular night Yasumasa thought they were shooting swans again.[14]

Katō Yasumasa only appreciated the significance of the gunfire when Nabeshima's troops came rushing into his camp for protection from the pursuing Chinese, who were loosing hundreds of arrows towards the Japanese lines. Having been advised by their scouts that the Japanese defences were still incomplete, a flying squad had been sent on ahead of the main body to do as much damage as possible. Fire arrows hit the temporary barracks buildings, which soon caught fire. Keinen was fortunate in being inside Ulsan castle when the dawn attack happened. 'At the Hour of the Dragon smoke was rising on the eastern side of the castle, and I could hear the sounds of gunfire. Chinamen had advanced and set fire to the huts of the troops from Chūgoku.'[15]

The brunt of the assault was taken by the soldiers under the command of three of Mōri Hidemoto's subordinate generals. The account in *Taikōki* tells of a certain Reizei Motomitsu who 'wielded his naginata like a water wheel,

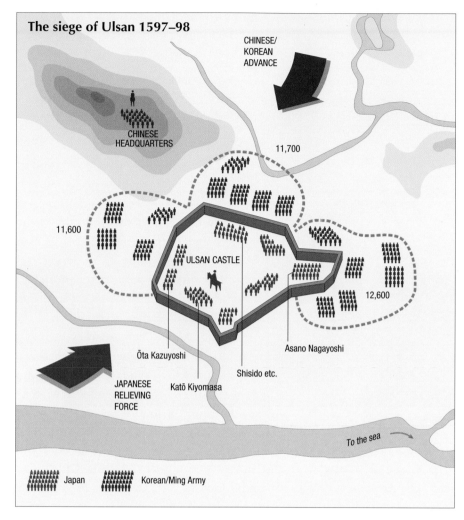

The siege of Ulsan 1597–98

CHINESE/
KOREAN
ADVANCE

CHINESE
HEADQUARTERS

11,700

11,600

ULSAN CASTLE

12,600

Ōta Kazuyoshi

Asano Nagayoshi

Shisido etc.

Katō Kiyomasa

JAPANESE
RELIEVING
FORCE

To the sea

Japan   Korean/Ming Army

Map of the siege of Ulsan.

slaying fifteen or sixteen of the nearby enemy', before being cut down, to the great distress of his followers:

> Because Shiromatsu Zen'emonnojō, Igazaki Matabeinojō and Yoshida Tarōbei were by chance somewhere else, they regretted that they had not been there with him to be killed in battle, so when they took possession of Motomitsu's corpse they performed the act of cutting open their bellies in the shape of a cross on that very spot.[16]

The chronicler notes approvingly how impressed the rest of the army were by this exemplary act of bushidō, and adds that their ihai (funerary memorial tablets) were installed beside Motomitsu's in the family temple in Izumi province, an institution later to become richly endowed in their memory.

At some stage early in the campaign (the date is unclear) Asano Nagayoshi sent a messenger to Sŏsaengp'o to inform Katō Kiyomasa of the situation.

After despatching a message to Pusan for reinforcements, Katō made ready to assist Ulsan in person, and Ōkōchi Hidemoto describes the grand departure of Japan's great hero general:

> Kiyomasa put on his black laced armour, tightened the cords of his helmet . . . and taking along fifteen pages, fifteen messengers, twenty guns and thirty-five foot soldiers, jumped into a small boat, set up his standard and shouted 'Ei! Ei! . . . [17]

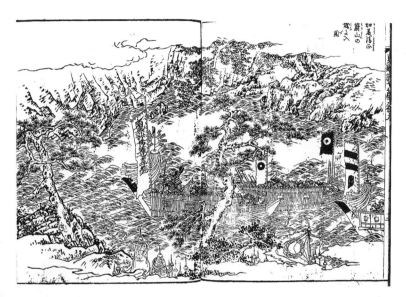

Great heart was put into the defenders of Ulsan by the arrival of Katō Kiyomasa, who sailed from Sŏsaengp'o like a war god coming to their rescue. (ETK)

To Ōkōchi, Katō, standing on a coil of rope and 'pointing his naginata as if it were a cane', resembled the god Tamonten, and it was indeed as if he were a gift from heaven that the Ulsan garrison greeted him on his arrival.

The survivors of the night attack had taken refuge within Ulsan's incomplete walls while rearguard actions held off the attackers. The casualties included Mōri Hidemoto's general Shishido Bizen no kami, whose standard of a white swan was snatched from his standard bearer's hands as Shishido was cut down. One other samurai 'mentioned in despatches' was the brave young Yoshimi Hiroyuki, aged fifteen in one account and eighteen in another, who 'excelled in the Way of Bow and Arrow'. Ordering his ashigaru to draw the enemy on but not to waste their arrows, he led an impetuous charge that covered the retreat:

> After a short while Yoshimi returned to the safety of the castle, and seeing that the gateway of the section of the defence works for which he was responsible was looking in a poor state, he ordered his retainers to construct a low wall by using the various large and small swords that had been collected, thus producing a rampart of spikes. [18]

Ōkōchi Hidemoto's *Chōsen ki* relates how several of the units which had been based within the comparative safety of the castle mounted a counterattack. Ōta Kazuyoshi was among them as they advanced about six or seven chō away from the castle, drew up their lines, and engaged the enemy in combat. Suspecting that their opponents might be only the vanguard of a greater host, Ōta sent out scouts to investigate, but before they returned the presence of a huge Chinese army was confirmed by a massive cloud of black dust 'as large as Mount Atago in Japan' stirred up by the horses' hooves. It indicated the approach of 500,000 horsemen according to *Taikōki*, or 800,000 horsemen in *Chōsen ki*, a figure that was in reality nearer to 50,000, which was itself sufficient to outnumber the Japanese many times over. As the Japanese army withdrew combats continued where the two armies overlapped, and some of the retreating garrison got cut off from the castle and were slaughtered beside the river.[19]

The pursuit of the stragglers continued up to the unfinished gates of Ulsan. Foot soldiers fired arquebuses from the ramparts to cover the withdrawal, but the Chinese 'were not discouraged by this and, trampling over the corpses, forced their way in', and the bar of the gate broke under the weight of the soldiers climbing over it. To divert the Chinese attack another gate of the castle was opened and a sally was made onto the Ming flank:

> But as friend and foe were all mixed up we could not fire our guns. A soldier who had sallied out and taken a head half-way down the slope had achieved the exploit of yarishita [first to take a head with a spear], then our troops, without the loss of a single man, began to pull back.[20]

Inoue Nagayoshi, a retainer of Katō Kiyomasa, shows his great strength by using a heavy-calibre arquebus in the defence of Ulsan.

As the two armies separated firing began again, which finally drove back the Chinese. 'No brush could be equal to the task of painting a picture of this particular battle,' wrote Ōkōchi, who added a note of sadness that this great battle fought in a distant land could not be personally witnessed by Hideyoshi himself. His master Ōta Kazuyoshi, naturally, comes in for the most effusive praise:

> Afterwards they performed the head inspection ceremony for the men's eleven meritorious heads. Katō Kiyomasa's men had taken one head. Asano Nagayoshi's men had taken one head, but Ōta Kazuyoshi's men had taken a total of nine heads. Everyone inside the castle noticed this and praised him, saying, 'While Kiyomasa owns half of Higo province, and Nagayoshi owns the whole province of Kai, they only took one head each, yet Kazuyoshi is a person of low degree and has taken nine heads. Indeed, he conducts himself as a fine, brave samurai.'[21]

Keinen adds that Ōta received a bullet through his arm, which caused him great pain.[22]

The Chinese made no further advance against Ulsan that day, but contented themselves with burning down the temporary barracks and then withdrew. The situation was not encouraging. The garrison had no more than three days supply of food, and another major attack was expected.

At about 4.00 a.m. on 1m 23d the Ming gathered their forces for the first assault on Ulsan castle itself. Asano Nagayoshi, wielding an arquebus out of choice instead of a spear, led the counterattack on the eastern side of the walls. Keinen was now in the thick of the fighting for the first time, and gives us a vivid eyewitness description of how 'the castle was surrounded by countless numbers of troops, who were deployed in a number of rings that encircled us. There were so many of them covering the ground that one could no longer distinguish between the plain and the hills.' Because the gateways were still incomplete the Chinese were able to swarm inside, and began loosing fire arrows from outside the walls. The result was that the bedding, storage boxes and many other 'treasured possessions' went up in flames. The smoke was so dense that the defenders could not keep their eyes or mouths open, and thousands of labourers who were late returning to the castle were caught in the conflagration and died.[23]

By now thousands of Chinese soldiers were climbing up the walls, so both Keinen and his fellow priest Ryōshin prepared themselves for death. As that day was the eve of the Memorial Day for Shinran, the Patriarch of Jodō Shinshū, how fitting it was that they should die and be reborn in bliss! But it was not to be. Shifting their efforts to the west, the Chinese succeeded in breaking down the outer palisade on the north-western corner by about 11.00 a.m. They were eventually driven back, but at the cost of 660 Japanese casualties. That night Keinen did not sleep, convinced that if he died on Shinran's Memorial Day he was certain to be reborn in paradise. A fierce attack came with the dawn, but was again driven off by gunfire. 'It now appears', wrote Keinen, 'that they want to lay siege to the castle and stay on the defensive until it falls.'[24]

Keinen was right, because the Ming set up siege lines round Ulsan, and in between the Chinese assaults the defenders reflected on their enemies' tactics. The fighting always appeared to be controlled by two mounted men who sat motionless on their horses even in the middle of a freezing night, leading some Japanese to suspect that they were

One of the most prominent defenders of Ulsan was Asano Nagayoshi (also known as Yukinaga), who is shown here using his sharp sword to lop off a Chinese arm. (ETK)

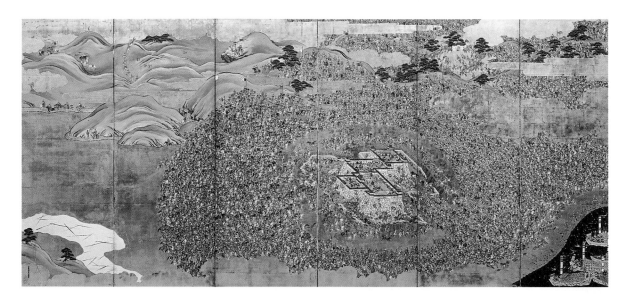

not real men at all but straw dummies. The actual assaults were terrifying, because as one human wave of Chinese was driven back another swept up to replace them, the dead bodies of their predecessors taking the place of scaling ladders as they clambered up the huge mound of corpses. 'They would put a large hook up on the wall and fifty or even a hundred men would take hold of the attached rope to pull the wall down,' wrote the author of *Matsui Monogatari* in some amazement. 'When this happened we fired on them from the side, but out of fifty men five or ten still hung on and pulled to the end. It has to be said that they are extremely brave warriors.'[25] On one occasion a detachment of Koreans carrying shields and bundles of brushwood approached the outer bailey to make an arson attack on the palisade, but they were spotted and received volleys of arquebus balls for their pains.[26] Cannon were also very much in evidence:

> The Chinamen fired a cannon. It hit Kiyomasa's bodyguard, cutting him in half at the waist, so that only that part of his body below the waist was left.[27]

Concern was also expressed that the Japanese arquebus fire was being stopped by the solid Chinese shields, so to test them arquebuses were trained on the middle of the shields and it was noted at which range they could be pierced, as shown 'by the blood flowing'.[28] The chronicler of *Matsui Monogatari* also noticed a strange pattern of behaviour associated with the Chinese shields:

> Furthermore, when the vanguard troops went forward they carried wooden shields on their back plates tied with two cords. They carried these on the back and walked backwards. The men behind them walked

The siege of Ulsan, from a painted screen in the collection of the Nabeshima family. The unfinished nature of the wajō of Ulsan is clearly depicted, as it has stone walls but only rudimentary turrets. The flower mon on the curtains is associated with Katō Kiyomasa. Thousands of Chinese troops attempt to scale the walls.

A battle at Ulsan between South Chinese troops, whose black and yellow battle flag is described in the chronicles, and a samurai identified as Ayukawa. The Chinese horseman has caught Ayukawa's sword between his own two sword blades. (ETK detail)

along carrying half-bows, flexing their fingers and blowing on them. When they drew near and we fired arquebuses in a volley, they discarded the shields and fled away. After a short while they returned to the shields they had fetched. They looked at the name written on it and took their own ones, then went back. Even though arquebuses were being fired at them they took the shields with their own names on them and looked for a way back. It seemed that they prized their names up to the higher ranks of soldier.[29]

As Ulsan had no well within the castle the torments of thirst were soon added to the intense discomfort of the Chinese attacks. Water-gathering parties slipped out of the castle by night and brought back supplies from ponds choked with corpses. 'But just when we were really craving for water,' writes Keinen, 'it began raining heavily and everyone in the castle could wet their mouths.'

'Japan is the Land of the Gods
And by their mercy
Rain falls to benefit men'

wrote Keinen in the one poem in his diary to make use of the expression that so many other chroniclers had used to provide justification for Japan's aggression. 'The water fell like shed tears onto their helmets,' he continues, 'and we washed our hands in the water that cascaded over us'.[30] When the temperature dropped below freezing that night a strong wind arose that brought about a wind-chill factor so severe that it affected the fighting spirit on both sides. The pause in the attack, and the intense cold, made the defenders realise how tired they were. By now all food was practically exhausted, and foragers had been reduced to searching the bodies of dead Chinese for scraps of food. Now the men forced themselves to improvise by roasting strips of meat cut from dead horses over fires made from broken arrows, piles of which lay several feet deep. The following morning, fooled by the deceptive warmth of a brief spell of winter sunshine, the exhausted soldiers huddled in the sunny places on the ramparts and fell asleep. The *Chōsen ki* tells us:

> . . . both friend and foe are silent. Nevertheless inside the castle we have maintained our defences by day and night without any sleep. Here and there inside the castle, at the sunny places on the walkways and at the foot of towers, with no distinction between samurai, ashigaru or labourers, fifty men at a time may be found crumpled under the unbearable hunger, thirst and cold. In addition there are a number of men who have let their heads drop and lie down to sleep. Other soldiers go on tours of inspection with their spears, and when they try to rouse men who have not moved all day by using the butt end of a spear, the ones who stay completely bent over have been frozen to death.[31]

The conditions made both sides ready to parley, and the resulting offer by the Ming of a ceasefire was accepted by Katō Kiyomasa as a way of buying time, because the plight of Ulsan was now known to the rest of the Japanese army. On 12m 27d Mōri Yoshinari, accompanied by ten samurai, had sailed round from Sŏsaengp'o and rowed up the river as far as was possible, where they waved their banners towards the ramparts, hoping that they had been seen. Two days later a large scouting force that included Mōri Hidemoto and Kuroda Nagamasa arrived in the estuary to identify a suitable landing place for a relieving army. They disembarked

The starving defenders of Ulsan go foraging among the Chinese dead, rifling their pockets for scraps of food, and drinking water from ditches polluted by corpses. (ETK)

briefly on some high ground and again waved flags towards the castle. This time they were definitely noticed, and the garrison waved back to them. While this was going on the relieving army arrived at Sŏsaengp'o. The list of names. is long, and includes almost every general of note except Konishi, Shimazu and Tachibana, who were needed in their own wajō further to the west.

The relieving army, which had been placed under the overall command of Mōri Hidemoto, left Sŏsaengp'o on Keichō II, 1m 2d (7 February) 1598. After camping overnight they took up a position on the high ground that had previously been identified, planting as many flags as possible. 'I was resigned

The Japanese army marches to the relief of Ulsan, from a painted screen in the collection of the Nabeshima family. The steady progress of the relieving army across the frozen river is clearly shown.

to my fate,' writes Keinen, 'when at early dawn we saw the tips of the banners, and there was much rejoicing.'[32] Greatly relieved at the sight, Katō Kiyomasa broke off his negotiations with the Ming, who resolved to make one final attempt to take Ulsan before the new army advanced upon them. Keinen watched in some excitement as the night attack unfolded:

> From early dawn they attacked anew, loosing fire arrows and firing arquebuses and cannon, and set up scaling ladders at places where they could climb the stone walls. We threw down pine torches, cut down their climbing implements and fired at them.[33]

Soon intelligence reached the Chinese command of the huge relieving army that was approaching from behind them. The Japanese quickly fell on their rear, and the result was a considerable Japanese victory. 'They returned to drag away the bodies,' wrote Keinen, 'They were a broken army.'[34] As dawn broke the following morning the defenders of Ulsan were heartened by the welcome sight of flocks of scavenging birds descending upon the now abandoned Chinese camp. The siege of Ulsan was over, and the chronicler of the Asano family summed up the situation:

> From the 22nd day of the 12th month to the 4th day of the 1st month we were defending against a total of 100,000 of the enemy, fighting without distinguishing between day or night. Inside the castle practically all are either wounded or dead and buried.[35]

There was only a brief pursuit. The garrison from Sŏsaengp'o took the places of the defenders of Ulsan, and for some there was a welcome return home. Ōta Kazuyoshi was one of the lucky ones. He sailed for Japan that same day accompanied by Ōkōchi Hidemoto and the monk Keinen, the latter's Korean nightmare now finished forever.

THE BATTLE OF SACH'ŎN

As the winter of 1597 gave way to the spring of 1598 the two foreign armies that were now camped on Korean territory began to review their respective positions. The relief of Ulsan had been a major setback for the Chinese army, who had looked upon a siege of an incomplete castle as a minor matter to be disposed of easily. To the Japanese the success at Ulsan had been very welcome, but they were not prepared to allow this triumph to blind them to certain facts of arithmetic. The Ming now had about one hundred thousand troops on Korean soil, and this, together with the native Korean army and its volunteers, meant that for the first time since the war began the Japanese expeditionary force was outnumbered. Admiral Yi's navy had also grown in numerical strength from the twelve ships that had humiliated the Japanese at Myŏngyang, and had now been joined by a Chinese fleet. Finally, the superiority in hand-held firearms which the Japanese had always enjoyed was also being quickly eroded as the Korean army developed its own arquebus squads.

The wajō were still Japan's trump cards. Protected by shore batteries from Admiral Yi's incursions, and having demonstrated so convincingly at Ulsan how they could stand up to assaults by land, they remained the symbol of a continuing Japanese presence. In addition, Korea's major port of Pusan had never left Japanese control, and was defended as stoutly as the other key communication outlets. Yet there was a limit to the garrison size that the wajō could hold, so in June 1598 Hideyoshi ordered the return to Japan of approximately half the troops who had taken part in the second invasion. Seventy thousand men under Kobayakawa Hideaki, Ukita Hideie, Mōri Hidemoto, Asano Nagayoshi and others left Korea for the last time, leaving 64,700 men behind in the wajō, which were now stretched along a 125-mile

Table 6: Commanders and garrisons of the wajō, 1598

Ulsan	Katō Kiyomasa	10,000
Sŏsaengp'o	Kuroda Nagamasa	5,000
Pusan	Mōri Yoshinari	5,000
Chukdo & Ch'angwŏn	Nabeshima Naoshige & Katsushige	12,000
Kŏje	Yanagawa Tsunanobu	1,000
Kosŏng	Tachibana Muneshige	7,000
Sach'ŏn	Shimazu Yoshihiro	10,000
Namhae	Sō Yoshitomo	1,000
Sunch'ŏn	Konishi Yukinaga	13,700
Total		64,700

belt from Ulsan to Sunch'ŏn. The list in Table 6, which may be compared to the names in Chapter 8, now sheltered half as many men again as the comparable fortress line had done during the occupation, and several of the larger wajō also supported a number of small communications forts in their immediate vicinity.[36]

In common with the Japanese commanders, the Ming regarded the three major fortresses of Ulsan, Sach'ŏn and Sunch'ŏn as the key to the continued presence of Japanese troops on Korean soil, and after a prolonged period of consolidation after Ulsan, the Chinese and Korean armies moved back on to the offensive against these bases in October. While the Chinese fleet sailed down the Yellow Sea coast to join Admiral Yi at his new base on Kokŭm island (Yŏsu was now too close to Sunch'ŏn for comfort), three Chinese armies marched from Seoul towards their respective objectives. The eastern force passed through Ch'ungju, Andong and Kyŏngju and headed for Ulsan. The central force went via Ch'ŏngju, Sangju and Sŏngju to rendezvous at Chinju for an attack on Sach'ŏn, while the western army marched through Kongju, Chŏnju and Namwŏn to attack Sunch'ŏn. This was to be the last major troop movement of the war, and the slowness of contemporary communications ensured that the operation was conducted without the possession of a vital piece of military intelligence, because on 8m 18d (18 September) 1598 Toyotomi Hideyoshi had died peacefully in his sleep at Fushimi castle.

On Hideyoshi's death the administration of Japan fell into the hands of the five senior daimyō (Tokugawa Ieyasu, Maeda Toshiie, Ukita Hideie, Mōri Terumoto and Uesugi Kagekatsu), whom he had appointed to ensure the succession of his infant son Hideyori. These men knew that one of the greatest obstacles to progress in this regard (and progress, in several instances, was a metaphor for the exercise of their own personal ambitions), was the presence of Japanese forces in Korea. But the troops had to be brought home safely, and one factor in ensuring that this happened was to keep the news of Hideyoshi's death secret for as long as possible. For a few days they even managed to keep it a secret from the commanders of the wajō in Korea. A letter to Nabeshima Naoshige seven days after Hideyoshi's death reassured him that the Taikō was recovering from his illness, and that two emissaries would shortly be arriving in Pusan and would instruct Nabeshima further. Shimazu Yoshihiro in Sach'ŏn received a similar letter, which added that the purpose of the emissaries' visit was to bring about a settlement of the war by negotiation. All the Japanese now wanted from Korea in return for their departure were some token tribute goods such as tiger skins. It was a far cry from the conquest of China, the partition of Korea and a Ming princess.

Oblivious of the deal which they were shortly to be offered, the Ming army began the three-pronged campaign again Ulsan, Sach'ŏn and Sunch'ŏn. Ulsan was the first to be attacked in an attempt that was both brief and feeble compared to the herculean operation of January. The Chinese army, which set up a base on a hill to the north of Ulsan on 9m 20d, tried to entice the garrison out for a pitched battle, but Katō Kiyomasa was not tempted, and when any soldiers came near he blasted them with gunfire. By 9m 28d rumours of a relieving army approaching from Pusan were enough to make the Ming withdraw.[37]

The Sach'ŏn operation was a far more serious undertaking. There were two castles at Sach'ŏn. The 'old castle' was a Korean fortress taken over by the Japanese, while the 'new castle' was a wajō built on a promontory two miles to the south-west, where it overlooked the harbour and provided a safe anchorage. It was actually built on the same high ground occupied temporarily by the Japanese prior to the naval battle of Sach'ŏn in 1592, and was defended by the Shimazu of Satsuma province in southern Kyushu under Shimazu Yoshihiro and his son Tadatsune (later to be known as Iehisa), while other Satsuma retainers held four small outposts to the north, including the old castle.

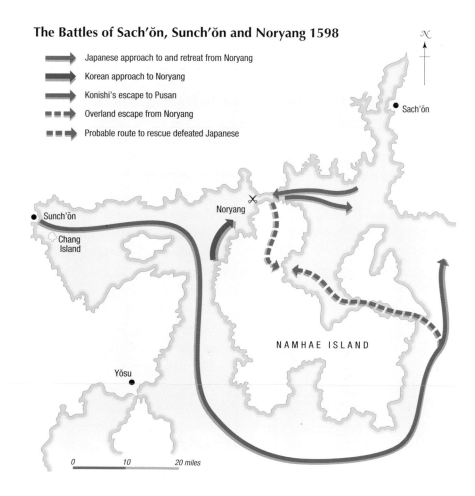

The Battles of Sach'ŏn, Sunch'ŏn and Noryang 1598

- Japanese approach to and retreat from Noryang
- Korean approach to Noryang
- Konishi's escape to Pusan
- Overland escape from Noryang
- Probable route to rescue defeated Japanese

N

- Sach'ŏn
- Noryang
- Sunch'ŏn
- Chang Island
- NAMHAE ISLAND
- Yŏsu

0   10   20 miles

Map of the battles of Sach'ŏn, Sunch'ŏn and Noryang in 1598, showing the escape route used by Konishi Yukinaga.

There is an amusing anecdote concerning the building of Sach'ŏn in *Jōzan Kidan*, which tells of an argument between the veteran Chōsokabe Motochika and a younger samurai about where to place the gunports in the castle's gatehouse. Chōsokabe maintained that gunports should be inserted 'at a level between a man's chest and hips'. His colleague disagreed, saying that gunports should be placed high up on the walls, because low gunports would allow enemy scouts to peer into the castle. 'Let them!' was Chōsokabe's reaction, 'Then they can see how strong it is!'[38]

In preparation for their attack on Sach'ŏn, the Chinese army advanced as far as Chinju, where they sent out scouts across the Nam river. Hearing of their approach, Shimazu evacuated the three forward positions, and pulled them back to the new castle, so the Chinese completed their preliminary advance by burning these three forts to the ground. At midnight on 27d the Ming advanced on the old castle. Its commander had received orders to evacuate it, and was planning to do so the following morning. On being disturbed by the Ming, he calmly opened the gates and drove the vanguard away in classic Satsuma style. As dawn broke on 28d they made another sally out, but were themselves driven away, not into their own castle, but prudently and at speed into the new castle.

Having seen four outposts lost to the Chinese, young Shimazu Tadatsune was for making an immediate attack, but his father forbade it. He reasoned that the Chinese army would wish to waste no time in attacking anyway, and the men of Satsuma were ready for them in their wajō. This assumption proved to be correct, and the Ming army, in three units of right, left and centre, moved in for an attack at about 6.00 a.m. on 10m 1d (30 October) 1598 with a total of 36,700 troops. The Shimazu father and son monitored their movements from the two towers that flanked the eastern gate. Under strict orders from Yoshihiro, the Japanese held their fire, and as one or two men fell dead from Chinese arrows Tadatsune was again for launching an attack, but once more his father urged caution.[39]

By now the Chinese were approaching the walls, and were also attacking the main gate with a curious siege engine. *Seikan roku* calls it a 'wooden lever', while the chronicler of Kawakami's Korean campaign talks of 'gunpowder jars'.[40] It was probably a combination of an iron-tipped battering ram mounted on a

The decisive moment of the battle of Sach'ŏn, when the Satsuma troops sallied out and destroyed the combined battering ram and cannon that had broken down the gate. (ETK)

carriage with a cannon, which is how it is illustrated in *Ehon Taikōki*. The joint effects of cannonball and ram smashed the gate, and soon thousands of Chinese soldiers were milling round the entrance and climbing up the castle walls. 'Lord Yoshihiro, who saw this, gave the order to attack without delay,' writes a commentator in behalf of the Shimazu, 'and all the soldiers as one body fired their arquebuses and mowed down the enemy soldiers who were clinging on to the walls.'[41] At this precise moment the Japanese managed to destroy the combined ram and cannon, causing its stock of gunpowder to explode with great fury right in the middle of the Ming host. A separate Shimazu chronicle implies that the engine was destroyed by a fire bomb thrown from a mortar or a catapult, because 'We flung fire against the gunpowder jars, many of which had been placed within the enemy ranks. It flew from one jar to another, and the tremendous noise was carried to our ears. Consequently the alarming sound terrified all the enemy who were in the vicinity.' [42]

This dramatic action, which is depicted on the painted screen of Sach'ŏn in the Shōko Shuseikan in Kagoshima, proved to be the turning point of the battle. Seeing the confusion in the Chinese ranks, Shimazu Yoshihiro led out his men in a tremendous charge. Many Chinese were cut down, but showing admirable organisation and discipline the army regrouped on a nearby hill and took the fight back to the Japanese. Some Japanese units had now become detached from the main body, and although temporarily spared from Chinese attack, quickly realised their responsibility and the tactical problems they faced. A certain Terayama Hisakane suggested a way out of their difficulty: 'I have no doubt that in the rear ranks of the enemy there are low-ranking soldiers and servants. If we fire bows and arquebuses into their midst it cannot fail to unsettle them. In that case it is unlikely that even the enemy's front ranks will be able to attack.'[43] The plan was carried out rapidly, and soon the Ming

The Chinese burial mound at Sach'ŏn, where are interred the noseless remains of over thirty thousand men killed during the battle. Even today the sheer size of the mound, as indicated by the nearby trees and telegraph poles, has the capacity to shock any visitor.

baggage carriers had broken and were causing unintentional havoc in their own ranks. Yet still the fight continued, and the Shimazu remained outnumbered by three to one until the approach of a relieving army from Tachibana's wajō at Kosŏng tipped the balance in Japan's favour. Thousands of Chinese were killed or pursued back as far as the Nam river, where very few stragglers managed to cross and reach the safety of Chinju.

Sach'ŏn was China's worst defeat at Japanese hands. Pyŏkje had only produced 6,000 Chinese heads, but Sach'ŏn resulted in a casualty rate of over five times that number. The site is now marked by a massive burial mound containing the remains of more than 30,000 Ming troops killed by the Japanese and interred here without their noses, because these important trophies were to be among the last contributions to be lodged within Kyoto's Mimizuka. A few hundred yards further on lies the bluff on which Sach'ŏn castle stood. It is a popular place for cherry blossom festivals in the spring, and contains two prominent memorials to the great struggle fought there in 1592 by Admiral Yi, but has no mention of the disaster of 1598.

The site of the wajō of Sunch'ŏn. The castle occupied the whole of the hog's back in the far distance. On the other side steep cliffs fall down to the sea. The base of the keep can be seen on the horizon.

SHOWDOWN AT SUNCH'ŎN

If modern means of communication had existed in 1598 the catastrophe at Sach'ŏn would have resulted in the proposed attack on the wajō of Sunch'ŏn by the Chinese western column being called off. Instead, as night fell on the battlefield of Sach'ŏn, the battle of Sunch'ŏn was just about to begin.

The presence of Konishi Yukinaga as commander of the wajō of Sunch'ŏn ensured that Japan's Korean War was to end as it had begun, with the leader of the vanguard of 1592 acting as the commander of the fighting rearguard in 1598. Sunch'ŏn castle lay 35 miles due west of Sachŏn and formed the end of the Japanese line. Like Sach'ŏn, Sunch'ŏn was built on high ground overlooking a bay, but in Sunch'ŏn's case the harbour side of the wajō faced east over the bay of Kwangyang from a long hog's back of a hill that is today the finest of all the preserved wajō sites. The natural slopes of the hill, surrounded by sea on all sides except the west, had been cleverly utilised in the traditional Japanese way by cladding them in walls of shaped cyclopean stone, and a similar mound was added on the top to take a rudimentary keep. Sunch'ŏn held 13,700 men, and was well supplied with food and ammunition. Almost five hundred ships lay at anchor in the harbour, waiting for the moment when they could safely evacuate the Japanese army.

The operation against Sunch'ŏn was designed to be a combined land and sea operation between the Chinese Western army and the naval commands of Admiral Yi and his Ming ally Chen Lin. Relations between the two admirals had not always been cordial. The Ming admiral was a bad-tempered bully who intimidated his own men, and even though the combined fleets had achieved some small victories over the Japanese in isolated skirmishes, Chen Lin remained highly sensitive whenever Korean sailors were acknowledged as having fought more effectively than Chinese ones. More seriously, his men were also given to raiding and looting Korean villages with as much impunity as the Japanese pirates, and not even Admiral Yi's own followers had been spared. After a fierce argument the Chinese sailors had been disciplined, and the overall command of joint operations was ceded to Yi Sun-sin.

The naval arm of the Sunch'ŏn attack was therefore to be masterminded by Korea's most skilled and experienced leader. On the morning of 9m 19d a vanguard fleet of 500 Korean ships under Admiral Yi sailed into Kwangyang bay and secured Chang island, which lay within sight of Sunch'ŏn castle and on which the Japanese had stored some equipment and provisions. The fleet then proceeded to surround Sunch'ŏn, and sat there as a floating siege line while the Ming army made similar preparations on land. 'Tonight the ships were brightly illuminated,' wrote Yi in his diary, 'and the enemy must have been very frightened.'[44]

The other arm of the attack on Sunch'ŏn was to see the employment by General Liu Ding of a weird and wonderful collection of Chinese siege engines, including movable shields, siege towers and the so-called 'cloud ladders', wheeled vehicles from which a hinged ladder could be folded out to hook on to a wall. The assembly and installation of these heavy contraptions took several days, but by 9m 28d all was ready, and with this array surrounding Sunch'ŏn from the land, and Yi's ships, now augmented by 1,000 Chinese vessels, on the sea, the combined operation was ready to be set in motion. Supremely confident, Liu Ding offered sixty gold pieces to any Chinese soldier who brought him a Japanese head.

During the daylight hours of 10m 1d, while tens of thousands of their fellow countrymen were being slaughtered 35 miles east of them at Sach'ŏn, the two forces made their final preparations for an attack at dawn the next day. 'At 6.00 a.m. we opened an all-out attack,' wrote Yi. 'Our naval craft advanced to the very front and fought the enemy until noon, inflicting countless casualties

The base of the keep at Sunch'ŏn. Like most of the wajō sites, Sunch'ŏn was built in traditional Japanese style by excavating the natural hill to give a series of overlapping baileys reinforced with stone. A rudimentary keep would have stood upon this carefully shaped stone mound.

upon him. In this battle we also suffered some losses. Sado Commandant Hwang Se-dŭk was hit by an enemy bullet and fell dead.'[45]

While the two navies bombarded Sunch'ŏn from the sea, the Chinese soldiers slowly heaved the cloud ladders and siege towers towards the land walls. Fierce and accurate arquebus fire meant that few of these lumbering monsters got through to clamp their hooks against Sunch'ŏn's parapets, and those that did were met by desperate resistance. Realising how much faith the Chinese were placing in their siege machines Konishi's men dared to sally out of the gates and take on the operatives in hand-to-hand fighting. The lack of an alternative plan of assault was soon made plain. With their siege engines stranded and useless the Chinese pulled back to their lines, while on the sea the turn of the tide provided its own contribution to a temporary allied withdrawal, and the bombardment ceased.

Frustrated by this reversal on land, Liu Ding sent a message to Admiral Chen Lin suggesting a night attack on Sunch'ŏn from the sea. Admiral Yi had grave misgivings about the proposal, but Chen Lin was determined, so Yi was forced to provide support for the Chinese advance. Timing the assault to coincide with the incoming tide just after midnight, Chen Lin rowed in and opened up a close-range bombardment with heavy cannon, which knocked out a considerable section from the Japanese palisades. But within a hour the tide turned, and thirty Chinese ships ran aground. The result was one of those farcical moments that sometimes occur in the bitterest of battles. Not realising that the beaching of the Chinese ships was a mistake, the Japanese troops interpreted the accident as a dramatic attempt at an amphibious landing that had no doubt been timed to coincide with a night attack from the land. The Chinese soldiers on board, however, had no such intentions, and sat there in great fear while they waited for the tide to rise and free them.[46]

The Japanese unit nearest to the site of this unexpected amphibious incursion was commanded by a certain Utsunomiya Kunitsuna. Not daring to wait for confirmation of a land-based attack, he ordered his samurai on to the beach to deal with the seaborne landing. No one was moving on board the Chinese ships, but Utsunomiya's officer Koyama Umanosuke noticed that they were full of troops:

> Whereupon he went round to the stern and saw a rope hanging down. Umanosuke grabbed hold of the rope and climbed up into the ship where, with low thrusts at the enemy who appeared before him, he took some heads. While he kept going Nagasaki Heizō climbed on board and also took some heads. Those on board, thinking that a Japanese army had attacked the ships in large numbers, ended up jumping down one by one from the bows and running away.[47]

The battle of Sunch'ŏn involved the use of Chinese siege equipment such as the 'cloud ladder'. This crude illustration shows how the hinged ladder was swung forward from the wheeled frame to enable soldiers to attack a wall. (From Werner, 1932)

Utsunomiya's unit succeeded in capturing five Chinese ships, an unusual prize for a land-based soldier! The account continues:

> One of them was requested by Matsuura Hōin [Shigenobu]. Two were sent to Japan and placed beside the Kōrai Bridge in Osaka, where they were moored from the first to the third month of the Year of the Snake and became a popular spectacle. The remaining two were burned.[48]

When the tide rose Utsunomiya took the opportunity to launch raids against other Chinese ships as they pulled back. More Japanese units quickly joined in, including Matsuura Shigenobu 'who took 36 helmeted heads', while his retainers 'took as prizes from the enemy's greatest ship the big drum, the bell and other military equipment'.[49]

Writing later in his diary, Admiral Yi expressed regret at the failure of Chen Lin's precipitate action, which had resulted in the loss of 19 Chinese vessels. 'It was a great pity to see him shaken by the shock on his flagship,' he noted.[50] Throughout the operation Yi had provided rear support, and the Japanese were only driven off when Yi's ships went to Chen Lin's rescue. The following morning Yi prepared for an attack of his own, but a strong westerly wind blew up and prevented any approach being made for the next two days, and in his diary entry for 10m 6d Yi notes his disgust at hearing that General Liu Ding, who had no doubt been informed of the simultaneous disaster at Sach'ŏn, had abandoned Sunch'ŏn and retreated north. Now deprived of all support by land, and with two Chinese defeats within two days to demoralise them, Yi and Chen Lin also left Sunch'ŏn a few days later and sailed back to the base on Kokŭm island, leaving a small blockading force in place around Sunch'ŏn.

THE BITTER FAREWELL

With Hideyoshi dead and the Chinese defeated, the Japanese garrisons were now heading for home all along the south coast of Korea. The Ming army of the east, which was monitoring local movements after withdrawing to its base at Kyŏngju, became aware of troops moving out of Ulsan, Sŏsaengp'o and Chukdo and heading for Pusan. There was less movement over in the west because the allied navies were keeping Konishi confined to barracks, but then, on 11m 7d, the news of Hideyoshi's death finally came to the ears of Yi and Chen Lin. It was now certain that Konishi would attempt to escape from Sunch'ŏn, but the allied blockade was tight, so for the last time in the campaign Konishi Yukinaga turned to negotiations to ensure a safe passage. Chen Lin proved quite amenable to his advances, particularly as Konishi's request was backed up with bribes in the form of 'two pigs and two bottles of wine' according to Yi's contemptuous diary entry.[51] By contrast, Admiral Yi Sun-sin was not to be bought at any price and would not agree to lift the blockade.

The Chinese had clearly had enough of war, and as Chen Lin was willing to let the Japanese go without further bloodshed, he proposed to Yi that he, Chen Lin, should conduct an operation against Sō Yoshitomo's small wajō on Namhae island. Apart from the inherent promise of a final portion of military glory, Chen Lin also hoped that Konishi might take advantage of his absence and settle the matter by default by running the blockade. Yi, however, was greatly indignant at the suggestion of an attack on Namhae, which had long been within his sphere of influence. He knew that many Korean civilians were virtual prisoners of the Japanese there, and he feared that the Chinese would be unable to discriminate between them in a raid. Chen's subsequent and outrageous comment that any such Koreans should be regarded as collaborators, who deserved to die anyway, confirmed Yi's worst suspicions about his ally and roused him to fury.[52]

Nevertheless, the result of Konishi's determined pressure on the Chinese admiral ensured that one boat at least was able to escape from Sunch'ŏn. Its commander made contact with Sach'ŏn to coordinate an escape. 'Yesterday two blockade captains . . . chased a medium-sized Japanese vessel fully loaded with provisions that was crossing the sea from Namhae,' wrote Admiral Yi in what was to prove the last diary entry of his life.[53]   The ship was apprehended on its return, but a chain of signal fires then sent plumes of smoke from one wajō to another to inform Konishi that the message had succeeded in getting through. The troops stationed in Sach'ŏn, Kosŏng and Namhae quickly gathered at the agreed rendezvous point in the bay of Sach'ŏn, where they would be joined by Konishi for the voyage home. But when two days had passed and Konishi had not appeared, Shimazu realised that Konishi was still being prevented from leaving. The decision was therefore made to send 500 ships to Sunch'ŏn to run the blockade. The shortest route between the two bays was to head due west, and pass between Namhae island and the Korean mainland through the narrow strait of Noryang.

Scouts and local fishermen informed Admiral Yi of what was happening. Anticipating that the Japanese fleet would take the direct route through the Noryang straits Yi drew up his fleet in the open sea just to the west of the narrow stretch of water. Late at night on 11m 18d Yi was told that the Japanese fleet had sailed into the Noryang strait and were anchored for the night. It was the perfect opportunity for a surprise attack, which was launched at 2.00 a.m. on 11m 19d (17 December) 1598. The battle, most of which took place in the narrow sea area that now lies under the Namhae suspension bridge, was conducted in perfect Korean style, and within hours almost half the Japanese fleet was either broken or burned. Admiral Yi was in the thick of the fighting, and personally wielded a bow when he rowed to the aid of Chen

Lin, whose flagship came under attack from a group of Japanese ships. By the time the dawn was breaking the Japanese ships were retreating and, sensing that this could be the last time for them to come to grips, Yi ordered a vigorous pursuit. It was at that moment, when victory was certain, that a Japanese arquebusier put a bullet into Yi's left armpit. He was dead within minutes. Only three close associates saw the incident, and with his dying breath Yi asked them to keep his death a secret, so his body was covered with a shield and the battle of Noryang continued towards its victorious conclusion.

The death of Admiral Yi Sun-sin, killed on board his flagship at the moment of his final victory like Nelson at Trafalgar, was a tragedy that deprived Korea of its ablest leader and greatest hero. Out of 500 Japanese ships only 50 survived to limp home. Shimazu Yoshihiro himself narrowly escaped death while Tachibana and Sō provided protection from the Chinese ships who harassed them for a considerable distance.[54]

There was only one act left to play in the drama of the Korean evacuation. Many Japanese soldiers and sailors had escaped to land on Namhae island and took temporary refuge in Sō's now deserted wajō. The allied fleet burned any Japanese ships remaining in Noryang, so the survivors faced a long trudge across the mountains to its eastern coast. Five hundred of them were eventually rescued, probably by Konishi's fleet, who took advantage of the battle to slip out of Sunch'ŏn on the morning of 11m 19d. They headed for Kŏje island round the southern end of Namhae and docked at Pusan, Japan's last continental possession, on 11m 20d. Three days later the final evacuation began, and by the beginning of the 12th month, in the dying days of 1598, all the Japanese had disembarked at Hakata, where many heard for the first time the news that Hideyoshi was dead.[55]

The death of Admiral Yi at Noryang, 1598. This painting in the Chesungdang on Hansan island shows Yi dying – like England's Lord Nelson – from a bullet wound as his final victory is secured. In the background a Japanese ship is on fire.

Back in Korea the Chinese and Korean forces began to enter and occupy the now deserted wajō of Ulsan, Sŏsaengp'o, Sach'ŏn and Sunch'ŏn. Admiral Chen Lin even discovered some Japanese stragglers on Namhae island who had not managed to make it to the eastern coast to be rescued by Konishi. They were all beheaded with great glee, and their heads taken to the Korean court as proof of the valuable role played by Korea's Chinese allies, but certain Korean officials suspected that in Chen's desire for a final glorious flourish, the Koreans on Namhae whom he had labelled collaborators had also been cut down, the tragic outcome that the late Admiral Yi Sun-sin had so feared. It was a suitably sad ending to a long and terrible war.

chapter eleven

THE HIGH PRICE
OF KOREAN POTTERY

THE samurai of Japan who followed Toyotomi Hideyoshi's orders to invade Korea were men of war who had inherited a long ancestral tradition of military service and had carried out their leader's commands to the letter. Yet these men who, by accident of history, had been born into their warrior families during the third quarter of the sixteenth century, had in fact taken part in an operation that was unique in Japanese history, because the invasion of Korea was the sole act of aggression mounted by Japan against a foreign country within the space of a thousand years, a remarkable feat of peaceful coexistence that puts most of sixteenth-century Europe to shame.

The war may also have been terrible in its execution, but the events of the seven years in Korea were little different to the depredations wreaked during the Dutch Revolt or the Thirty Years' War. In 1593, for example, soldiers were marching through Ireland committing similar acts of violence to those Korea was witnessing at precisely the same time.[1] The sack of Antwerp in 1576 was an orgy of rape and plunder, and when Maastricht fell in 1579 one third of the city's women and children were slaughtered on the spot or died from the brutalities inflicted upon them.[2] Namwŏn was by no means unique in its horror, and Ōkōchi Hidemoto would have felt quite at home if he had witnessed Turkish troops parading the severed heads of the defenders of Nicosia under the walls of Famagusta in 1571.[3]

To the Katō Kiyomasas of this world, however, the Korean operation was another war under Hideyoshi and another glorious victory. In the absence of newly conquered territory the rewards may have been somewhat intangible, but that was not how the affair was regarded or even recorded, and the years which followed the return to Japan of the invading armies saw the compilation of the chronicles, diaries and family histories concerned with the campaign that provided the bombastic quotations used in the previous chapters.

With the exception of the monk Keinen's remarkable work, these accounts are unashamedly heroic, telling the story of the Korean War in a style that echoes the gunkimono (war tales) of a previous age. Individual prowess, particularly in terms of single combat, is cited and praised so often that one has to look very carefully to discover passages that adequately describe the reality of contemporary warfare, which involved such mundane matters as the marshalling of large infantry squads.

Nor is there any expression of regret or contrition for the devastation the subjects of these tales had unleashed. Passages which at first sight might imply an attempt at justification turn out upon inspection to be merely background colour, or a reminder to the reader of the traditional circumstances of Korea's place in the world with regard to Japan. Japan is 'The Land of the Gods', and it was this myriad of benevolent deities who caused the rain to fall in Manchuria to cover Katō's withdrawal from the Orangai and in Korea during Hosokawa's strategic retreat after the first siege of Chinju. Moreover, the warriors of 1592 were doing no more than following in the footsteps of the Empress Jingū, who had subdued the peninsula a millennium before, carrying in her womb the greatest warrior kami of all, Hachiman Dai Bosatsu, whose presence was felt everywhere, and whose name was invoked by Ōkōchi Hidemoto as he broke into the courtyard at Namwŏn.

Yet the invading troops were also guided, if not actually led, by a man whose military reputation alone had made him into a living legend. To the samurai who had followed Toyotomi Hideyoshi from the siege of Inabayama in 1564 to the stunningly bloodless triumph over the Hōjō at Odawara in 1590, he was already a god of war, with the stature of a deified super-Napoleon, yet a Napoleon who had never known defeat. The image of him that they carried with them to Korea was of the all-conquering figure who had reviewed his troops in Nagoya accompanied by a banner representing every single one of Japan's provinces. Yet to the vast majority of the men in his army their great leader was from then on to become a shadowy and remote figure.

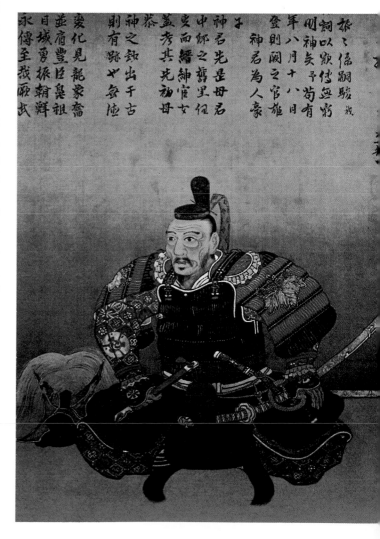

Toyotomi Hideyoshi as a general, the image cherished by all the samurai who followed him so loyally. His paulownia crest is prominently displayed on the shoulder guards of his armour. From a painted scroll in the Hōsei Nikō Kenshōkan, Nagoya.

Throughout the whole of the seven years Hideyoshi never even ventured as far as Tsushima, and the select few of his generals who were actually admitted to his august presence saw only an echo of the hero of Yamazaki, even if he was still the tiny man with the wizened face who believed in his own celestial conception that gave him a destiny that was to lead to India and beyond.

The daimyō who stayed in Japan, however, had ample opportunity to judge Hideyoshi's decline. To them it soon became clear that his glory days were over, that he now preferred to a muddy battlefield the scented chambers of Fushimi castle, where he raged at ambassadors, read despatches and framed orders, and was endlessly tormented by concerns over his succession. When not so occupied he was entertained like the bored monarch he had become, drinking sake and indulging in his passion for the Noh theatre through numerous command performances. Otherwise it was endless tea ceremonies, cherry blossom viewing, and one bizarre fancy dress party held in the gardens of Nagoya castle where Hideyoshi appeared as a melon seller and Maeda Toshiie was attired as a begging monk. As Maeda Gen-i Munehisa had to dress up as a nun on this occasion the situation may have been considerably more trying for them than was the position of their comrades occupying the wajō in Korea.[4]

Yet so strong and unquestioned was this image of Hideyoshi as the great general he had once certainly been, that throughout the seven years of conflict overseas there was no rebellion and no murmur of discontent, because through the medium of conquest his followers were exercising the purpose for which they were fit. The samurai were Hideyoshi's men, who had gone to do their duty and had returned with the proof of it, which mundanely consisted of bringing back to Japan tens of thousands of Korean noses. Ōkōchi Hidemoto provides the best example of the contemporary attitude when he concludes his *Chōsen ki* with a simple balance sheet. One hundred and sixty thousand Japanese troops had gone to Korea, where they had taken 185,738 Korean heads and 29,014 Chinese ones, a grand total of 214,752.[5] The account had therefore ended in credit, in accordance with Hideyoshi's wishes. In a similar vein runs the account of Motoyama Yasumasa, who, like Ōkōchi, refers to the enduring monument to Japanese savagery which is the Mimizuka in Kyoto. Unlike Ōkōchi, however, the Motoyama account does not fail to mention that many of the noses interred therein were not of fighting soldiers but ordinary civilians, because 'Men and women, down to newborn infants, all were wiped out, none was left alive. Their noses were sliced off and pickled in salt.'[6]

Of those who were not slaughtered, the monk Keinen's diary had recorded the sight of Korean captives being led away in chains and bamboo collars by Japanese slave traders. Between fifty and sixty thousand captives are believed to have been transported to Japan. Most were simple peasants, but there were also some men of learning and numerous craftsmen including medicine makers and gold smelters; however, particularly well represented were the potters. The Japanese enthusiasm for the tea ceremony had ensured that at least one aspect of Korean culture was respected when the country was invaded, and it would certainly have astounded some anonymous Korean potter to hear that a simple peasant's rice bowl he had once made was doing service as a treasured and priceless tea vessel, handled by the greatest in the land. Even before the war Hideyoshi had hired two brothers, sons of a Korean-born potter, to make the tiles for the roof of his palace of Jūrakutei, and under the guidance of the famous tea master Sen Rikyu these ceramic craftsmen had developed the unpretentious but highly prized raku style of tea bowl.

When the conquerors prepared to return home the opportunity to enrich their own pottery tradition at so little cost was too good to miss. The Shimazu brought seventy Koreans with them to Satsuma, including several potters, who began ceramic production in three areas, and two centuries later visitors to Satsuma noted the distinctive Korean dress and language of the communities. Not all the kilns were as successful as these, and the low-quality clay that was available for one of the Korean kilns established by Kuroda Nagamasa led to some of his potters being sent back to Korea.[7]

Most of the imported workers, however, were to be associated with successful and continuing production for many years to come, and it is no coincidence that the daimyō who established Korean-operated kilns in their provinces were all passionate devotees of the tea ceremony. Kuroda Nagamasa, who brought back to Japan the Korean stone lantern still standing in the Daitokuji in Kyoto, set up a successful kiln at Takatori using potters brought from Kyŏngsang province. Hosokawa Tadaoki, whose aesthetic sensibilities led to his Korean souvenir collection being enriched by the inclusion of a stone from the Namdaemun gate of Seoul for a garden feature, put his captives to work at Agano. Mōri Terumoto established a kiln at Hagi, while the famous name of Arita porcelain is associated with Imari, a town within the fief of Nabeshima Naoshige, the conqueror of southern Hamgyŏng. Here, in 1616, a Korean potter called Yi Sam-pyŏng discovered deposits of kaolin-rich clay which led to the first production of porcelain in Japan. Karatsu, which, under the name of Nagoya castle, had provided the departure point for the invasions, boasted several kilns in the domains of Nabeshima and Terazawa.[8]

THE FATE OF THE VICTORS

Connoisseurs or otherwise, the daimyō who had fought their way through Korea returned home in 1598 to a Japan that was changed forever. The great Toyotomi Hideyoshi, who had led them to victory in Japan and then sent them to their deaths in Korea, was no more, and had left an infant son to

232 of Samurai Invasion

inherit his domains. The infant in question was not, however, his firstborn son Tsurumatsu, the baby who had been born in 1589 when Hideyoshi was 53. Tsurumatsu, who distinguished himself by urinating in front of the Korean ambassadors in 1591, had died later that same year. This tragic loss had plunged Hideyoshi into profound grief, a state of mind which some historians have blamed for the excesses of the Korean campaign. Fearing that he was too old to produce another heir, Hideyoshi adopted as his successor his nephew Hidetsugu, to whom he passed on the title of Kampaku as preparations for war got under way. Hidetsugu was then 23 years old, and had distinguished himself in many of hs uncle's battles including Nagakute (1584), Negoro (1585), Shikoku (1585) and the final campaign of unification conducted against Kunoe in northern Japan in 1591. As will be recalled from an earlier chapter, it was to Hidetsugu that Hideyoshi had addressed the famous and enthusiastic letter promising him the position of Kampaku of China once victory was secured.

Like Hideyoshi himself, Hidetsugu never crossed over to Korea to inspect his new domains, a matter which apparently irked his uncle, and Hideyoshi soon had other reasons to complain about his nephew's behaviour. With a complete disregard for protocol Hidetsugu had organised a hunting expedition while the nation was still in mourning for the recently deceased Emperor Ogimachi, and had also dared to take his wife and daughter with him on a visit to the monastery of Hieizan, a sanctuary barred to women. In 1593, while receiving such complaints about Hidetsugu's conduct, Hideyoshi was delighted to be informed that his own wife had given birth to a son, and from that moment on Hidetsugu's position grew increasingly perilous.

Tokugawa Ieyasu was but one among several daimyō who correctly anticipated Hidetsugu's ultimate fate and hurried to distance themselves from his interests. Ieyasu's son Hidetada declined an invitation to visit Hidetsugu in case he should be taken and held as a hostage, while Hosokawa Tadaoki borrowed money from Ieyasu to repay his financial debts to Hidetsugu, thus removing a particular element of obligation that might later be brought against him. Perhaps seeking to ingratiate themselves with Hideyoshi, two of the 'Chiefs of Staff' in Korea, Ishida Mitsunari and Mashita Nagamori, then accused Hidetsugu of plotting treason. Taking no chances, Hideyoshi had Hidetsugu confined within the Seiganji, part of the monastery complex on Kōyasan, which was the traditional place of political exile in Japan. One day in 1595 the temple was unexpectedly surrounded by 10,000 men under Fukushima Masanori. Hidetsugu, who still protested his innocence, was ordered to commit seppuku, and when the army returned to Kyoto with the news of a successful conclusion to the operation Hideyoshi ordered the arrest of Hidetsugu's wife, concubines and children, some thirty persons in all, and had them beheaded at the common execution ground.[9]

All the hope of a Toyotomi succession now lay on the shoulders of young Toyotomi Hideyori, because Hideyoshi's half-brother Hashiba Hidenaga, whom Hideyoshi had once considered for the post of Kampaku, was already dead, and Hashiba Hidekatsu, who was the son of Oda Nobunaga and had also been adopted by Hideyoshi, had died in Korea in 1593 after sterling service as commander of the Ninth Division. Anticipating the rivalries that might arise during Hideyori's minority, Hideyoshi had taken great pains to set up a structure for a regency and had ensured that the daimyō swore fealty to it. To this end he nominated not one regent (tairō) but five: Tokugawa Ieyasu, Maeda Toshiie, Uesugi Kagekatsu, Mōri Terumoto and Ukita Hideie, of whom only the last two had seen service in Korea. To assist in the administration he retained the services of the five bugyō he had appointed over a decade before. They were Ishida Mitsunari, Mashita Nagamori (both of whom had gone on to perform similar administrative duties in Korea), Nagatsuka Masaie, Maeda Gen-i Munehisa and Asano Nagamasa. The latter had been one of Hideyoshi's inspectors in Korea, and his son Nagayoshi had fought heroically at Ulsan. Finally, to ensure that there was no friction between the tairō and the bugyō, three so-called chūrō, Nakamura Kazuuji, Horio Yoshiharu and Ikoma Chikamasa, were appointed to an intermediate rank between the two groups, while Katagiri Katsumoto and Koide Masahide were put in charge of Hideyori's education. Having made all parties swear loyalty to Hideyori, Hideyoshi died in the confident belief that his family name would continue.

In 1599 Toyotomi Hideyori, the heir to the most complete empire Japan had seen for four centuries, was just five years old. On the death of Hideyoshi the boy's mother took him to the safety of mighty Ōsaka castle, the most massive of his late father's impregnable fortresses. Ōsaka dominated the east-west lines of communication through Japan at the place where the roads were squeezed to their closest by the narrowness of the neck of navigable terrain, and from within these colossal walls young Hideyori watched helplessly as his inheritance quickly crumbled around him. Within two years of his succession the house of cards that had been the structure of tairō, bugyō and chūrō had collapsed into civil war, and in October 1600, on the muddy fields of Sekigahara, thousands of samurai who had fought for Hideyoshi in Korea now died defending his infant son's inheritance.

It is tempting to see the triumph of Tokugawa Ieyasu, who crushed his rivals among the tairō, bugyō and chūrō at Sekigahara, and was proclaimed Shogun in 1603, as a victory of eastern Japan over the west, or as a defeat of those weakened in Korea at the hands of those who had avoided its bloodletting. The politics of 1600 were, however, far more complex than this, and several prominent names mentioned in previous chapters may be found on both sides of the epic encounter at Sekigahara, although many of the most notable do in fact appear under the list of the dead, defeated or disgraced.

Leading the so-called Western Army, the pro-Hideyori coalition of daimyō who were still nominally loyal to the dying wishes of the great general who had sent them to Korea, was Hideyoshi's bugyō Ishida Mitsunari, who had first attracted Hideyoshi's attentions through his skill at the tea ceremony. Fighting beside him was his former fellow 'Chief of Staff' Ōtani Yoshitsugu, together with Ankokuji Ekei, who had tried to invade Chŏlla province three times. Ukita Hideie, commander in chief during the first invasion, was also a Westerner, as was the loyal and long-suffering Konishi Yukinaga, who had fought the length and breadth of Korea for the entire seven-year operation. Tachibana Muneshige, one of the heroes of Pyŏkje, provided a great service to the Western Army by his capture of Ōtsu castle, but the result was nullified by the defeat at Sekigahara.

Within the ranks of the Eastern Army facing them were Fukushima Masanori of the Fifth Division, Hosokawa Tadaoki of Chinju fame, the erstwhile admirals Katō Yoshiaki and Tōdō Takatora, Asano Nagayoshi of Ulsan and Kuroda Nagamasa, commander of the Third Division, while other Korean veterans provided service to the Tokugawa many miles away. The most notable of these was Katō Kiyomasa, who absorbed the domains of his defeated and disgraced neighbour Konishi as a final settlement of their long rivalry. With his experience at Ulsan still fresh in his mind, Katō Kiyomasa then set out to ensure that his castle at Kumamoto would benefit from the lessons of Chinese siegecraft that he had experienced, raising huge stone walls and adding such ingenious features as floor mats stuffed not with straw but with vegetable stalks that could be eaten in cases of dire emergency. He was not to live to see his ideas tested, but in 1870 Kumamoto withstood a siege from an army wielding modern European weapons, an achievement that would have given the shade of Katō great satisfaction.

Of the waverers at Sekigahara, to whose reluctance and indecision the Tokugawa side owed an acknowledged debt, Mōri Hidemoto had the largest army, and did very little. Being stationed at a distance from the fighting, the closest Mōri got to the action was the sight of Shimazu Yoshihiro, the victor of Sach'ŏn, fleeing across his flanks on the beginning of a long journey back to Satsuma. Hidemoto's uncle Mōri Terumoto was in Ōsaka castle during the battle, and tried to curry favour with Ieyasu by executing the son of Konishi Yukinaga. Wakizaka Yasuharu, the admiral defeated at Hansando, also changed sides from West to East during the battle, but the most dramatic act at Sekigahara was performed by Kobayakawa Takakage's heir Hideaki, the commander in chief during the second invasion. Hideaki had been appointed to this elevated post at the age of twenty and had been denounced as incompetent by the bugyō Ishida Mitsunari. Hideaki's resentment at this treatment received its final expression at Sekigahara, where he abandoned Ishida at a crucial moment in the battle and, when the victory was secured, went on to burn Ishida's castle of Sawayama. Ishida Mitsunari, Konishi Yukinaga and Ankokuji Ekei were captured and eventually beheaded, but few others received such drastic treatment.

THE RESTORATION OF DIPLOMATIC RELATIONS

Personally secure because of his geographical remoteness, Sō Yoshitomo, daimyō of Tsushima, declared his support for Ieyasu's faction prior to Sekigahara, but wisely stayed on his island while the campaign was fought to its conclusion. None felt the effects of the lack of contact with Korea more acutely than Sō, but with the opportunism that had characterised his family for centuries Yoshitomo had begun sending peace feelers to Korea in 1599, only to have three successive messengers taken captive and sent to Beijing by the Chinese troops still stationed in the peninsula. In 1601 an ambassador from Sō succeeded in reaching Seoul, and returned to Tsushima with the message that Korean captives should be sent back to Korea if Japan really sought peace. For her part, Korea saw the normalisation of relations with Japan as an essential step in getting rid of the Chinese armies, who were causing as much devastation as had the Japanese. Sō Yoshitomo responded to the letter by sending home some Korean prisoners, an act that was acknowledged in 1603 when two envoys from the Korean court came to Tsushima. Sō accompanied them on to Kyoto where, in the spring of 1604, they were received by Tokugawa Ieyasu. The meeting was cordial, and led to the repatriation of a further 3,000 Koreans.[10]

In 1606 Korea stepped up its diplomatic efforts by means of a note to Sō Yoshitomo that contained two further demands. It requested a formal letter to be sent from the Shogun asking for peace with Japan, and the extradition to Korea of some Japanese soldiers who had desecrated the royal tombs in Seoul during the invasion. Just as had happened in 1590, Sō found himself placed in the position of being the bearer of an unacceptable demand, and, as also had happened before, he resorted to forgery to solve the problem. His counsellor Yanagawa thereupon sent to Seoul a fabricated letter appearing to come from Ieyasu and asking for peace, together with a group of criminals whose youthful appearance made it most unlikely that it was they who had actually perpetrated the sacrilege in 1592. Nevertheless, as Korea was so desperate for peaceful relations, both deliveries were accepted at face value. The criminals were executed, and the letter was received.

In 1608 a reply was prepared, and a fine Embassy consisting of three officials and an entourage of 270 men arrived at Tsushima. Yanagawa carefully altered the wording of the Korean letter so as not to disclose the existence of the previous forgery, and hastily added a number of expensive presents to the diplomatic gifts that were soon on their way to Edo. By now Ieyasu had retired as Shogun in favour of his son Tokugawa Hidetada, and it was he who received the Embassy that summer. The gifts from Korea to Japan included ginseng and the inevitable tiger skins, and those from Japan to Korea began with silver and fine swords. On the way back the Koreans called in to visit Ieyasu at Shizuoka, then proceeded home after some very satisfactory exchanges. One result was the return to Korea of hundreds more prisoners, and the repatriation of some Japanese who had been taken captive at the end of the war. As a result of his efforts Sō Yoshitomo received an increase in his revenue and a promotion to court rank, and was allowed by Korea to send twenty trading vessels a year from Tsushima. As for the inventive Yanagawa, it is recorded that in 1624 he again tried to tamper with state correspondence between Japan and Korea but was found out and exiled.[11]

Relations between Japan and Korea stayed cool for several more years following the 1608 visit. Then in 1614 the Tokugawa war machine turned against Toyotomi Hideyori in his late father's fortress of Ōsaka, which he had packed with tens of thousands of disaffected samurai who had been dispossessed by the Tokugawa. The subsequent fall of Ōsaka castle in 1615, the death of Hideyori and the extermination of Hideyoshi's remaining descendants prompted the victorious Tokugawa Shogun to send an extraordinary message to Korea that the last survivor of the family who had been Korea's enemy had now been destroyed, and that Korea should congratulate him for it. This brazen effrontery did the trick, and until 1763 Korea continued to send ambassadors to Japan on the occasion of the appointment of a new Shogun. Japan also sent envoys to Korea when there was a change in the Korean monarchy. The appointees to these ambassadorial posts were usually from Tsushima.

THE MANCHU INVASION OF KOREA

The Japanese invasions had left Korea in a sorry state. As much as five-sixths of the cultivable land in Kyŏngsang province alone had been reduced to waste ground and, as the long process of recovery began, Korea suffered another invasion. This one did not come from across the sea but from the old direction of the northern mountains. The Jurchen tribes had united under their leader Nurhachi (1559–1626), who declared war on the Ming in 1616. The Koreans were closely allied to the Ming dynasty who had helped them so much against the Japanese, so they supported the 'parent' nation as China had once helped the child. Despairing of ever persuading the Koreans to change their allegiance,

Nurhachi's heir the Manchu Emperor invaded Korea in 1627 and forced the King to flee to Kanghwa island. The Korean King then pledged allegiance, and the Manchus withdrew, but with the accession of a new King the Koreans repudiated their promise and began preparing for war. Fortresses on Kanghwa and the mountain castle of Namhansansŏng to the south of Seoul were repaired and extended.

In January 1636 the Manchus, who now called themselves the Qing dynasty of China, invaded Korea again, crossing the frozen Yalu on the ice with perhaps as many as 100,000 men. Their advance was so rapid that Kaesŏng fell within five days. The King sent the royal family to Kanghwa island, intending to follow himself, but the Manchus cut the road and forced the King to flee south to Namhansansŏng. The mountain fortress was surrounded, and after a 45-day siege, with starvation looming, the King surrendered. No Korean king had ever surrendered to a foreign enemy before, be they Mongol, Ming or Japanese, but in 1637 the present incumbent had no choice. When the news reached Kanghwa island the women of the court threw themselves into the sea to avoid capture, and in a brave gesture a loyal retainer called Kim San-yong took the ruling family's ancestral tablets into the pavilion over the south gate. Here he ignited a cache of gunpowder and blew everything to smithereens.

The Qing proved to be generous overlords, and allowed Korea to retain its own national identity and its own sovereign dynasty of Chosŏn, which lasted

A Korean official weeps as he visits the countryside and sees the havoc wreaked by the invasion. (ETK)

until 1910. King Hyojong, who reigned from 1649 to 1659, took a keen interest in his country's defence, encouraging the development of muskets and cannon and the construction of walls. In 1654 and again in 1658 the Qing demanded Korean musketeers to help them fight the Russians. The strength of the Korean navy was also maintained, with the inclusion of several turtle ships among the fleet. The construction of walls was a particular concern of the reformer Yu Hyŏng-wŏn, but, as with his namesake Yu Sŏng-nyong, difficulties of meeting the enormous demands on labour greatly restricted such development until 1794, when work began on the fortress of Hwasŏng, which encircles the city of Suwŏn. The intention was to move the capital from Seoul to Suwŏn, and although this was never done the result was the production of one of the world's finest walled cities. The walls snake up the central mountain and then complete a defensive ring at a lower level. Many excellent defensive features may be noted. There are artillery bastions and stone lookout towers reminiscent of European models, together with floodgates and a unique beacon tower with its beacon chimneys built into the top of the wall. It is interesting to note that Hwasŏng is essentially a development of the native Korean style of fortification that the Japanese so despised, while the invaders' own coastal wajō began to crumble back into the Korean fields on which they had been raised.

Back in Japan the transformation of its society that was to produce two more centuries of the 'Pax Tokugawa' continued to wipe from the collective memory the experience of an ill-judged and ill-planned overseas adventure. In time all the memoirs and family histories were completed, and the emphasis shifted to the achievements of the Tokugawa rather than the failure of the Toyotomi. The overcoming of the Shimabara Rebellion of 1638 finally ensured that the concept of a Christian daimyō, as expressed so well by Konishi Yukinaga, no longer existed, and the closing of Japan to European trade in 1639 marked a very real gesture of a nation turning its back on the outside world. It was to be two hundred years before a new Japan would lift its eyes again towards conquest in Korea and China, a time when the exploits of such heroes as Katō Kiyomasa would be rediscovered and used as exemplars, just as Katō himself had believed in the myth of Empress Jingū.

Finally, in the year 1662, there went as a guest to the White Jade Pavilion Ukita Hideie, the commander in chief during the first invasion of Korea seventy years before. This remarkable man, who had been adopted by Hideyoshi and had once been a candidate for Kampaku of Japan, had escaped from the field of Sekigahara to distant Satsuma, where he was protected by the Shimazu until 1603. Old Shimazu Yoshihiro, the victor of Sach'ŏn, had also fled from Sekigahara and was forced to cede his domains to his son Tadatsune, who had fought beside him in Korea. When Tokugawa Ieyasu became Shogun in 1603 Tadatsune was required to pay homage, and submitted so completely to Ieyasu that he even took Ieyasu's former surname of Matsudaira and one syllable of his given name, becoming Matsudaira Iehisa. Having escaped so lightly and been restored so fully, there was no room for a Sekigahara fugitive in Kagoshima, so Ukita Hideie was betrayed.

On being handed over to the Tokugawa, Hideie shaved his head and accepted exile on the tiny island of Hachijō, where he had much opportunity for reflection on his momentous contribution to the history of East Asia and the changes in Japanese society that had followed it. All that Japan now saw of marching armies were the interminable processions of the daimyō on their way to pay their respects to the fourth Tokugawa Shogun, Ietsuna, whose contribution to Japanese culture was the banning of any written material that contained the slightest reference to the government of Japan. Meanwhile vessels still arrived in Nagasaki bringing Korean tea bowls, and exiles from that country still gathered to weep in front of the mound of noses in Kyoto. Through all these years Ukita Hideie, who had once effectively acted as King of Korea, stayed on Hachijōjima, unknown and forgotten, living a life of quiet meditation to the ripe old age of ninety, and eventually dying in 1662 as the last survivor of Japan's Korean War.

The Mimizuka from a painted screen in the Watanabe collection, Tottori. People dressed in Korean costume are shown riding nearby.

appendix I

ORDER OF BATTLE FOR THE FIRST INVASION

FIRST DIVISION		18,700
Konishi Yukinaga	7,000	
Sō Yoshitomo	5,000	
Matsuura Shigenobu	3,000	
Ōmura Yoshiaki	1,000	
Arima Harunobu	2,000	
Gotō Sumiharu	700	

SECOND DIVISION		22,800
Katō Kiyomasa	10,000	
Nabeshima Naoshige	12,000	
Sagara Nagatsune	800	

THIRD DIVISION		11,000
Kuroda Nagamasa	5,000	
Ōtomo Yoshimune	6,000	

FOURTH DIVISION		17,000
Mōri Yoshinari	2,000	
Shimazu Yoshihiro	10,000	
Takahashi Mototane	2,000	
Akizuki Tanenaga	1,000	
Itō Yūbei	1,000	
Shimazu Tadatsune	2,000	

FIFTH DIVISION		25,100
Fukushima Masanori	4,800	
Toda Katsutaka	3,900	
Chōsokabe Motochika	3,000	
Hachisuka Iemasa	7,200	
Ikoma Chikamasa	5,500	
Kurushima Michiyuki	700	

SIXTH DIVISION		15,700
Kobayakawa Takakage	10,000	
Mōri Hidekane	1,500	
Tachibana Muneshige	2,500	
Takahashi Munemasa	800	
Chikushi Hirokado	900	

SEVENTH DIVISION		30,000
Mōri Terumoto	30,000	
Kikkawa Hiroie		
Mōri Motoyasu		

EIGHTH DIVISION		10,000
Ukita Hideie	10,000	

NINTH DIVISION		11,500
Hashiba Hidekatsu	8,000	
Hosokawa Tadaoki	3,500	

TENTH DIVISION		12,000
Miyabe Nagahiro	2,000	
Kinoshita Shigekata	850	
Kakiya Tsunefusa	400	
Kamei Korenori	1,000	
Nanjō Motokiyo	1,500	
Saimura Hirohide	800	
Akashi Norizane	800	
Bessho Yoshiharu	500	
Nakagawa Hidemasa	3,000	
Inaba Sadamichi	1,400	[1]

appendix II

ORDER OF BATTLE FOR THE SECOND INVASION

COMMANDER IN CHIEF   Kobayakawa Hideaki

THE ARMY OF THE RIGHT		
Mōri Hidemoto	30,000	
Katō Kiyomasa	10,000	
Kuroda Nagamasa	5,000	
Nabeshima Naoshige/Katsushige	12,000	
Ikeda Hideuji	2,800	
Chōsokabe Motochika	3,000	
Nakagawa Hidenari	2,500	
Total:	**65,300**	

APPOINTED AS INSPECTORS TO
THE ARMY OF THE RIGHT:
Kobayakawa Nagamasa
Kakimi Kazunao
Kumagai Naomori

THE ARMY OF THE LEFT

Ukita Hideie	10,000
Konishi Yukinaga	7,000
Sō Yoshitomo	1,000
Matsuura Shigenobu	3,000
Arima Harunobu	2,000
Ōmura Yoshiaki	1,000
Gotō Sumiharu	700
Hachisuka Iemasa	7,200
Mōri Yoshinari/Katsunari	2,000
Ikoma Kazumasa	2,700
Shimazu Yoshihiro	10,000
Shimazu Tadatsune	800
Akizuki Tanenaga	300
Takahashi Mototane	600
Itō Yūbei	500
Sagara Yoriyasu	800
Total	**49,600**

APPOINTED AS INSPECTORS TO THE ARMY OF THE LEFT
Ōta Kazuyoshi
Takenaka Shigetoshi

NAVAL COMMAND

Tōdō Takatora	2,800
Katō Yoshiaki	2,400
Wakizaka Yasuharu	1,200
Kurushima Michichika	600
Mitaira Sa'emon	200
Total	**7,200**

**COMMANDERS OF THE WAJŌ AT THE TIME
OF THE SECOND INVASION**

Sŏsaengp'o	Asana Nagayoshi	3,000
Pusan	Kobayakawa Hideaki	10,000
Angolp'o	Tachibana Munetora	5,000
Chukdo	Mōri Hidekane	1,000
Kadŏk (first wajō)	Chikushi Hirokado	500
Kadŏk (second wajō)	Takahashi Munemasu	500 [2]

appendix III
THE LIST OF HEADS AT NAMWŎN

The record of heads taken during a battle was a very important document. The following extract from the *Chōsen ki* of Ōkōchi Hidemoto, which refers to the siege of Namwŏn, is an excellent example. The heads are listed in four sections relating to the four walls of Namwŏn, and it is not surprising to find that Ōkōchi begins with the exploits of his own unit under Ōta Hida no kami Kazuyoshi, or that there is considerable more detail included for these warriors. The Japanese names are listed exactly as given in Ōkōchi's record, where the surnames are accompanied by various honorary titles rather than the more familiar given names listed in Appendix II. For example, Konishi Settsu no kami is Konishi Yukinaga. There is one mistake. The 'Magistrate of Kyŏngju, general of 20,000' was in fact Yi Ch'un-wŏn, the Magistrate of Kwangju.

FIRST
The retainers of Ōta Hida no kami in the vanguard:
Resident in Echizen province – Kutsumi Heizō – two heads taken
Resident in Mikawa province – Ōkōchi Shigeza'emon – three heads,
    including the General and Magistrate of Kyŏngju, a general of 20,000 horsemen
Resident in Ōmi province – Kiyomizu Yaichirō – one head

Resident in Ise province – Toyoshima Kinza'emon – one head

Resident in Kii province – Danzuka Genshirō – one head

The first head at Namwŏn (was taken by)

Resident in Kii province – Kishi Rokudayū – one head

Hida no kami's total heads – 119.

SECOND

The retainers of Tōdō Sada no kami in the vanguard:

Resident in Ōmi province – Tōdō Niza'emonnojō – two heads

Resident in Ōmi province – Tōdō Shinshichirō – three heads

Resident in Mino province – Tōdō Yo'emonnojō – three heads

Resident in Ōmi province – Tōdō Sakubeinojō – three heads

Sada no kami's total heads – 260.

Number of heads – 622 – (Ukita) Bizen Chūnagon.

(Together with) Hida no kami and Sado no kami, the grand total of heads taken on the southern side by the above three leaders is 1,001.

NUMBER OF HEADS:

64 – Takenaka Iyo no kami

879 – Konishi Settsu no kami

91 – Wakizaka Chūmushōyū

The grand total of heads taken on the western side by the above three leaders is 1,034.

NUMBER OF HEADS:

51 – Katō Samanosuke

421 – Hashiba Hyōgo no kami

461 – Kurushima Izumo no kami

18 – between Suga Saburoheinojō and Sa'emon Hachirō of the same name.

The grand total of heads taken on the northern side by the above five leaders is 951.

NUMBER OF HEADS:

40 – Mōri Hyōbudayū		35 – Sagara Sabeisa
468 – Hachisuka Awa no kami		17 – Shimazu Matashichirō
11 – Ikoma Gagaku no kami		35 – Akizuki Saburō
8 – Ikoma Sanuki no kami		25 – Takahashi Kurō
50 – Mōri Iki no kami		21 – Itō Hyōbudayū
30 – Mōri Buzen no kami		

The grand total of heads taken on the eastern side by these eleven leaders is 740.

The number of all the above heads, in total, is 3,726, as checked by the bugyō.

Note – As for the head of the Magistrate and General, this head (has been kept) as it was. For all the others only the noses have been kept, and they have all been put into salt and lime.[3]

appendix IV

THE TURTLE SHIP

THE exact size and appearance of Yi Sun-sin's famous turtle ship has been a matter of controversy ever since the illustrious admiral's death. Apart from brief descriptions in his own diaries, we are largely dependent upon an eyewitness account by Yi's nephew Yi Pun, who produced a biography of his uncle. In it he writes:

> He invented a warship of the same size as a p'anoksŏn. On its upper deck were driven iron spikes to pierce the feet of any enemy fighters jumping on it. The only opening was a narrow passage in the shape of a cross on the surface for its own crew to traverse freely. At the bow was a dragon head in whose mouth (on either side?) were the muzzles of guns and another gun was at the stern. There were six gun ports each, port and starboard, on the lower decks. Since it was built in the shape of a big sea turtle it was called kŏbuksŏn. When engaging the enemy wooden vessels in a battle, the upper deck was covered with straw mats to conceal the spikes. It rode the waves swiftly in all winds and its cannon balls and fire arrows sent destruction to the enemy targets as it darted at the front, leading our fleet to victory.[4]

In 1795 was published *Ch'ungmu-kong Chŏnsŏ* (The Complete Works of Admiral Yi) which combined Yi's War Diaries and Memorials to Court. The editor added some details about the turtle ships, though even he admitted that the material available to him was sparse. Much confusion has been caused ever since by the fact that he included not one but two drawings of a turtle ship which differ in certain details from each other. The vessels illustrated are identified as the 'T'ongjeyŏng Turtle Ship' and the 'Chŏlla Chwasuyŏng Turtle Ship' respectively. According to a book by Sang-woon Jeon published in 1974 the description and drawing of the T'ongjeyŏng ship is said to be based on information the author possessed about the turtle ships of the fifteenth century, while the Chwasuyŏng model is based on an existing turtle ship still around in 1795 and said to be

very close to Yi's first 'revival' turtle ship of 1592. Chŏlla Chwasuyŏng (Left Naval Station of Chŏllado) is Yŏsu, which was Yi's headquarters until 1593, when he moved to Hansando island.[5]

It would appear that Yi took this earlier model and re-designed it to produce the turtle ship that he used in the war against Japan. Supplementary comments in the *Ch'ungmu-kong Chŏnsŏ* indicate that the ships were of a similar size overall except for a small increase in height of the bulwarks in the Chwasuyŏng ship. The main points of difference between the two are essentially the improvements that Yi introduced when he revived the design. The first difference lies in the number of oars, of which there are ten each side for the T'ongjeyŏng ship and eight for the Chwasuyŏng. The design of the 'turtle shell' roof in the earlier T'ongjey'ŏng ship is of overlapping planks, while the Chwasuyŏng ship has a smooth surface covered with something which has a pronounced hexagonal pattern. On the T'ongjey'ŏng ship the bulwarks are a single line, while the Chwasuyŏng ship has an additional narrow layer allowing extra weapon or ventilation slits above what are clearly cannon ports, hence the increased height of the bulwarks.

In 1933 the Turtle Ship received the attention of the missionary and antiquarian Horace Underwood, who devoted several pages to it in his book *Korean Boats and Ships*. Underwood made scale drawings of the turtle ship based on the information in the *Ch'ungmu-kong Chŏnsŏ*. He was not a naval architect, nor was he aware of the important distinction between the T'ongjeyŏng ship of 1414 and Yi's improved Chwasuyŏng ship of 1592. He appears to have concluded that both drawings were different attempts to reconstruct the same ship, and his own plans are therefore something of a compromise between the two, augmented with some speculation. Unlike more recent reconstructions, Underwood roofed his turtle ship from bow to stern, making the end of the 'tail' like a pair of fins.[6]

Underwood also acknowledged in particular a major problem with the location of the oars, because both drawings in the *Ch'ungmu-kong Chŏnsŏ* are very ambiguous. If the oars project outwards and almost horizontally from the sides of the ship then the location of the rowers must be near the ship's bottom. If they project downwards from the ship's deck then this would require a certain amount of overhang by the deck and bulwarks, a factor that is not mentioned in the account of the dimensions quoted in the *Ch'ungmu-kong Chŏnsŏ*. Underwood favoured the former model, largely because to place the oarsmen in with the fighting men would have crammed too many people into a small space.

This was the conclusion shared by the makers of the first scale model of a turtle ship, which was produced in 1969 and is now on show in the Hyŏnch'ungsa Shrine to Admiral Yi. It has eight oars low down on each side projecting outwards, and is at a scale of 1:6. A very similar model with ten oars was produced at about the same time in North Korea, and is displayed in the Central Historical Museum in P'yŏngyang. Both models take all their other details from the drawing of the Chwasuyŏng ship, including the flush 'turtle shell' and the presence of two heads at the bow – the raised dragon's head, and the smaller 'devil's face' below.

In 1975 the subject was tackled afresh by Korean scholars, who produced detailed scale drawings of the Chwasuyŏng ship. The major difference from Underwood's earlier reconstruction is that they decided that the oars must project downwards from an overhanging deck. This allows much more deck space for gunners and oarsmen, thus overcoming Underwood's objections. The absence of oarsmen from below decks also allows space for the cabins which are a feature of the historical record, and is more likely in view of the water which lower oar holes would probably allow to enter the ship.

The 1975 drawings based on the Chwasuyŏng ship have now become accepted as the most likely model for Yi's turtle ship, and have therefore been used as the template for every subsequent reconstruction. Nowadays a model of scale 1:5 may be seen at Noryang on Namhae island. In the War Memorial in Seoul (opened in 1994) is a magnificent turtle ship at a scale of 1:2.5, while at Yŏsu visitors can go on board the superb 1:1 turtle ship lying at anchor. All are practically identical in their features, being based on the Chwasuyŏng model with oars projecting downwards from an overhanging deck. Smaller models may also be found in several museums in Korea and around the world.

The most cherished belief of all about the turtle ship is that it was the world's first ironclad battleship. It is accepted by all authorities that the curved 'turtle shell' of the roof was covered with spikes to discourage boarding, but this is all in the historical record that implies armour plating except for the iron reinforcements noted above between joints in the bulwarks. These are, however, little more than large-scale versions of the iron brackets to be found at the corners of Korean and Japanese chests of drawers, so it is unlikely that these would lead to claims of the turtle being an ironclad ship. However, the claim that the turtle ship was the world's first ironclad battleship has long been supported in Korea, and such a belief may also have been shared by the Japanese who suffered its attacks, as shown in the words 'covered in iron' in the Angolp'o account quoted earlier. Also, in February 1593 the Japanese government ordered the daimyō to supply iron plate for use in building warships, possibly as a reaction to such reports. Tokugawa Ieyasu's provision of iron plates for this purpose was his main contribution to the war effort.[7]

It is also fascinating to note that when Korea found itself under threat from the French Navy at the end of the nineteenth century because of the persecution of Christians, an unfortunate official was commissioned 'to build an ironclad ship like the turtle ship'. In spite of enormous expense and a genuine fear for his life should the project fail, the vessel very unobligingly refused to float! As we do not know how much of his 'turtle' the unfortunate designer tried to cover in iron, his experience should not be allowed to rule out a limited amount of armour plating in 1592. The strongest evidence for an armoured turtle shell is found in the 1795 drawing of the Chwasuyŏng ship, where the turtle shell roof is shown as having a very distinctive hexagonal pattern, implying that some material has been overlaid on to the planking. One interpretation of this has been to see each hexagon as a metal plate from the centre of which the spikes protrude. This has been reproduced in the full-scale replica at Yŏsu and the ship in the War Memorial in Seoul. As a result, the two most prominent modern reconstructions are therefore of a partially ironclad vessel, but it is impossible to tell whether this is a result of original research or just wishful thinking. Nagging doubts must remain, particularly because neither Yi nor his nephew mention iron plates around the spikes that both so proudly describe. However, as the very concept of an ironclad battleship is a modern idea unknown to contemporary Korea they may simply have accepted the existence of these plates without feeling the need to make a particular comment.

NOTES

WEIGHTS AND MEASURES

1 monme	3.75 gm
1 shaku	30.3 cm
1 ken	1.8 m
1 chō	109 m
1 ri	3.93 km
1 koku	180 l

REFERENCES

References are cited in the notes using the Harvard system, with fuller references being included for most primary sources, both to their original authorship and their location in published work. The following abbreviations are used:

CNE   Kuwada *et. al* (eds.), 1965, *Chōsen no eki*
          (Nihon no Senshi Vol. 5)
TASJ   Transactions of the Asiatic Society of Japan
TKBRAS   Transactions of the Korean Branch of the
          Royal Asiatic Society
ZGR   *Zoku gunsho ruijū* Series (Zoku Gunsho
          Ruijū Kanseikai, 1933)
ETK   Takenouchi, Kazusai, 1802, *Ehon Taikōki*
          (cited in picture captions as 'ETK detail'
          where not all of a page opening has been used)

GENERAL SOURCES

To the popular mind, the Hideyoshi invasion is proof that Korea has no real military tradition of its own, being merely a pawn in the power game between the great military blocs of China and Japan. An eternally weak and backward Korea is seen as being subject to repeated invasions from Chinese, Mongol, Japanese and tribal armies, each of which lays Korea waste in a short time with little resistance. This erroneous attitude, which overlooks the fact that Korea was independent for most of its recorded history, was once also held by respected scholars; one of the few articles in English ever published about Korean weapons and armour begins with the words, 'The story of Korean arms is a tragedy', and describes the relationship between the Koreans and warfare as 'a people driven in desperation to a task for which they

had no heart, forced to learn an art for which they had no natural aptitude' (Boots 1934:1).

This caricature of Korea as a land of incompetent victims was nurtured for political reasons during the Japanese occupation between 1910 and 1945, and it is only since World War II that Korean researchers have had the opportunity to question the myth of Korean weakness and reveal the military skills that lay behind Korea's long independence and its successful resistance to invasions. Foremost among these efforts has been the establishment of the War Memorial Museum in Seoul, whose superb collections have provided the basis for careful study and much reflection.

In my translations from primary sources I have used Korean place names rather than the Japanese versions of the names that were used in the old Japanese chronicles and continued during the Occupation. So, for example, my translations from *Kuroda Kafu* refer to the siege of 'P'yŏngyang' rather than 'Heijō' as it reads in the original.

The paucity of accounts of the war in western languages reflects the overall neglect of the topic. The chapter by Griffis in his book of 1882, the works of Hulbert (1895), Murdoch (1925) and the series of articles by Aston (1878–83) have long provided the main sources of information in English. Modern western scholarship on the Korean War is almost exclusively provided by Jurgis Elisonas (George Elison) whose chapter in Volume IV of Hall's *The Cambridge History of Japan* (1991) is the finest overall account of the war to have been published in English. His even-handed treatment of the subject, and in particular his introduction to the West of Keinen's *Chōsen Nichinichi ki* (Elison, 1988) broke new ground.

Early Japanese works such as Ikeuchi (1936) inevitably took a strongly imperialist line, reflecting the sentiments contained in the contemporary diaries and chronicles of the Korean Invasions, many of which appeared in printed form during the 1920s and 1930s in the series *Zoku gunshō ruijū*. In 1965, however, there appeared the work *Chōsen no eki*, volume 5 in the series *Nihon no Senshi* by the Japanese General Staff (cited here as CNE), which relates the events of the war in a straightforward, unglorified style, and includes an extremely valuable compilation of primary source material selected from the contemporary chronicles.

It was not until the 1970s that Korean sources became generally available to western scholars. In 1972 Bacon published the first part of what was intended to be a complete translation of Yu Sŏng-nyong's *Chingbirok*. Sadly, he did not live to finish this important work. However, in 1978 Park published *Admiral Yi Sun-shin and his Turtleboat Armada*, the first work in English to be written from the Korean point of view, which, although a popular work, contains numerous quotations from *Chingbirok*, as does Palais (1996). The most valuable primary source material translated at this time is undoubtedly the *Imjin Changch'o* (Memorials to Court) and *Nanjung Ilgi* (War Diaries) of the famous Admiral Yi Sunsin, two vital compendia giving highly detailed coverage by a reliable eyewitness.

NOTES TO CHAPTER 1:
KOREA AND JAPAN

1. Covell & Covell (1984).
2. See Palais (1996), which provides much of the material for this chapter. For information on the slave system in Korea see Peterson (1985) and Salem (1978).
3. See the general works on Korean history such as Henthorn (1971).
4. Bacon (1972:9).
5. Kim (1978:16).
6. Bacon (1972:18).
7. Bacon (1972:18).
8. Bacon (1972:18).
9. Bacon (1972:21).
10. Bacon (1972:19).
11. Palais (1996:516).
12. Ha (1981:4).
13. Ha (1981:8).
14. Ha (1981:14).
15. Ha (1981:5).

NOTES TO CHAPTER 2:
JAPAN AND KOREA

1. The standard biography of Toyotomi Hideyoshi is Berry (1982). For selections from his personal correspondence see Boscaro (1975).
2. Most of the material on the Japanese pirates has been drawn from the works of Hazard (1967a, 1967b) and the chapter by Elisonas in Hall (ed.) (1991).
3. Tanaka (1977:159-178).
4. The full text is in Tsunoda *et. al.* (1958:321).
5. Bacon (1972:13).
6. In addition to Bacon's translation of *Chingbirok*, much material concerning the Korean embassy has been drawn from the interesting article by Stramigioli (1954).
7. Bacon (1972:14).
8. As translated by Stramigioli (1954:88).
9. Bacon (1972:17).

NOTES TO CHAPTER 3:
THE YEAR OF THE DRAGON

1. Nukii (1992:24).
2. Cooper (1974:136).
3. The additional information about the quotas is from Park (1978:61).
4. Elisonas in Hall (ed.) (1991:269).
5. Elisonas in Hall (ed.) (1991:273).
6. The data appears in CNE (1965:77). I have grouped the types into the two categories shown here.
7. Asakawa (1929:333).
8. Asakawa (1929:393).
9. Shimoyama (1990:34).
10. *Matsuura Hōin Seikan Nikki* in CNE (1965:252).
11. *Matsuura Hōin Seikan Nikki* in CNE (1965:252) .
12. *Taikōki* in Yoshida (1979:102).
13. *Yoshino Jingoza'emon oboegaki* in ZGR (1933:379).
14. *Yoshino Jingoza'emon oboegaki* in ZGR (1933:379).
15. CNE (1965:255).
16. From the captions to the pictures in the Ch'ungnyŏlsa Shrine at Tongnae.
17. From the extraordinary collection of Korean tales assembled by Ha (1983:1676).
18. Kondō (1977:102;111).
19. CNE (1965: 115).
20. Ha (1981:52).
21. *Kuroda Kafu* in CNE (1965:255).
22. Park (1978:102).
23. Park (1978:102).
24. *Taikōki* in Yoshida (1979:104).
25. CNE (1965:118).
26. CNE (1965:123).
27. CNE (1965:122).
28. Park (1978:104) from an unidentified source.
29. *Taikōki* in Yoshida (1979:111).
30. *Taikōki* in Yoshida (1979:112).
31. *Taikōki* in Yoshida (1979:113).
32. *Taikōki* in Yoshida (1979:114).

NOTES TO CHAPTER 4:
A SLOW MARCH TO CHINA

1. Tsunoda *et.al.* (1958:318).
2. Tsunoda *et.al.* (1958:319).
3. Park (1978:110).
4. CNE (1965:132).
5. *Wakizaka ki* in ZGR (1933: 439).
6. *Kuroda Kafu* in CNE (1965:257).

7. *Kuroda Kafu* in CNE (1965:257).

8. *Kuroda Kafu* in CNE (1965:258).

9. Park (1978:118).

10. Shimokawa (1907:299). The chronicle *Kiyomasa Kōrai no jin oboegaki* in Shimokawa (1907), together with Ikeuchi (1936) and CNE (1965) are the major sources for the campaign.

11. Shimokawa (1907:300).

12. Shimokawa (1907:300).

13. Shimokawa (1907:300).

14. Shimokawa (1907:300).

15. Ikeuchi (1936:14).

16. Shimokawa (1907:302).

17. Ikeuchi (1936:15).

NOTES TO CHAPTER 5:
THE DEFEAT OF THE JAPANESE ARMADA

1. The main sources for this chapter are *Nanjung Ilgi: The War Diary of Admiral Yi Sun-sin*, translated by Ha, Tae-hung and edited by Sohn Pow-key, cited here as Ha (1977), and *Imjin Changcho: Admiral Yi Sun-sin's Memorials to Court*, translated by Ha Tae-hung and edited by Lee Chong-young, cited as Ha (1981). The latter volume includes the biography of Yi written by his nephew Yi Pun.

2. Ha 1981:19.

3. Ha 1981:22.

4. Ha 1981:23.

5. Ha 1981:25.

6. Ha 1981:26.

7. Ha 1981:27.

8. Ha 1981:29.

9. Ha 1981:27.

10. Ha 1981:29.

11. Kim (1994:278).

12. Kim (1994:281).

13. Kim (1994:280).

14. Examples of these cannon and missiles are illustrated in the catalogue of the War Memorial, Seoul (where they are on display) and in Udagawa (1993a:117-18).

15. Ha (1981:30).

16. Ha (1981:31).

17. Ha (1981:32).

18. Ha (1981:34).

19. Ha (1981:36).

20. Ha (1981:37).

21. Ha (1981:37).

22. Ha (1981:38).

23. Ha (1981:40).

24. Ha (1981:40).

25. Jeon (1974:215).

26. Ha (1977:7).

27. Ha (1977:14).

28. Ha (1977:16).

29. Ha (1981:41) See also the account by Yi's nephew quoted here in Appendix IV.

30. Ha (1981:42).

31. Ha (1981:42). The account of the battle of Sach'ŏn given by Sadler (1937b:188) is unfortunately completely wrong, because the account he quotes from *Taikōki* is in fact from *Ehon Taikōki*, a historical romance based on the life of Hideyoshi, which has many embellishments, including a passage claiming that Wakizaka Yasuharu actually boarded and captured a turtle ship.

32. Ha (1981:43).

33. Ha (1981:44).

34. Ha (1981:43).

35. Ha (1981:47).

36. Ha (1981:48).

37. Ha (1981:51).

38. Ha (1981:49).

39. Ha (1981:54).

40. *Wakizaka ki* in ZGR (1933: 440).

41. Ha (1981:57).

42. Ha (1981:58).

43. *Wakizaka ki* in ZGR (1933:440).

44. Ha (1981:58).

45. Ha (1981:59).

46. Ha (1981:59).

47. *Wakizaka ki* in ZGR (1933:440).

48. *Wakizaka ki* in ZGR (1933:440).

49. *Wakizaka ki* in ZGR (1933:440).

50. Ha (1981:60).

51. *Kōrai Funa Senki* in CNE (1965:262).

52. Ha (1981:61).

53. *Kōrai Funa Senki* in CNE (1965:262).

54. *Shima Gunki* in CNE (1965:262).

55. *Shima Gunki* in CNE (1965:262).

56. *Shima Gunki* in CNE (1965:262).

57. Ha (1981:62).

58. Ha (1981:63).

59. Park (1978:170).

NOTES TO CHAPTER 6:
SOUTH TO THE NAKTONG – NORTH TO
THE YALU

1. Most of the following details about Kwak's life are from Kim (1993a). The article by Nukii (1993) is the other most useful source for the irregular armies.
2. This is another gem from Ha's collection of Korean legends! (1983:173).
3. Nukii (1993) and Kim (1993a).
4. Nukii (1993:94).
5. Kim (1993b:157).
6. Kim (1993b:157).
7. Most of the material on the monk-soldiers is taken from the PhD thesis by Kim (1978).
8. Kim (1978:26).
9. Kim (1978:27).
10. Kim (1978:88).
11. CNE (1965:138-40).
12. References to this well-known passage appear in many of the early English-language works on the Korean invasions. This translation is based on Udagawa (1993b:136).
13. Udagawa (1993b:136).
14. There are examples of both mortars and shells in the War Memorial, Seoul.
15. Ha (1981:71).
16. Ha (1981:72).
17. Ha (1981:73).
18. Ha (1981:76).
19. Ha (1981:75).
20. CNE (1965:141-42).
21. *Taikōki* in Yoshida (1979:153).
22. *Taikōki* in Yoshida (1979:153).
23. *Taikōki* in Yoshida (1979:155).
24. CNE (1965:137).
25. CNE (1965:138).
26. As depicted in a painting at the shrine to Kwŏn Yul at Haengju, and related also at the site of Toksan castle.
27. Ikeuchi (1936:17).
28. Ikeuchi (1936:19).
29. CNE (1965:235).

NOTES TO CHAPTER 7:
THE YEAR OF THE SNAKE

1. CNE (1965:148).
2. *Yoshino Jingoza'emon oboegaki* in ZGR (1933:383).
3. CNE (1965:148).
4. *Yoshino Jingoza'emon oboegaki* in ZGR (1933:384).
5. Wyatt (1982:104).
6. Kim (1978:93).
7. *Yoshino Jingoza'emon oboegaki* in CNE (1965:273).
8. *Yoshino Jingoza'emon oboegaki* in CNE (1965:274).
9. CNE (1965:235).
10. *Kuroda Kafu* in CNE (1965:275).
11. Most of the details of the battle of Pyŏkje are from the full account in CNE (1965:150-3), together with the primary source material also presented in CNE.
12. CNE (1965:285).
13. CNE (1965:285).
14. CNE (1965:153).
15. Kim (1978:94).
16. From the pamphlet produced by the Haengju Memorial Shrine.
17. CNE (1965:234).
18. CNE (1965:236).
19. CNE (1965:235.
20. Park (1978:181).
21. CNE (1965:236).
22. Ha (1981:89).
23. Ha (1981:89).
24. Ha (1981:90).
25. Ha (1981:91).
26. Ha (1981:94).
27. *Wakizaka ki* in ZGR (1933:443).
28. Ha (1981:93).
29. Ha (1981:90).
30. Ha (1977:29).
31. Ha (1981:91).
32. CNE (1965:235).
33. CNE (1965:155-159).
34. CNE (1965:290).
35. CNE (1965:290).
36. *Taikōki* in Yoshida (1979:155).
37. *Taikōki* in Yoshida (1979:155).
38. *Kuroda Kafu* in CNE (1965:290).
39. *Kuroda Kafu* in CNE (1965:290).
40. CNE (1965:291).
41. *Kuroda Kafu* in CNE (1965:290).
42. Shimokawa (1907:325).
43. CNE (1965:159).
44. *Taikōki* in Yoshida (1979:156).
45. From the shrine to Nongae in Chinju castle.
46. Ha (1981:105).
47. Ha (1981:107).
48. Ha (1981:107).

NOTES TO CHAPTER 8:
THE STRANGE OCCUPATION

1. CNE (1965:93-4).
2. CNE (1965:94) and Palais (1996:83).
3. CNE (1965:95).
4. Ha (1981:118).
5. Ha (1981:122).
6. Ha (1981:145).
7. Ha (1981:145).
8. Ha (1981:123).
9. Ha (1981:123).
10. Ha (1977:180).
11. Ha (1977:193).
12. Ha (1977:196).
13. Ha (1977:233).
14. *Wakizaka ki* in ZGR (1933:449).
15. *Jōzan Kidan* in CNE (1965:294).
16. *Jōzan Kidan* in CNE (1965:294).
17. Quoted by Elisonas in Hall (ed.) (1991:286).
18. *Jōzan Kidan* in CNE (1965:300).
19. Ha (1981:163).
20. Ha (1977:46).
21. Ha (1977:305).
22. Ha (1977:670).
23. Ha (1977:66).
24. Ha (1981:166).
25. Ha (1981:167).
26. Ha (1977:80).
27. Ha (1977:117).
28. Ha (1977:123).
29. Ha (1977:124).
30. Ha (1977:126).
31. Ha (1977:144).
32. Cary (1936:12).
33. Cary (1936:41).
34. Cary (1936:42).
35. Cary (1936:43).
36. Cary (1936:43).
37. Cary (1936:14).
38. Cary (1936:41).
39. Cary (1936:14).
40. Cary (1936:44).
41. Palais (1996:516).
42. Palais (1996:519).
43. Palais (1996:520).
44. Palais (1996:87).
45. Palais (1996:529).
46. Palais (1996:532).
47. Stramigioli (1954:106).
48. Elisonas in Hall (ed.) (1991:282).
49. Stramigioli (1954:108).
50. Elisonas in Hall (ed.) (1991:283).
51. Stramigioli (1954:111).

NOTES TO CHAPTER 9:
THE KOREAN WAR

1. Park (1978:191).
2. CNE (1965:181).
3. *Tōdō ke oboegaki* in CNE (1965:302).
4. CNE (1965:304).
5. CNE (1965:304).
6. CNE (1965:184).
7. The existence of Keinen's work was brought to the attention of the West by an article by Elisonas (Elison, 1988) and his briefer account in Hall (ed.) (1991:292-3). The full text appears in Naitō (1965). I wish to acknowledge my debt to Professor Elisonas for his helpful comments in dealing with this difficult but important text.
8. Naitō (1965:69).
9. Naitō (1965:70).
10. Naitō (1965:70).
11. Naitō (1965:70).
12. Naitō (1965:71).
13. Naitō (1965:71).
14. Naitō (1965:72).
15. Griffis (1982:132).
16. Dimensions as given in the souvenir booklet of the Namwŏn Shrine.
17. Naitō (1965:72).
18. *Shimazu ke Kōrai gun hiroku* in ZGR (1933:313).
19. *Wakizaka ki* in ZGR (1933: 448).
20. *Matsuura Hōin Seikan nikki* quoted in Takahashi (1965:231).
21. This part of *Chōsen ki* by Ōkōchi Hidemoto contains some particularly vivid writing on contemporary warfare. It may be found in ZGR (1933:267-353).
22. *Chōsen ki* in ZGR (1933:281).
23. *Chōsen ki* in ZGR (1933:281).
24. *Chōsen ki* in ZGR (1933:282).
25. *Chōsen ki* in ZGR (1933:282).
26. *Chōsen ki* in ZGR (1933:285).
27. *Chōsen ki* in ZGR (1933:287).
28. Naitō (1965:72).
29. Naitō (1965:73).
30. Naitō (1965:73).
31. Naitō (1965:73).

32. Naitō (1965:73).
33. *Wakizaka ki* in ZGR (1933:448).
34. CNE (1965:191).
35. CNE (1965:192).
36. CNE (1965:192-3).
37. *Kuroda Kafu* in CNE (1965:305).
38. *Kuroda Kafu* in CNE (1965:305).
39. Park (1978:209-14).
40. CNE (9165:192).
41. Ha (1977:314).
42. Ha (1977:315).

NOTES TO CHAPTER 10: THE WAJŌ WARS

1. Naitō (1965:98).
2. Naitō (1965:98).
3. Naitō (1965:99).
4. Naitō (1965:100).
5. Naitō (1965:102).
6. Naitō (1965:102).
7. Naitō (1965:103).
8. Naitō (1965:104-5).
9. Naitō (1965:103).
10. Naitō (1965:103).
11. Naitō (1965:104).
12. Naitō (1965:105).
13. Naitō (1965:118).
14. *Matsui Monogatari* in CNE (1965:305).
15. Naitō (1965:128).
16. *Taikōki* in Yoshida (1979:180).
17. *Chōsen ki* in CNE (1965:311).
18. *Angei Monogatari* in CNE (1965:318).
19. *Chōsen ki* in CNE (1965:309).
20. *Chōsen ki* in CNE (1965:309).
21. *Chōsen ki* in CNE (1965:309).
22. Naitō (1965:127).
23. Elison (1988:35).
24. Elison (1988:37).
25. *Matsui Monogatari* in CNE (1965:312).
26. CNE (1965:198).
27. *Kiyomasa Kōrai no jin oboegaki* in Shimokawa (1907:325).
28. *Kiyomasa Kōrai no jin oboegaki* in Shimokawa (1907:328).
29. *Matsui Monogatari* in CNE (1965:312).
30. Naitō (1965:130).
31. *Chōsen ki* in CNE (1965:331).
32. Naitō (1965:132).
33. Naitō (1965:133).
34. Naitō (1965:133).
35. CNE (1965:235).
36. CNE (1965:202).
37. CNE (1965:202).
38. *Jōzan Kidan* in CNE (1965:307).
39. CNE (1965:204).
40. *Seikan roku* in CNE (1965:316).
41. *Shimazu ke heihō* in CNE (1965:316).
42. *Shimazu ke Kōrai gun hiroku* in ZGR (1933:367).
43. *Seikan roku* in CNE (1965:316).
44. Ha (1977:340).
45. Ha (1977:340).
46. CNE (1965:209).
47. *Utsunomiya Kōrai Kijin Monogatari* in CNE (1965:321).
48. *Utsunomiya Kōrai Kijin Monogatari* in CNE (1965:321).
49. Kondō (1977:102,111).
50. Ha (1977:340).
51. Ha (1977:340).
52. Park (1978:240).
53. Ha (1977:343).
54. CNE (1965:212).
55. CNE (1965:213).

NOTES TO CHAPTER 11: THE HIGH PRICE OF KOREAN POTTERY

1. Hale (1985:184).
2. Hale (1985:195).
3. Hill (1948:987).
4. Sadler (1937a:179).
5. *Chōsen ki* in ZGR (1933:352).
6. *Motoyama Buzen no kami Yasumasa oyako senkō oboegaki* in ZGR (1933:391).
7. Maske (1994:47).
8. Maske (1994:51).
9. Sadler (1937:181).
10. Yamagata (1913:5).
11. Yamagata (1913:8).

NOTES TO APPENDICES

1. Data from Park (1978:59) and CNE (1965:119).
2. CNE (1965:184-7).
3. Chōsen ki in ZGR (1933:287-8).
4. Ha (1981:210).
5. Jeon (1974:218).
6. Underwood (1933:fig.47).
7. Watanabe (1935:588).

BIBLIOGRAPHY

Asakawa, K. *The Documents of Iriki: Illustrative of the Development of the Feudal Institutions of Japan*, Greenwood, Westport, Conn. 1929 (reprinted 1974)

Aston, W.G 'Hideyoshi's Invasion of Korea', *TASJ* 9-1878–83

Bacon, Wilbur D. 'Fortresses of Kyŏnggi-do', *TKBRAS* 37, pp. 1–64 1961

Bacon, Wilbur D. 'Record of Reprimands and Admonitions (*Chingbirok*) by Yu Sŏngnyong', *TKBRAS* 47 pp. 9–24 1972

Ballard, G.A. *The Influence of the Sea on the Political History of Japan*, John Murray, London 1921

Berry, Mary E. *Hideyoshi*, Harvard University Press 1982

Bird, Isabella *Korea and Her Neighbours* (reprinted with an introduction by Pat Barr 1985), KPI, London 1897

Bonar, H.A.C. 'On Maritime Enterprise in Japan', *TASJ* 15, pp. 103–23 1887

Boots, J.L. 'Korean Weapons and Armour', *TKBRAS*, 23, 2 1–37 1934

Boscaro, A. *101 Letters of Hideyoshi*, Sophia University, Tokyo 1975

Boxer, C.R. 'Notes on early military influence on Japan', *TASJ (2nd Series)* 8, pp. 68–95 1931

Chan, A. *The Glory and Fall of the Ming*, University of Oklahoma Press, Norman 1982

Cho In-bok *Han'guk ko hwagi togam*, Seoul 1974

Cooper, Michael *Rodrigues the Interpreter: An Early Jesuit in Japan and China*, Wetherhill, New York 1974

Cory, Ralph M. 'Some notes on Father Gregorio de Cespedes: Korea's first European visitor', *TKBRAS* 27, pp. 1–45 1937

Covell, J.C. and Covell, A. *Korean Impact on Japanese Culture: Japan's Hidden History*, Hollym, Elizabeth, N.J. 1984

Elison, George 'The Priest Keinen and His Account of the Campaign in Korea, 1597–1598: An Introduction' in Motoyama Yukihiko Kyōju taikan kinen rombunshū henshū iinkai, (ed.), *Nihon Kyōikushi ronsō: Motoyama Yukihiko Kyōju taikan kinen rombunshū*, Kyoto Shibunkaku pp. 25–41 1988

Fujiwara Yasumoto *Wakizaka ki in Zoku gunsho ruijū*, XX-2 Tokyo Zoku Gunsho Ruijū Kanseikai, (1933) 591 pp. 431–53 1642

Griffis, W.E. *Corea: The Hermit Nation*, Scribner, New York 1882

Ha, Tae-hung *Nanjung Ilgi* (The War Diaries of Admiral Yi), Yonsei University Press, Seoul (1977)

Ha, Tae-hung (trans.) & Lee, Chong-young (ed.) *Imjin Changch'o (Admiral Yi's Memorials to Court)*, Yonsei University Press, Seoul (1981)

Ha, Tae-hung *Behind the Scenes of Royal Palaces in Korea (Yi Dynasty)*, Yonsei University Press, Seoul 1983

Hale, J.R. *War and Society in Renaissance Europe 1450–1620*, McGill–Queen's University Press 1985

Hall, J.W (ed.) *The Cambridge History of Japan: Volume 4, Early Modern Japan*, Cambridge University Press, Cambridge 1991

Hazard, Benjamin H. 'The Formative Years of the Wako, 1223–63', *Monumenta Nipponica* xxii 3, 4 pp.260–77 1967

Hazard, Benjamin H. *Japanese Marauding in Medieval Korea: The Wako Impact on Late Koryŏ*, Unpublished Ph.D thesis, University of California, Berkeley 1967

Henthorn, W.E. 'Some notes on Koryŏ Military Units', *TKBRAS* 39 pp. 67–75. 1959

Henthorn, W.E. *Korea – the Mongol Invasions*, Brill, Leiden, 1963

Henthorn, W.E. *A History of Korea*, The Free Press, New York 1971

Hill, Sir George *A History of Cyprus Volume III The Frankish Period 1432–1571*, Cambridge University Press 1948

Hori, K. *The Mongol Invasions and the Kamakura Bakufu*, (Unpublished Ph. D thesis, Columbia University 1967

Hulbert, H. *A History of Korea*, Seoul 1895

Ikeuchi, Hiroshi *Bunroku Keichō no Eki*, Toyo Bunko, Tokyo 1936

Ishihara, Michihiro *Bunroku Keichō no Eki* (Hanawa Senshi 31), Tokyo 1963

Jeon, Sang-woo *Science and Technology in Korea: Traditional Instruments and Techniques*, MIT Press, Cambridge, Mass. 1974

Jho, Sung-do *Yi Sun-shin, A National Hero of Korea*, Choong moo-kong Society, Naval Academy, Korea

Joe, Wanne J. *Traditional Korea: A Cultural History*, Chung'ang University Press, Seoul 1972

Kani, Masano 'Yi Sun-sin senjō o yuku', *Rekishi Gunzō* (Magazine) 17, pp 88–90 1995

Katano, Tsugio *Yi Sun-sin to Hideyoshi, Bunroku Keichō no Kaisen*, Tokyo 1983

Kim, Samuel Dukhae *The Korean Monk Soldiers in the Imjin War: An Analysis of Buddhist Resistance to the Hideyoshi Invasion 1592–1598*, Unpublished Ph. D dissertation Columbia University, New York 1978

Kim, Yan-gi 'Kwak Chae-u' in *Bunroku Keichō no eki (Rekishi Gunzō Series Volume 35)*, Gakken, Tokyo, pp.152–4 1993a

Kim, Yan-gi 'Ko Kyŏng-myŏng' in *Bunroku Keichō no eki (Rekishi Gunzō Series Volume 35)*, Gakken, Tokyo, pp.157–8 1993b

Kim, Zae-gun 'An Outline of Korean Shipbuilding History', *Korea Journal 29*, 10 pp. 4–17 1989

Kim, Zae-gun *A study of Korean Shipbuilding History*, (in Korean with English summary) Seoul 1994

Kondō, Giza'emon *Ikitsuki shi kō*, Sasebo 1977

Kuno, Y.S. *Japanese Expansion on the Asiatic Continent*, University of California Press, Berkeley 1937

Kuwabara, Yaza'emon *Motoyama Buzen no kami Yasumasa oyako senkō oboegaki*, in *Zoku gunsho ruijū*, XX-2 Tokyo Zoku Gunsho Ruijū Kanseikai, (1933) 591 pp. 388–95 1636

Kuwada, T. and Yamaoka, S. (eds) *Chōsen no Eki (Nihon no Senshi 5)*, Tokyo 1965

Lee, Kenneth B. *Korea and East Asia: The Story of a Phoenix*, Praeger, Westport, Conn. 1997

Lee, Ki-baik *A New History of Korea*, Harvard University Press, Cambridge, Mass. 1984

Marder, A.J. 'From Jimmu Tenno to Perry – Sea Power in early Japanese history', *American Historical Review* 51 pp.8–31 1945

Maske, Andrew 'The Continental Origins of Takatori Ware. The Introduction of Korean Potters and Technology to Japan through the Invasions of 1592–1598' *TASJ* 4th Series 9 pp. 43–61 1994

McKenzie, F.A. *Korea's Fight for Freedom*, Simpkin, Marshall, London 1920

Murdoch, James *A History of Japan Volume II*, London 1925

Naitō, Shunpo *Bunroku Keichō no eki niokeru hiryonin no kenkyu*, Tokyo 1976

Nakanishi, Takeshi 'Ryō eki ni hatashita wajō no yakuwari', in *Sengoku Kassen Daizan (ge) (Rekishi Gunzō Series Volume 51)*, Gakken, Tokyo 1997

Needham, Joseph *Science and Civilisation in China Vol. 5 Pt 7 Military Technology; The Gunpowder Epic*, Cambridge, Cambridge University Press 1986

Needham, Joseph and Yates, Robin D.S. *Science and Civilisation in China Vol. 5 Pt 6 Military Technology: Missiles and Sieges*, Cambridge, Cambridge University Press 1994

Nukii, Masayuki 'Bunroku Keichō no eki', in *Hideyoshi Gundan (Rekishi Gunzō Series Vol. 30)* pp. 24–5, Gakken, Tokyo 1992

Nukii, Masayuki 'Gōshi shishu', in *Bunroku Keichō no eki (Rekishi Gunzō Series Vol. 35)* pp. 92–7, Gakken, Tokyo 1993

Ōkōchi, Hidemoto *Chōsen ki*, in *Zoku gunsho ruijū* XX-2 Tokyo Zoku Gunsho Ruijū Kanseikai, (1933) 590b pp. 267–353 1662

Palais, J.B. *Confucian Statecraft and Korean Institutions: Yu Hyŏngwŏn and the Late Chosŏn Dynasty*, Seattle, University of Washington Press 1996

Paludan, A. *The Imperial Ming Tombs*, Yale University Press, New Haven 1981

Park, Y. *Admiral Yi Sun-shin and his Turtleboat Armada*, Hanjin, Seoul 1978

Paske-Smith, M. *Japanese Trade and Residence in the Philippines before and during the Spanish occupation*, *TASJ* xlii Nov 1914 685–710 1914

Peterson, Mark 'Slaves and Owners; or Servants and Masters? A Preliminary Examination of Slavery in Traditional Korea', *TKBRAS* 60 pp. 31–41 1985

Saccone, Richard *Koreans to Remember: 50 famous people who helped shape Korea*, Hollym, New Jersey 1993

Sadler, A.L. *The Maker of Modern Japan: The Life of Tokugawa Ieyasu*, Allen and Unwin, London 1937a

Sadler, A.L. 'The Naval Campaign in the Korean War of

Hideyoshi', *TASJ (2nd Series)* 14 179–208 1937b

Salem, E. *Slavery in Medieval Korea,* Unpublished Ph. D thesis, Columbia University 1978

Satō, K. 'Nazo no kaishō "Konishi Yukinaga" no jitsuzō ni seru', *Rekishi Gunzō* (Magazine) 17, pp 91–106 1995

Satow, E. 'The Korean Potters in Satsuma', *TASJ* (1st Series) 6 pp. 193–203 1878

Shimokawa, Heidayū 'Kiyomasa Kōrai no jin oboegaki', *Zokuzoku gunshō ruijū Vol. 4* (Tokyo: Kokushō kankōkai) pp. 273–305 1907

Shimoyama, Haruhisa 'Masamune no Chōsen shuppei', in *Date Masamune (Rekishi Gunzō Series Vol. 19)* pp. 34–5 Gakken, Tokyo 1990

Stramigioli, Giulina 'Hideyoshi's Expansionist Policy on the Asiatic Mainland', *TASJ* 3rd Series 3 pp.74–116 1954

Tae, Hung-ha *A Trip Through Historic Korea,* Yonsei University Press, Seoul 1958

Takahashi, K. *Hata Sashimono,* Akida Shōten, Tokyo 1965

Takekoshi, Y. *The Story of the Wako,* translated by Hideo Watanabe, Kenkyusha, Tokyo 1940

Takekoshi, Yosaburo *The Economic Aspects of the History of the Civilisation of Japan,* London 1930

Takenouchi, Kazusai *Ehon Taikōki,* (Woodblock printed edition – Kobayashi Rokubei, Osaka); (Printed edition – Yuhodo Bunko Series no. 81 – 1917) 1802

Tanaka, Taneo 'Japan's Relations with Overseas Countries', in Hall and Toyoda (eds) *Japan in the Muromachi Age* University of California Press, pp. 159–78) 1977

Tsunoda R., de Bary W., Keene, D. (eds.) *Sources of Japanese Tradition Volume I,* Columbia University Press 1958

Turnbull, S.R. 'War, trade and piracy: military and diplomatic relations between China, Korea and Japan and their influence on Japanese military technology', *Royal Armouries Yearbook* 2, pp. 149–55 1997

Turnbull, S.R. 'Chinese influence on Japanese siege warfare', *Royal Armouries Yearbook* 3 pp. 145–58 1998

Udagawa, T. Chōsen ōcho shuryoku kaki sōran, in *Bunroku Keichō no eki (Rekishi Gunzō Series Volume 35),* pp.117–19. Tokyo, Gakken 1993a

Udagawa, T. Nichō no shuryoku kaki 'teppō' to 'jūtō', in *Bunroku Keichō no eki (Rekishi Gunzō Series Volume 35),* pp.134–6. Tokyo, Gakken 1993b

War Memorial *A Comprehensive Pictorial Guide to the War Memorial,* The War Memorial, Yongsan, Seoul 1996 (revised 1998)

Watanabe, Yosuke 'Chōsen eki to waga zōsen no hattatsu', *Shigaku Zasshi* 46, 5 pp. 551–97 1935

Werner, E.T.C. 'Chinese Weapons', originally in the *Transactions of the North China Branch of the Royal Asiatic Society,* and reprinted in 1972 by Ohara Publications 1932

Wyatt, D.K. *Thailand: A Short History,* Yale University Press 1982

Yamagata, I. 'Japanese-Korean Relations after the Japanese invasion of Korea in the XVIth Century', *TKBRAS* 4, 2 pp. 1–11 1913

Yang, Jwing-ming *Ancient Chinese Weapons: A Martial Artist's Guide,* YMAA Publication Center, Boston, Mass. 1999

Yi, Hyŏngsŏk *Imjin Chŏllansa* (3 vols), Sinhyŏnsilsa, Seoul 1974

Yi, Wŏn-jin *Han'gug-ŭi Pae,* Daewonsa, Seoul (1990)

Yoshida, Y (ed.) *Taikōki* (Volume 3), (Volume 9 in the series I) Kyōikusha Shinsho, Tokyo 1979

Yoshino, Jingoza'emon *Yoshino Jingoza'emon oboegaki,* in *Zoku gunsho ruijū* XX-2 Tokyo Zoku Gunsho Ruijū Kanseikai, (1933) 591 pp. 378–88 1636

INDEX